AF478080

Rita Roos critique

Rita Roos (1956–1996) in Helsinki, July 1996

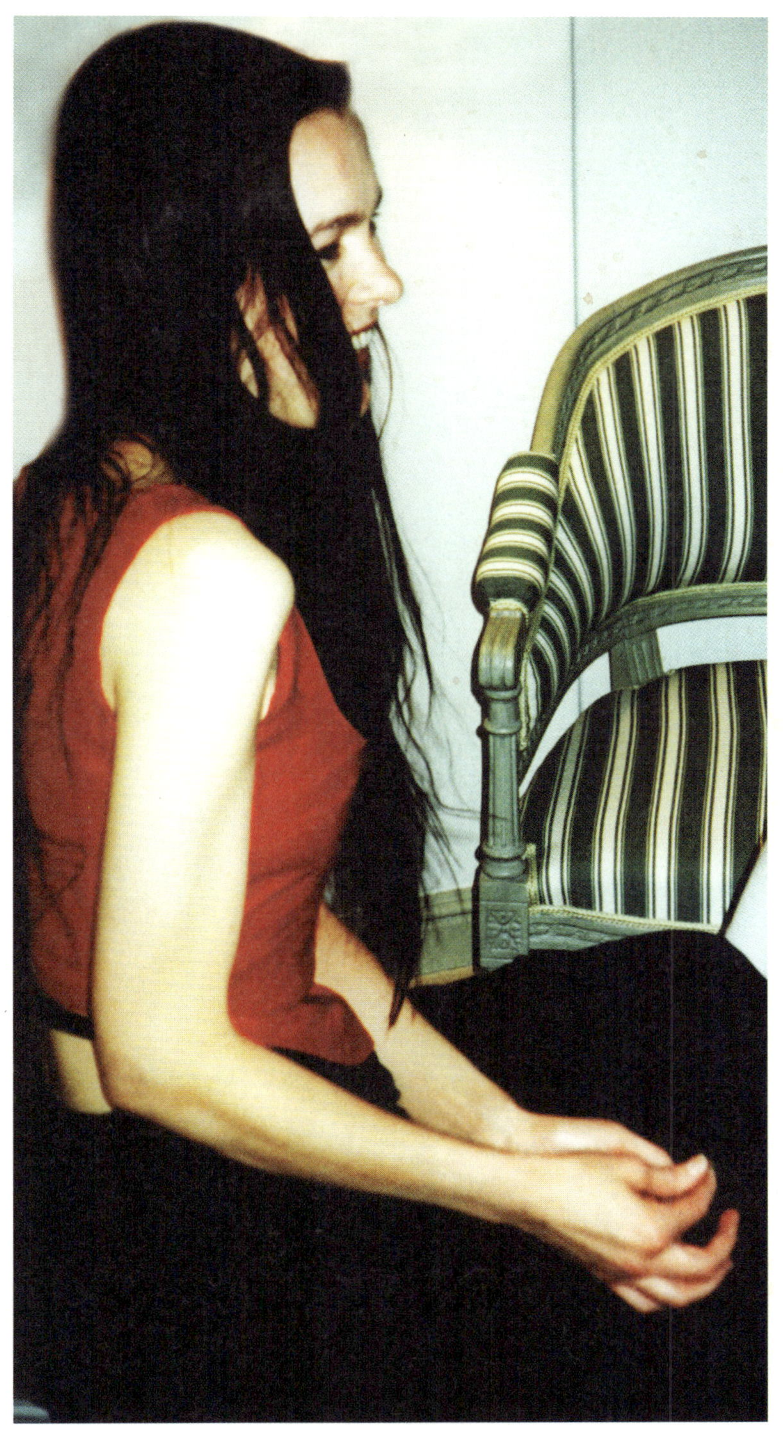

Ten years ago, in the middle of an intensely active period, Rita Roos hastily and unexpectedly passed away. She was an art critic at *Hufvudstadsbladet* in Helsinki and the Finnish editor for *Siksi. The Nordic Art Review*. She lectured in art theory at the Trondheim Art Academ in Norway. She was a passionately attentive observer, reader and conversation partner.

This book is published in memory of a beloved sister, close friend and admired colleague. Yet it is not intended only for those who were fortunate to know Rita Roos and followed her work in newspapers, art journals, exhibition catalogues and monographs.

Rita Roos's texts, like herself, communicate empathy and curiosity, but also critical distance and listening, as well as her ability to actually see. She had an unusual gift for the intensive encounter, and she used it in her writing. She approached art and artists with clear-sighted intellect and an intelligent eye. Rita Roos's texts invite us to be together with her as she sees and experiences and thinks. Her language is a tools that she used to write herself into art, to write together with art rather than about it.

This is a book of art criticism, but it also gives us insight into how writing can become a form of continuous thinking. In her texts Rita Roos tests and interrogates thoughts and ideas that are important to her and develops them further in her encounters with works of art. We experience an unusually close dialogue between the writer and the artwork, between what is observed and its expansion in thought. This approach yields penetrating, uncompromising texts that manage to convey with precision how meaning is created in art.

This selection of Rita Roos's texts is offered in the original Swedish and in English translations. We hope the book also will find readers with no prior knowledge of one of Scandinavia's finest art writers, and that her texts will be appreciated for what they tell us about art and about Rita Roos herself.

We have arranged a selection of Rita Roos's published texts as an open circuit. Fragments from her texts serve as chapter headings. The book focuses on areas of special importance to her that might be formulated like this: 'boundary', 'voice', 'image', 'method', 'transgression', 'world', 'verticality'.

Lund, September 2006

Anders Kreuger and Nina Roos

colophon

Rita Roos. Critique

Text: Rita Roos
Editing: Anders Kreuger, Nina Roos
Translations: Anders Kreuger, Mike Garner, William Jewson, Philip Landon
Language Editing: Fiona Key
Photography: Marianna Uutinen
Design: Daiva Kišūnaitė
Printing: Logotipas, Vilnius 2006

Publisher:
Veenman Publishers/Gijs Stork
Sevillaweg 140
NL-3047 AL Rotterdam, The Netherlands
Tel. +31 10 2453333, fax. +31 10 2453344

ISBN: 9086900399
EAN: 9789086900398
© Nina Roos

Thanks to: Kristin Bergaust, Yane Calovski, Anne-Karin Furunes,
Maaretta Jaukkuri, Iréne Kreuger, Pyry Nykyri, Ann-Mari Roos,
Gertrud Sandqvist, Mikko Zenger

This book was supported by the Finnish Cultural Foundation,
the Swedish Cultural Foundation in Finland, Trondheim Art Academy

Distribution:

D.A.P.
155 Sixth Avenue, 2nd floor
New York, NY 10013, USA, dap@dapinc.com

Idea Books
Nieuwe Herengracht 11
1011 RK Amsterdam-NL, the Netherlands, idea@ideabooks.nl

Art Data
12 Bell Industrial Estate
50 Cunnington Street
W4 5HB London, UK, info@artdata.co.uk

table of contents

what is officially stated

turned into a waking reality

Identity – the Self
Museum of Contemporary Art, Helsinki

An Assigned Identity

After the lively hairsplitting around themes like identity, the self and the subject in the 80s, today's attempts at summarising issues of identity tend to come across as slightly simplistic, which becomes particularly clear when we consider that this notion is based on multiplicity.

Anyway, the exhibition at the Museum of Contemporary Art with Russian and Finnish artists has *Identity – the Self* as its theme, and this topicalises once more, like many of the thematically constructed exhibitions of the 80s, the relation between art and theory. Theory is not art and art is not theory. This sounds self-evident, but it is precisely the point missed by some of the 80s exhibitions, to the extent that the work of art was treated like a clear-cut object of knowledge, excluding qualities that did not fit the assigned interpretative frame.

The tricky thing about the current exhibition relates to the question: on what level does the concept of identity and the self operate? In a way the answer is simple, and even too simple. First, the artists in question are working conceptually with emphasis on the cerebral and some of the works seem to be made with the exhibition's theme in mind. Partly as a consequence of this, the works illuminate the theme in a way that functions as a confirmation of the Lacanian conception of the self and in this respect the take becomes predictable; the works reach exactly as far as Lacan thinks it is possible for us to reach in our quest for knowledge about our self. According to Lacan, what we know about the self can hardly even be called knowledge, rather constructions around something that shows through its disguises, like a symptom that forever escapes our self-awareness. What the *Identity* exhibition enlarges is consequently the barrage of constructions, what does not fit within the frame is the quality that a work of art has the potential to realise; to anticipate, to pre-empt given knowledge, to make constructions crack.

For an artistic investigation to achieve a revealing crack-up is in itself nothing new. We only need to refer to Marcel Duchamp's glass works, which are particularly interesting for the notion of the self since

Duchamp's method can be understood as an extreme application of the principle of construction, but in such a way that the result is not about logical structure but the opposite, a void beyond our structured conscious-ness that the disguises manage to hide, in a supreme but at the same time illusory fashion. An artistic investigation on this level is thus possible without excluding multiplicity. Therefore it is also no coincidence that Duchamp's glass works could be analysed using the vocabulary of the last decades on the self and identity: male, female, desire, lack, the relation of the self to convention etc.

What makes *Identity* a good exhibition is first and foremost the exacti-tude and accuracy of the individual works. Of the artists Eija-Liisa Ahtila is the one who has managed to create a kind of break or discontinuity in relation to a normalised understanding of reality, provided that her three three-minute films *Okay*, *We* and *Gray* are shown in their designated con-text, inserted into the content of a commercial TV channel. Ahtila's andro-gynous woman who paces back and forth in a flat, speaking in both a man's and a woman's voice, would be well suited for the commercial break in *The Bold and the Beautiful*, and her three women in a lift, preoccupied by a nuclear disaster, would be suitable for viewing after the advertisement for detergent where the women almost obsessively analyse the mystery of the dirt stain.

If identity is understood as culturally and socially constructed, then we can say that Yuri Leiderman's gaming table is its live metaphor. Every day during the exhibition various objects change places on a numbered, grid-ded playing field. If two of the objects happen to become placed on the same number a mouse is released from its hiding place under the table.

Maximising and minimising an assigned identity – Pekka Niskanen's reconstruction of the media phenomenon Stefan Lindfors by way of a fic-titious interview and a collection of Lindfors's designer furniture becomes the point where the anchorage of identity in a real person is obliterated and the self moves on a surface from which all the qualities that are neces-sary for medialisation can be freely selected. And what about minimising? In Juha-Pekka Hotinen's *Second Hand Man* it is a slight defect in one of the artist's arms that is the answer to the question: What is wrong with me? Through diagnosing the damage and analysing the symptoms the subject is closed with a therapeutic manicure session in the professional manicure chair that is placed in the middle of the room.

In the room next to Lindfors's exhibitionism Gia Rigvava's video installation focuses on live eyes. The effect of the eyes moving on the video screens is somehow puzzling. Although the material is not manipulated I do not think of these eyes as mirrors of the soul but they seem more clinical, like live organs.

When most things have been said and resaid about identity and the self without anyone feeling a bit wiser it is time to have a look at Pentti Koskinen's melon head, i.e. one half of a melon head fixed to the wall in the rear room, accompanied by a photograph on which Koskinen's head has been transformed into the melon's other half.

Hufvudstadsbladet 16 December 1993

Zacheta National Gallery, Warsaw

Where Is Abel, Thy Brother?

Zacheta, the Museum of Contemporary Art in Warsaw, is housed in one of the few buildings that were spared destruction during the Battle of Warsaw. The Germans, who occupied the city from 1939 to 1944, used it as a house of entertainment, a casino.

The Jewish ghetto never recovered. Anda Rottenberg, Zacheta's Director and curator of the exhibition *Where is Abel, Thy Brother?*, takes me round Warsaw by car. The city is laid out like an open book on methodical cruelty; only a few of the buildings in the ghetto survived the violence, here and there inexplicably empty areas, junctures, and reconstruction projects are set side by side like strangers.

> And the Lord said unto Cain, Where is Abel thy brother? And he said, I know not: Am I my brother's keeper? And he said, What hast thou done? the voice of thy brother's blood crieth unto me from the ground.

What kind of exhibition today is called *Where is Abel, Thy brother?* – with the art of the 1990s inundated by confessions: I am homosexual, I have AIDS, I am black, I am 'white trash', plus a theoretical discourse centred on the shaky foundations of the 'I'-sign and the question of who is speaking? The exhibition at Zacheta is not easy to describe, nor to explain. It is one of those exhibitions that have succeeded, it has the quality of requiring that you enter, walk through the galleries, move among the works. Once you notice that Abel, the murdered brother, is the more present of the two, then you know that the theme works, that the exhibition is able to bring the apparatus of symbols and metaphors back down to earth, to a situation that is given concrete mental form in the works on display. Only to be cast out again into the critical context that the biblical questions push to the fore.

Miroslaw Balka's corridor with its pale-yellow, soap-scented walls is more than its outward appearance. It marks the site for a ritual, one that is either terrifying or voluptuous. It spans the distance between extreme poles, to wash yourself as befits human dignity or to wash yourself to be worthy of death. In Christian Boltanski's installation, *Neighbours*, a voice reads anonymous names from a telephone catalogue, as you see your own face reflected in the shiny black surfaces. Lists of names. A list of prize-winners, the chosen, the condemned, winners, losers. A name that could be anyone at all. Lawrence Weiner's text on one of the walls is a long-awaited prologue to the tablets of the law (in my imagination they are always blocks of stone): *Wet sand and small stones placed in the sun to dry (All mixed together)*.

The writing in the Bible is refined to the point that the writer's problem, of constantly finding himself drifting away from the presence of the meaning he sought, is eliminated. Limits are set on the multiplicity of the writing through the way that the Bible comprises a whole in which the context functions like dogma, a dogma that even embraces the history of The Scriptures themselves. And the crucial feature that makes the Bible the Bible is that, beyond the sign, a presence is created of something that exists outside the play of differences: God. A conversation with the Lord thus always takes place in terms of the Lord's discourse.

The exhibition at Zacheta is an adaptation of another possibility. The question the Lord asks Cain is excised from the Book, and tested out in a visual language that, in contrast, neither demands nor punishes, i.e. one that is devoid of ethical imperatives. The works at Zacheta, in the presence of the Biblical question, apply a kind of 'ethics of neutrality', if I can be permitted a free borrowing from Barthes here. He spoke of Writing as norm, of the Text as a field of seduction. Then at the end of the 1970s to introduce the expression 'the ethics of neutrality', by which he meant a language that does not desire, but which loves; non-aggressive, non-genital, wanting to live without possessing. The works at Zacheta demand nothing, but they awaken a great deal.

Who is my brother? Imagine, just for a change, we can ask a question that is not about identity, but about community and togetherness. We have, and have had, systems that operate according to the principles of solidarity and unity, but the result is often that the other's brother is annihilated or reduced to silence. Tomasz Kizny's work *The Verdict* consists of two sequences of black-and-white photographs: of condemned people from the KGB central archive and of passengers on the Moscow underground at that same tired afternoon hour. When filed, the portraits of the condemned were annotated with exact personal details. The person's name, profession, date of execution and the reason for this: killed in 1938 for undesirable political activities. What more can be added when even the questions have fallen silent?

Siksi 3/1995. Translated by Mike Garner

Muu Gallery, Helsinki

Jouni Kujansuu

In the window of Muu Gallery, Jouni Kujansuu displayed a black-and-white, naturalistic photograph of a man in jeans with his arms set in a promising 'gesture of desire', the one in which a T-shirt is pulled up to expose the torso. In this case, the gesture in the photograph had a different function – the mid-section of the body was encased in a mass of dough, which the man was trying to stretch and pull up towards his shoulders like a layer of malleable fat. At around the same time, Calvin Klein's new advertising placards were first launched on the city, a bunch of young people (Kate Moss & Co) with empty stares and anorexically thin arms and legs. The same gesture, the man seductively pulling up his T-shirt, also appeared in Klein's adverts.

Who is he, this man who exposes himself as a desirable object? Some are born to be men, others to be women, of course, we know that. And yet, what I am, and what it means for me to be a man or a woman, is a question that is asked incessantly, and one which cannot be satisfied by one or other natural, definitive conclusion. And this is given in the culture (or in the unconscious), in which there is an incomplete script that poses questions about our mental gender identity. And what we do, each in our own way, is to try again and again to inscribe ourselves into this, so as to find there our own specific place.

Finding our way through the jungle of uncertain self-definitions, living with them, is different from what is manifested by confessional art. Having had enough of the aesthetics of ego-excess that makes assertions about areas that actually reveal themselves in the shadow of their symptoms, skeptical about the tendency that promotes a multi-national, mass-media visual language that is supposed to express the self – I find relevant 'anti-points' in Kujansuu's exhibition, which are more a matter of relating to a black, sick area than of the conviction that the self knows.

Apart from the photograph mentioned earlier, there is another one with a similar naturalism. A young man heroically and at the same time ingenuously directs his gaze upwards with dough forming an awkward wig (echoes of the British legal system where the law is enacted by characters in wigs). The photograph is not just awkward, but also personifies shame, believing that everything is fine and not oneself noticing that something is amiss (despite the fact that everyone is already laughing). The shame of the stigma is visible; the forbidden, repulsive, nauseating, and the dirty. Either as with anorexics who try to keep their bodies clean through control of the oral-anal passage. Or like bulimics, who intermittently burst the bounds of the body so as to vanish into emptiness, to become nothing, a vacuum.

What Kujansuu did in his other photograph was to present the dough as the distorted, forbidden object of comfort and compulsion. Taking care of and looking after what is most hated and repulsive has here been taken to a point where the dough participates in a ritual that purifies the abject. The dough is, among other things, interwoven into a pattern that evokes associations with gingham, the paints that have washed over it are pale green, as a tangible reminiscence of security. Another lump is synthetically green, a third warm brown. The mental state is one of regression, with a symptom-creating superiority, here represented by the aesthetics – in the reality of the father who has to cut the ties to the kitchen smelling of milk and dough, to the mother, the symbiotic. The photographs have an intrinsic dangerousness about them through the way their aesthetics counteracts this brutal cutting off, this schism between real and symbolic. They retain both centres of power that should substitute for one another, re-invoking both of them at the same time.

Siksi 4/1995. Translated by Mike Garner

Hans Hamid Rasmussen
Nordic Arts Centre, Helsinki

Stranger

Cold sweat and nausea in the early dawn. Hans Hamid Rasmussen's embroidered images of deformed foetuses on pale linen are cut out in a dream and transformed into dried-up lumps in a clinical hospital setting. They are thrown away in a silence filled with mute unease, someone has to touch these lumps in order to get rid of them.

Hans Hamid Rasmussen's history is far from the clinicality of the hospital. Born in Algeria in 1963, his mother Norwegian, his father an Arab; his parents political activities forced the family to flee via Hungary to Norway. Rasmussen was six years old. I find a picture of Algeria in my encyclopaedia. A man stands on a plateau above the town of El Hamel, which is set in the bottom of a long valley. My eye is drawn to the man, wrapped from head to foot in white cloth, with only his dark face visible.

At Rasmussen's exhibition *Stranger* at Galleri Augusta he shows three kinds of work: embroidery on white linen, drawings, and an installation in two parts – a 'honey wall' and a fragment of text written directly onto the wall. On first acquaintance, these different works seem to represent a 'normal' well-made whole. In contrast, the images that stay in mind point in another direction. The text on the wall, about honey, children, tears and warm milk, is a song of comfort, one that would need a person, a voice, so that the words were there more than simply as attractive constructions arising out of a culture-bound statement. And, on top of that, Rasmussen's drawings are samples of the ability of the gifted hand to conjure up mental images.

The embroidered images of the disfigured, foetus-like creatures exist differently from the rest, they are the one part of the exhibition that is in harmony with its technique, sewing something in, joining something together – a stranger?

The stranger is said (according to Kristeva) to safeguard his unconscious on the other side of the border. Here, Kristeva is referring to the new language that the stranger has learned, and which is doomed to function outside the unconscious. When I look at Hans Hamid Rasmussen's embroidery, I am convinced that its artistic quality is specifically linked with the way that, in his embroidering, Rasmussen succeeds in breaking into what is there on the other side, it acts as an umbilical chord, supplying life-sustaining substances. Thus, the actual 'strangeness' in the exhibition is not in the embroidery, but in the drawings and installations, in which the expression exists on a recognisable level of expression.

The nightmare of desiccated foetuses, the image of the cloaked shepherd above El Hamel, invisible Arab women, dismembered bodies, and much else is present in the unstructured mass that Rasmussen's embroidery has absorbed. Hans Hamid Rasmussen's foetuses are totally graspable, and strike like a sharp needle at the viewer's own inflamed sense of the uncanny.

Siksi 3/1995. Translated by Mike Garner

Jan Kaila
Painters' Union Gallery, Helsinki

Porkkala Blue Parenthesis

Why did the Russians on Porkkala favour a special blue? This somewhat heavy shade of blue was used both indoors and out during Porkkala's red parenthesis, from 1944 to 1956, when Finland's southern tip was transformed into a Russian military base. The population was evacuated, and ten times their number of Russians decked out the peninsula according to the principles of temporary military presence. Perhaps blue had become superfluous in a nation that signalised red. Another feature: the Russians (many of whom where young men doing military service) liked to put up wallpaper. In the old houses in Porkkala it is still possible to uncover layer upon layer of mostly floral wallpaper. Perhaps one more was added each time a new officer came to the territory, wanting to make his mark with a new choice of flowers for the wall.

In his exhibition about the Porkkala parenthesis, Jan Kaila makes the far-fetched near-fetched. Since 1990, Kaila has been going around his home area of Kirkkonummi, gathering material about Russian Porkkala, and about the Russians themselves, who for Finns are bearers of a double stigma: as both outsider and enemy. The exhibition is made up of 150 Russian objects, two still-films that the Russians left behind on Porkkala, some jottings by a Komsomol activist from 1951, and photographs from the album of Bertil Sjöholm from 1956. Kaila has thus not taken the photographs himself, but has selected them from a range of material, which he shows with subtle alterations, comparable to the fine adjustments made by a precision mechanic. The idea underlying the selection and format of the pictures is a coherent one. The way in which Kaila displays the documentary material is guided by a fruitful understanding of photography and of its possible uses as regards Porkkala. His choices are underpinned by a single factor, since the pictures expressly deal with photography as ritual. Kaila has subtly moulded this into an instrument that is capable of stripping off the taboo and the parenthetical, layer by layer. One stratum deals with the formal, 'discrete' discourse that is conducted within the theme (as a political topic, Porkkala has been handled disquietingly painlessly). Another layer is the dense jungle of the Finns' complex social fantasies about 'the Russians', and the border region, which around Porkkala has added yet another border within a border. When the Finns returned in 1956, they tried to remove all traces of the outsider, in a way that is specifically resurrected in Kaila's exhibition. Those returning families tore off layer after layer of the Russians' floral wallpaper.

Photographing becomes a ritual when it is done for a special reason, at one of those events that form life's peninsulas: a child's first step, major changes, moving in, moving out, getting married, birthday celebrations, an so on. Even very old people frequently look happy in photographs; as Kaila has noted during his wanderings around the Porkkala area. When the Finns were about to move off the peninsula they took out their cameras, the result being jolly, house-moving pictures of family and friends. In the photographs, the tragedy of leaving became just the opposite, through the way that the act of taking a picture came to be more a matter of the mutual relationship between photographer and object.

> Only by having our powers of imagination replace the zero point are
> we capable of seeing a face. (Walter Benjamin)

Through the way Kaila has managed to confine his exhibition solely to ritual material, no external discourse is introduced into the photographs. Instead, a contact is established between pictures and viewers, which shatters their historically and politically conditioned network of ideas about the Porkkala parenthesis. This effect arises through a kind of contrast; the outsider, the enemy, looks totally normal. There are no visible stigma.

The photograph that stays with us throughout the exhibition, where most of the pictures express camaraderie between men, is that of a woman with two children in her arms. What is special about it is not that she is probably the wife of a Komsomol activist, but that she is a woman who knows that she is loved. This is evident in the same way as the momentary significance of the photographic act is visible. One of the children is looking away from the camera, towards something that is happening outside the photograph.

Parenthetic life: camaraderie, love, everyday life as sticky as chewing gum. An excerpt from the Komsomol activist's notes:

> Simply can't get a letter written to Zorin.
> 1. Must write letter to Remiryasov's kolkhoz.
> 2. Must change books *How the Steel Was Tempered, Harvest, With All My Heart, Knight of the Golden Star, Living Water*.
> 3. Must organise agitation work. Must talk to people – where he is going.

When Bertil Sjöholm returned on a cold February the fifth, the day after civilians were permitted to visit Porkkala, he photographed the snow-covered houses. They look as if they had always looked the same.

Siksi 3/1994. Translated by Mike Garner

Change of Rules – a Break with Correct Distance

A change of rules is waiting to come through like a transit passenger who has lost her ID and thereby also her face. But the obstacles are nothing to do with possible problems at security or passport control, but with landing on territories, mental and social, that are not yet occupied by an already written, legitimising discourse. When everything typical of stable situations – that critical moments really are make-believe, not jeopardising anything or threatening anybody because they are the results of the system that has already foreseen them – when all of this is absent, where are we then?

Not in Västerås, anyway, in the sky bar of the SAS hotel which is the opposite, an ideal place for describing another sign of stability: correct distance. From above the town looks like the whole entity it is supposed to be. No pieces or readabilities can be seen; even the movement down there seems to correctly follow a given pattern, everything from the smoke belching out of industrial pipes to the municipal domestic helpers implementing care for the elderly and the cleaners engaging in sanitary activities. Rules and regulations, professional advice and assistance are available at each level, for everything and everyone.

Correct distance as an attitude. I come to think of the Royal Family's Ken and Barbie on a visit to one of the Baltic countries. The scenario was perfect, the crowds waved their flags in the face of the well-dressed royalty and Sweden became what it was in childhood fantasies: sponge cake, striped candy, liquorice boats... Dissonant cracks, voids between experience and experience.

In the centre of Vilnius there is a popular bar, NATO's, planned and decorated by architect Valdas Ozarinskas. The door to this place looks like any other front door in Vilnius. But inside! The music is aggressive, pumped up hard, the interior militant and brutal: rifles, metal, darkness and smoke. As you sit in one of the low chairs it feels like being in an officers' club where the drink provides temporary relief from planned destruction. I have no similar experience of changing roles in a social environment to refer to. I cannot establish what is irony, what is serious, where the boundary between staging and reality is drawn. Later I realised I had been looking for the wrong thing or, differently put, that the absence of what I was looking for was symptomatic for the situation in Vilnius. At present there is no system that could function according to 'correct' rules; you live in a state of change, right in its middle, lacking an above. Even a visitor loses her distanced tools. Aggressive music follows you to the toilet, an elegant metal cabinet where your own reflection frightens you.

What in Lacanian psychoanalysis is designated as the Discourse of the Lord is absent, i.e. the discourse that maintains the illusion that the world is whole and harmonious and guarantees stability. Thus it excludes threats of change and people can get on with their lives, with their preconceived notions about themselves. This discourse in fact contains no hatred, since no one actually identifies with the Lord or the Master. He is just there, and people defer to Him as a matter of course. In the NATO's bar there is no self-evidence, only mutations of liberated energy.

In his essay *The Enlarged Field – from High Modernism to Conceptualism* the philosopher Sven-Olof Wallenstein makes an interesting supposition, that the modern concept of art is undergoing a fundamental mutation. But if that is the case, in what direction? Wallenstein asks. 'A generalised theory of conscience, design, the media and communications, information technology, an æsthetics of social processes.'

The eleven artists from Vilnius who participate in the exhibition *Change of Rules* (in Norrtälje, Södertälje and Västerås) form a triangle of words: frames, tools, parts. In this case there is no need to mistrust the words. In Lithuania there is no reason at all to follow the restrictions of correct distance; survival comes first.

The main site of consumption in Södertälje, the shopping mall, has been extended. The place for art and culture, the kunsthalle, is transformed into a curious outlet, whose æsthetics and function is an aberration from the other shops. A sweater is crocheted from human hair (Eglė Rakauskaitė's work), who wants to buy? A football-patterned jacket in exquisite silk (by Sandra Straukaitė) is ready to catwalk. Gintaras Makarevičius stands naked with a gun larger than the man himself. With whom is he fighting? Is it the experience of chaos and disillusion that makes the Lithuanian artists so supremely adept at carrying with them, in their work, its context? As if they were in direct contact with the context, as if they knew that meaning is created out of connectedness, and that connectedness is without boundaries unless it is defined.

S & P Stanikas' installations rise with rarely seen agility from the ruins of a collapsed psyche. Often disturbing, incomplete and brutal, at the boundary of ugliness. To change is to lose control of old material; crimes committed, disillusions that made you drown, words thrown out in despair and hysteria. As a Phoenix of reality S & P Stanikas brush the ashes from their wings, dress up and put on a new record. A new day can begin, the banalities will be suffered this time as well.

Francesca Woodman
The Finnish Museum of Photography, Helsinki

The Camera as Soul-Mate

The data I have on Francesca Woodman's personal history are scanty. Woodman was born in 1958 in Denver to parents of Italian descent. She grew up in the USA and Italy. She started taking photographs at the age of 14 and in 1975 she began her studies at the Rhode Island School of Design. Three years later she moved to New York. In January 1981 she published the series *Some Disordered Interior Geometries*, a few weeks afterwards she committed suicide. The photographs at hand are thus made by a young woman, from 15 to 22 years of age.

Even if Woodman's photographs investigate women and femininity it is misleading to regard her as a pioneer of the staged conceptual photographic practice of the 80s that directs a conscious critique at the position of the second sex in our culture. Woodman does not manipulate the conventions inherent in the photographic medium – she is not concerned with the techniques of fixed vision, she is not using the camera to make visible the distance between subject and object. Her relation to the camera is another, it is a soul-mate, a nimble tool with almost magical qualities, allowing her to capture things that are not immediately accessible to the eye. Taking photographs becomes an act of constant psychological relevance.

If we wish to place Francesca Woodman's pictures in a photographical context we find allusions to Victorian photographers like Clementina Hawarden and Julia Margaret Cameron, with regard to the element of dream-like and romantic theatricality that can be found in the images. But the similarity to this tradition is deceptive, it offers only a visual framework in which the female body appears as signifier. In this context the female body is very little to do with traditional photographic beauty, the connection can rather be described as a break with the rhetoric of the beautiful. However, it is possible to see an influence from symbolism and surrealism where the unconscious is the object of artistic investigation.

When I study Francesca Woodman's photographs there is above all one question that preoccupies me: what was she trying to see or reveal with these depictions of herself? It is as if she would often start from a condition where the human being cannot be said to have *one* body – as if a critical boundary had been erased and the camera's task were to show the pictures of a body that moves at the boundaries between different states.

In the photographs there is an inherent ambivalence. Partly there is the striving to arrive without mediation at something raw and unrefined, something that is taking place before symbolisation; partly Woodman is expressly dependent in her practice on the picture as an intermediary and therefore many of her photographs will also be marked by a many-layered concept of the image. For instance in the series *Self-Deceit* we see how the naked woman is playing a kind of cat-and-mouse game with a mirror in an otherwise empty room. She tries in various ways, in vain, to escape the mirror or rather the mirror-image. Since Woodman in her photographs often handles mirrors and sheets of glass it is difficult not to associate to the drama of the mirror stage in which the child sees itself as a whole image through the mirror. Since the child does not grasp itself but the image of itself this image, like all others, becomes illusory. The *Self-Deceit* sequence comes across as an act of defiance directed at the self. 'The image is in my eye. But I am not in the image', to quote Lacan. In many of the photographs the depiction of the body is held back, the body seems to disappear and is replaced by a sign or a trace. It may be a burned impression of a body or a shadow-like figure.

Several of the exhibited photographs follow another route, and the problematic is elevated to the level of the symbol. The body is surrounded by fabrics, plants, scraps of fur, pearls. In these images Woodman establishes a personal symbolic order, an expression of the unconscious imagination. The capacity of the symbols to condense and corrupt meaning is underpinned by Woodman's accurate focusing. It is as if she had left part of the environment untouched. The location is often a messy or abandoned room. There somewhere emerges, conceived and carried out with crystal clarity, a scene that is strongly symbolically charged.

Hufvudstadsbladet 2 April 1993

Gerhard Richter
Moderna Museet, Stockholm

Shameless Freedom

At its opening in 1958 Moderna Museet showed Picasso's much-discussed work *Guernica*. The circle is closed, Gerhard Richter's retrospective exhibition, comprising some hundred works, will be the museum's last in the old building. After seeing the exhibition I am ready to call this man, educated in the classic art of painting, one of the most significant painters of our time, which of course raises many questions. What are the criteria for such a verdict, what motivates the nomination vis-à-vis Richter?

To begin with I cannnot refrain from speaking of the *experience*, wandering around among Richter's work does offer an unusually delicate experience. Also, the exhibition is exquisitely hung, as a result of the collaboration between the curator Kaspar König and Richter. Secondly, to analytically demonstrate Richter's significance is a multi-layered undertaking, and doomed to fail if it is not anchored in Richter's unique painterly qualities. Several of the tools used for analysing contemporary art suddenly become twisted and impossible to use as we face Richter's work. Already an expression like 'contemporary painting', or our habit of treating the 'development of painting' in a linear fashion, with headlines like Turn of the Century Painting, the Modernist Break-Through, Postmodern Disintegration, is threatened. This is one of Richter's many merits. The insight that the exhibition gives into painting is unpredictable and it is no doubt brought about by the artist's passionate relation to his medium.

It is impossible to demonstrate Richter's significance by referring to just one of the works as the summit of his painterly investigation. This circumstance hides Richter's uniqueness, the way in which he handles his medium implies an interesting touch of shamelessness; Richter paints in different styles, he goes in and out of them and he uses them in parallel. Photo-realism, landscape painting, abstract expressionism, portraits of people and 'portraits' of colours all occur. The controversial streak is therefore not visible in the expression, in the work itself, but it is manifested through the shameless freedom Richter has adopted in relation to the value-laden hierarchies of painting. He is moving transversally and therefore we need about a hundred works to discover Richter's destination: how his deep-rooted disbelief in aesthetic utopias is transformed into a puzzle laden with meaning but with several parallel solutions.

According to my interpretation Richter's use of styles is not an end in itself. I also do not subscribe to the opinion voiced by some writers when they talk about indifference as something typical of Richter's attitude, meaning that he empties his painting of meaning through variations of style and thus depletes his medium. I believe the opposite is true, that the various styles serve Richter as necessary passages for hunting down what he is looking for, that his painting is really to do with excesses around the desire for desire; what is left after you are struck by the insight that it is impossible to paint the object of desire.

Style provides some kind of necessary materialisation which compensates for the void left behind by the absent object. For this reason I do not agree with those who call Richter's attitude distanced. What is present in the paintings gains presence precisely because the whole undertaking is being carried out by one specific person in one specific situation. The beauty we see in Richter's work marks no final point, it seems to be driven onwards and come to life through some inherent wound or non-correspondence. The insight that there is a Richterian moment in the paintings, as strong as it is invisible, is, however, immensely difficult to analytically verify. 'Painting is pure lunacy, but still so meaningful' is what he himself says.

When Richter paints he often uses a photograph as a model. According to one statement he does not paint from the photograph but he wants to paint it. Is this about rehabilitating a memory of something past that would be lost without the act of painting? For instance his landscape paintings are preceded by thousands of photographs, in the final instance it is only very few of them that touch upon something he is looking for, something he did not know he was searching for.

The suite *18 October 1977* which is about the last days in the lives of the Red Army Faction members was painted only in 1988 after he had collected documentary material for years. The greyish-black photo-realist paintings with a specific blurred effect that makes the image fuzzy have been given a room of their own at Moderna Museet where they hang separately. What we see is death. Richter describes a tragic chapter of German contemporary history based exclusively on the fate of a few people.

That Richter has attained full mastery in finding the right level for his sensibility becomes obvious when we study the painting *Betty*, a colour portrait he painted of his young daughter as he was working on *October 18, 1977*. Betty does not show her face, she is sitting with her head half turned-away. Perhaps there is no other possibility than allowing the viewers to see the unsuspecting features of the young woman only in their imagination – after having seen the painting *Death* in which one of the RAF women is lying with a broken neck. When Richter had finished the suite he painted a number of abstract works in red.

Beauty that carries its own damage, concordance uniting disharmonious elements, forms the core of Richter's talent and it is precisely this characteristic that is reinforced by the hanging in the museum's room on the first floor. This little exhibition within an exhibition functions like a picture that leads us right into Richter's path. Down by the stairs, a large painting of a naked woman going down a staircase, next to it a small 'traditional' view of Venice with a boy sitting by a canal, looking into the water. As we mount the stairs we move towards an exquisite depiction of flowers. Inside the room we are directly confronted with the level that Richter's usage of given structures (the repertoire of styles) is aiming at – a temptation to see, search, listen, encounter is awakened.

Up here a well-chosen collection of discordant expressions are united and find a point where we can sense a context that carries meaning. A short description: the portrait of Betty next to 'portraits' of colours, as if taken from a colour chart, the colours are thereafter transferred to and transformed in a small, abstract, expressionist work. Right opposite *Betty* there is a rack carrying four glass panes that can be turned in any direction – Richter's newest work, the *Bach* series, represents another of the exhibition's absolute successes. Huge canvases with paint so thinly applied that we almost see through the coloured film. An analytic mind forgets itself, totally absorbed by *seeing*.

Hufvudstadsbladet 16 April 1994

Interview with the Psychoanalyst Iréne Matthis

Getting acquainted with old, lifeless words anew. Words whose content has stagnated and eventually faded away. In the introduction to her lecture *Strangebody* in Malmö Iréne Matthis immediately opened a forgotten door. What she said was that faith affects the body, that what we imagine and picture also resounds on the bodily level. Among others she refers to Claude Lévi-Strauss who, in his studies of myths, notes the healing power of the word in its ability to name what heretofore remained unaffected.

This was in May. When I went to Stockholm in September to talk with Iréne Matthis I had recently seen Catherine Bigelow's film *Strange Days*, which, at least to me, gave a premonition of the 'revolution of consciousness' that the cyber philosophy may lead to, not least in the relation between verbal language and vision. The main character produces and sells cyberspace tapes, that is, he provides his consumers with experiences that are on the cyber tapes and which are transferred to them by way of a helmet-like machine. The term experience is actually insufficient as a description of what is transferred to the recipient: he *is* the reality of the person who has had the recorder on his head (protected by a wig). As one of the customers in the film says after a trip to cyberspace: he was an 18-year-old girl in the shower; he saw what she saw, felt what she felt; he was identical with her body in the shower scenes. The result is that 'experiences' can be consumed anytime anywhere, and what is consumed can be anything from murder to love – and thereby the philosophical question whether I can feel what you feel loses its basis.

With crystal clarity Matthis analyses my questions about what virtual reality could mean from a psychoanalytic perspective.

Iréne Matthis The principle that material is stored is the same for the brain; what we experience in life is 'stored' in our brain. The decisive difference between what you say about the mechanics of cyberspace and the brain is that when a human being remembers there is movement in the recapitulation; the memory varies in relation to time, situation, place etc. However, we can relate to our memories in different ways, in short: as sign or as symbol. The sign works in the same way as the cyberspace tape, where the relation between the sign and what it refers to is direct. We could say that the sign adheres to the situation. The symbol, on the other hand, has taken a step further, to an abstract level: it does not revoke the situation as such but the concept. So, the symbol revokes the memory of the situation, which means that we can play with it, giving us a sense of distance. The sign is irrevocably fixed like a skin, whereas the symbol is like a dress that we can take on and off on our own accord.

Rita Roos What you say about the difference between sign and symbol makes me think of the tendency which is visible in art today: young artists are concerned with 'the real object', they are trying to establish a direct relation with reality. For example in what is called trash and slacker art. To my mind, the problem is that the project often fails; the work remains dumb, excludes dialogue. Could this come from the fact that the works adhere to something which doesn't open up to communication?

Matthis Yes, it is difficult to communicate with the sign. I'm thinking of the conceptual artist's pragmatic exercise in space, where he tries to find out why things should be in one particular way rather than in another, i.e. he has to find the exact way the work is going to function in space, because the sign is directly linked with the body; it speaks directly to us without our having to understand the work of art as such.

Roos Then one could say that what I called a failure in trash and slacker art is caused by the artist's not being able to make the sign communicate outside the body; it doesn't reach the spectator.

How do you think that cyberspace will affect our way of seeing and thinking? I recently heard someone describing time in virtual reality as 'dream time'.

Matthis That it will affect us is clear. If we enter virtual spaces as if they existed in real time they will, when we leave them, colour the way we see the world since what we experience stays in the brain. But it is of course difficult to imagine how this will be – just as it is difficult for us to imagine a completely oral culture. In his book *Orality and Literacy* Walter J Ong describes how such cultures function. Mnemonists in Africa, for example, worked by erasing and changing the story; the same story was never told twice. The way a historical event was described was different from what it is in our culture. Events could for example be described as flows, using the river as a model. Consequently time was thought of in spatial terms, since they knew space even if they could not grasp time itself. 'New virtual reality' will perhaps provide us with a new way of seeing and thinking, as

35

time becomes spatial again. We end up with a visual embodiment of memory and time.

Roos What are you currently doing in your theoretical work?

Matthis In short, it can be described as the relation between body and language; the leap or the gap between body and mind. For patients the psychosomatic symptom is a kind of sign that adheres to the body and directs the mental processes. If the sign is successfully transformed into a symbol there may be change, since the symbol has many values. Thus interpretation is an abstraction of the sign that brings it into the symbolic level, where there is change. It is this leap from body to language that I am trying to map. The leap can be seen on many levels, for example in the relation between the patient and the doctor, the man and the hysterical woman. Hysterical symptoms reveal the gap between body and mind. In hysteria, suffering is a negation, a sign of a denial to which the body has been exposed. To get hold of this and symbolise it is only possible in relation to others, when we aim at someone outside.

Paletten 2–3 1996. Translated by Philip Landon

Ars 95, Museum of Contemporary Art, Helsinki
Interview with Anish Kapoor

Extending the Moment of Trust

Anish Kapoor, born 1954 in Bombay, to an Indian father and a Jewish Iraqi mother. After his education as an artist in London in the 70s Kapoor worked in Great Britain, frequently appearing in the international context. Kapoor has added 'something' to sculpture; something at the same time simple and totally suggestive. Particularly in recent years we have encountered a deep blue, dark, unlimited hole in his work. At *Ars 95* we now have the opportunity to see his work *My Body Your Body* (1993).

Roos I have a simple example of the way in which your works evoke the fundamental verbs – to see, to look at, to perceive. Often we may wonder what the viewer actually sees and how he sees, but in front of your works we get the feeling it is possible to share something; what I see coincides with what you see.

Kapoor A large part of my works during the latest seven years have dealt with the membrane – the surface of an object – the point of contact between the object and the world. The confusion that exists about the relation between the body and the eye, the hand and the eye I connect precisely to the surface as skin, hide, envelope – something that looks very real but is not necessarily so in reality, or perhaps it looks unreal but is actually very simple. The question mark is always there: where is the beginning, where is the end? And we encounter linguistic problems; it is not possible to describe this in words since it contains a purely abstract dimension, illusory and evasive, which lives in our fantasy. What interests me is that abstraction on this level becomes impure, that it becomes vulgar when the body enters into the picture. And it is when the body enters that this becomes really interesting. Do you see what I mean?

Roos I remember a thought I had when I read a text about your works – discussions have mostly been about the void (the hole). In an interview you said that it is the viewer who must make the decisive choice: to descend or not into the enticing, sucking depth. But we do not descend, since where we will end up is unclear, descending into the hole presupposes an idea of what will come next, fantasies of a post-condition. Your works with a dark, infinite hole describe this without words. Somewhere you have said that you wish to tell 'another' story, a narrative without sequence; in a way we could say that the ideas about descending into the hole are about another kind of narrativity.

Kapoor A lot is being said nowadays about the void, as if the whole mythology of descent were a new discovery – the Platonic notion of Man in the cave, Christ's journey to limbo, or Edvard Munch's route to the brink of madness. These are, in a way, all images of what we see as the negative side of the psyche. I believe there is another form for this, which is as enigmatic but not as negative. It could actually be a question about a positive disappearance, a downward journey in the positive sense. But the problem is that when we speak like this we end up too close to a kind of religious language.

Roos A positive version of descending into the unknown? I cannot believe that anyone could imagine that possibility without relating the movement to a place, because what is built into the psyche from the very beginning is the insight that we have been dependent on another person. If we see things like this, we could possibly say that the fear is to do with a possible loss of our context that in some strange way is 'keeping us filled', giving us a concept of extension and duration in time.

Kapoor I once met a person in Greece whose father was a psychoanalyst who used LSD to bring people back to their experience before birth, and the son had also been there. I tried to talk to him about how it was.

At least this is a perfect idea of the return or descent. Finally he could only confirm that he really was unable to give real words to the experience although he knew what it felt like. And I did not understand more than earlier – what we can do is only to talk metaphorically about this subject.

Roos Yes, religion does that, and in different cultures there are different rituals to take care of this silent area. But on the other hand, this is not your problem since your area is visuality. You can for instance visualise the kind of experience that your Greek friend was unable to describe in words.

Kapoor First of all we lack a verbal language for this, and secondly we also have no visual language to stick to. The best we have is a kind of in-between, inexact space. What I try to suggest is that there is something more exact than inexactitude, and I think... When we think of all those stories by Dante, all the stories of dark descent; they become obvious the moment we start dealing with the subject physically. As a visual artist I really do not have to carry with me the mythological luggage, it appears by itself. I believe that as I become more secure in what I am trying to do I have less use for the mythological, since it is there anyway.

Roos But, referring to your works, is it plausible that you work after all with certain boundaries around abstraction? The visual process is not totally open; even if abstraction is given enormously free reins on one level, visualisation presupposes very exact boundaries.

Kapoor What is interesting with sculpture is that when it ends up in space it becomes theatrical. It becomes narrative out of necessity, because we have this or that moment and we are walking around in space and different sequences and moments occur. What I try to do is to limit this aspect as much as possible. Thus almost all the works I have made are frontal, we stand right in front of it and there it is, the work. What I have in mind is reducing the narrative moment to one single perspective, to a minimum. The reason is very simple. When we apply a limitation and use only one direction the time aspect enters into the picture. Time does not become symmetrical but it belongs to a state of mind. This state of mind is in turn anchored in a moment of presence, it is a question of a very, very present moment. The sublime is *now*, as Baudrillard was explaining in the 60s.

Roos Perhaps the primary basis of frontality is related to a psychological development, to a face-to-face contact, or more exactly to mirroring?

Kapoor A relation where we are face to face, not in front of or behind, is a receptive state, and that is important for my works. The sublime is here, right now, and thus the downward descent towards something else becomes embodied, it exists only in the relation and through the relation. Then we can say that the sublime does not exist in abstraction but only in a certain moment, for a certain time.

Roos A short summary of your work *My Body Your Body* (1993) here in Helsinki – as viewers we wonder: how far inside do we dare to go?

Kapoor My intention is to extend precisely this moment, since after a while we figure out how the void works technically, we turn it into something we can understand. I am immensely interested in trying to prolong the moment of trust in what we see, how long can it become? One moment of belief – we believe in what we see and forget to understand. It is approximately like catching a glimpse of a small child's magnificent face. We are positively struck by wonder, what a thing! Then, of course, we look at it as any child and the moment is gone.

Roos One last question. I am curious of how it was to be seventeen years old and come to London after having grown up in Bombay.

Kapoor I was nineteen really, because I spent two years in Israel. Quite difficult. I do not know why but it was rather disorienting. Everything felt surprisingly familiar and incredibly alien, confusing. I had grown up in a context where the only possibility, if you wanted to become an artist, would have been to follow some kind of western avant-garde model, but in terms of my own experiences there was no point in doing that. It felt external. It was only after I had figured out a way of dealing with the implications of being Indian that I could find a language that was meaningful to me and my experiences. Now I am in a position where the issue of being Indian or not is not decisive, it is totally irrelevant for what I am doing since language here has its own foundation.

Roos So you had no model whatsoever for how to act as an artist, no tradition to fall back on, when you came to London?

Kapoor That is true, there was simply no model to apply. There were, of course, artists like On Kawara, but On Kawara was working in the avant-garde tradition. There was Nam June Paik who had then made a few films, but still in that tradition. And then there was Naguchi who took a few steps outwards, but still very carefully. But the time was right for an opening that was to apply to the whole cultural frame. The hermetic view of culture was dissolved, and this happened everywhere, simultaneously, in music, theatre, visual art.

Siksi 1/1995

Lone Høyer Hansen
Nordic Arts Centre, Helsinki

Towards Unarticulated Form

An inspection of Lone Høyer Hansen's works reveals that a capacity for change is their dominant quality. The works look different from each other, they do not seem to be starting from a homogenous visual expression. If we want to look for a point of departure for her sculptural investigation it thus exists on another level than the formally visual. This, by the way, is something that characterises young Danish sculpture in general.

During the tour among Høyer Hansen's sculptures the same question constantly comes back. Is there a plausible starting point that could summarise the heterogeneous without forcing it into an analysis that reduces its complexity? At the same time it is difficult to ignore the fact that Høyer

Hansen's investigation of sculpture follows certain tracks, as if it was searching for something, possibly expressible as a kind of visualisation or concretion of the non-logical state of things.

In a recent interview Høyer Hansen says that she enrolled at the Art Academy in Copenhagen (1980–85) because Willy Ørskov was teaching sculpture there. She had read his book *Reading Objects* and liked it, partly because Ørskov gave sculpture a language and partly because his starting point was always in the real world. If we interpret the notion of the real completely literally it would connect more closely with what is visible in Høyer Hansen's works from the 80s, for instance in *Pascal* or *Still Life* where the building blocks consist of everyday objects. But in relation to her sculptural investigation as such the real has a relevance that transcends the recognisable objects. The sculptures do not engage in metaphysical speculations about bodies and forms but they can generally be related to the real world, because Høyer Hansen manages to put sculpture into an existence parallel to that of reality. Reality consists of bodies and voids, since perception in itself insists that bodies exist, and perception is the base from which we begin to draw conclusions when we are reasoning about the unknown, to quote a passage from Epicurean philosophy where the complexity of the real is summarised in a very non-dramatic way. In Høyer Hansen's works the sculpture becomes a body that equals our own body in space, but with the difference that the sculpture also embodies the unknown, the non-logical state of things, by making this seem like a reality among others.

The realisation, the embodiment of an immaterial state in Høyer Hansen's latest work, goes hand in hand with how her articulation of form has developed. In the works from the 80s with the everyday objects the articulation could be called a kind of redoubling, a repetition of a well known object placed in a context that pushes the significance in a certain direction. If we compare this to language we would be talking about the issue of submitting to the symbolic (in the Lacanian sense). After Høyer Hansen excluded everyday objects the development has been towards an unarticulated form, a form which does not univocally submit to the symbolic, which does not signify itself by clarifying itself but instead represents an undivided state where the subject is not given but generated.

The work *Fools' Portraits* (1990) consists of a constellation of extended shapes that we envisage as indications of long, bowed necks with heads whose faces remain constantly turned away. The frozen mimicry of the invisible faces appears to be skewed in relation to the connection between the figures' necks and heads. Despite the sculptures' persistent presence and concretion in space there is nothing to rule out the perception that the *Fools' Portraits* could just as well be seen as the reminiscence of a momentary quickly-passing sense of being lost, incapable of finding the redeeming words.

The *Puntello* works (1993) consist of two parts: regularly shaped iron boxes with a shining surface and softly shaped bronze lumps balancing next to, beside or on top of the iron box through a point of contact that makes the whole thing look unreasonably fragile. This frailty, the feeling that the bronze lump will be unsettled by the faintest shake, is the seed for a clash between the stable 'minimalist' form and the unarticulated disturbance. The minimalist body is subjected to something that is stronger than the objective, rational and measurable, as if a desiring subject were inserted to draw attention to the possibilities generated by a becoming.

Hufvudstadsbladet 16 October 1993

Jussi Niva and Nina Roos
Sara Hildén Art Museum, Tampere, 1994

A Shared Joy Is a Double Joy

Sharing Space

Even though spatiality has been a key word in analyses of Jussi Niva and Nina Roos's works, I now propose to set it aside. What interests me is the continuation, what will happen when their works share a space at the Sara Hildén Art Museum.

When Jussi Niva and Nina Roos meet to plan the exhibition, I have a question ready in my back pocket: What is the reason behind your putting on a show together? I, nevertheless, soon forgot to ask my question, absorbed as I was in listening, not so much to the content of what they were saying, but to the way they communicated. The medium was not really language, but their works, and I felt like an outsider. I noticed that, with time, the works had been given various designations and nicknames that were new to me. The situation was most reminiscent of one in which two people who have known each other for years spend time together in a common pursuit involving a to them self-evident plane of shared insights.

On the next occasion we saw each other I asked my question. Pause. Plus a laconic answer from Niva.

Jussi Niva Because we wanted to see our works together. Both Nina and I have a need to see our own works interacting with works that have, in a way, from the start lived in parallel with our own work. And then there is a satisfaction that may well await the viewer when the exhibition is ready, and the works have to cope and live on each other's terms. Nina is in fact the only artist whose works have sparked off an immediate desire to have them communicate with my own. Right from the start, we wanted to keep away from concepts, headings, themes, names, curators. We have been working on this exhibition in various different ways for two years now. As I said before there is a mutual need and desire to have the works spend time together.

Rita Roos So we will have to wait and see what happens. Since you both 'actualise' spatiality in your art, I imagine a kind of fruitful cross-current in the real space, which will accentuate the slippage between the physical dimensions of reality and the mental image's infinite potential for transformations.

Childhood

Rita Roos Tell me about a memorable episode from your childhood?

Jussi Niva I remember when my eyes were first opened to Nina's work. She was then in her final year at the Academy of Fine Arts, and was working with a bright green paint. Whenever I looked in she pointed to different parts of the paintings, and wondered with a feeble hopefulness whether it wasn't beginning to look 'wrong'? Isn't it slanting? Soon afterwards she abandoned the canvas, found the zinc sheet, and got a grip on 'wrongness'.

Nina Roos Your description must be about my attempts to find my own 'crime scene', i.e. a place for my paintings where I could to an extent break away from what I saw as a barrier, painting with a capital P, and to an extent could embark on an investigation on my own terms. By the way, Jussi, I associate your childhood works with paintings with organic motifs. They were flowers, weren't they?

Jussi Niva I very soon got tired of the organic shell and fungus shapes. The background, what was secondary, suddenly began to fascinate me, and I began to develop it as a separate visual object. The outcome was that the paintings in the form of wall panels invade the real space in a physical way.

One-Eyed

Rita Roos Now I want to hear the story about how you missed the coffee cup.

Jussi Niva On the journey I developed a bad eye inflammation, and while it was being treated my right eye was completely covered for a whole day. I had to manage with my wrong eye, wrong in the same way as if somebody right-handed had to write with his left hand. Suddenly I didn't understand familiar, safe three-dimensionality. With only one eye I could not get an idea of short distances. I was trying to get hold of objects before they were even in reach, I stepped into empty space on the stairs, and stumbled on level ground. These situations were like flashes of two-dimensio-nality, from which you had to try to construct the reality of space. In the same way as one-or-other-handedness determines the logic of doing things with your hands, one-or-other-sightedness plays an essential role in crea-ting three-dimensionality.

Rita Roos On that subject, I wonder whether the *I Spy With My Eyes* series is a kind of journey into the mysteries of perception? You especially produced monochrome paintings for authentic situations and then photographed the scene.

Jussi Niva I photographed the *I Spy* works using a panorama camera. The pictures it makes correspond to the situation of a viewer in motion, with the picture being formed equally by things that have already been seen and passed, as by the things in front of you. It is more of a sweep of the view, which at the same time coordinates distances and the relationships between sizes, rather than constructing details. The normal one-eyed lens focuses more while a panorama living room can be looked at as a picture in itself. It corresponds naturally to the situation when you are in the room. You know, for example, how to move around there. The paintings I made take up their own position in each room. They are actually one-eyed aids to forming an idea of distances by measuring or covering up, an attempt to change the situation.

The Eye and the Marianne Caramel

Rita Roos Jussi Niva's works contain an intermediary, the concept of an instrument is articulated. Visuality is handled pragmatically, despite the fact that there is no reason to use that word about the result, the actual works. Whatever the case, when Niva works he has no need of the unpredictability of practice, the process behaves relatively rationally and clearly. In this sense, you are both each other's opposite.

Nina Roos It is hard to make comparisons and to analyse differences, but there are dissimilarities. I could try to explain this by using a 'symptom' I have been thinking about. I don't have a driving licence, and I don't intend to get one. The reason is both very simple and complex. When you drive a car you are forced to react motorically to the surrounding world, by reading it through a certain set of codes, signal colours, traffic signs, patterns of movement. It would quite simply be impossible for me (and very probably dangerous) to conform to this kind of visual control. My painting is the opposite, to orient myself again and again in a spatiality in which there is no given place from which I myself or what is outside me can be zoomed in on. I can't separate or screen off visuality, what comes in through my eyes, from other kinds of sensory perception. That is why paint is my medium, paint in itself already contains an inexhaustible potential. And then comes the challenge of using it, and at the same time excluding and avoiding things that are visually recognisable. For example, the other day, when I was painting and was focusing on a red streak on white paint, I got a real taste of Marianne caramel in my mouth.

Rita Roos It sounds as though you were in a borderline situation of meaning. This usually refers to two types of situation, either a state in which there is not yet any meaning, or another in which it can no longer be expressed. I wonder whether in your painting this could involve a third variant, made possible precisely by the fact that your practice is not verbal, but that of painting. So, what interests me is that, even if we, as viewers faced with your paintings, can experience a 'borderline situation of meaning', it is at the same time possible to establish communication with the work. We are not left outside. My idea is that this is not a matter of a state before the sign or after the dissolution of the sign, but a third alternative, a parallel communication occurring alongside what happens on the symbolic level. A communication in which the symbols are replaced by handholds in the specific materiality of painting.

Nina Roos Sounds reasonable, but with the reservation that you are not going to refer to Julia Kristeva's ideas about the relationship between creativity and the mother's body, or rather to the loss of it. Despite the fact that it is not my job to interpret my paintings, this terminology makes me a shade sceptical?

Rita Roos In what way sceptical?

Nina Roos Quite simply because a term like, for example, the mother's body is far too visual and concrete (even if it is also an abstraction) when referring to painting. Then we are again stuck in the network of representation via language, on a level I try to get away from, i.e. from images in painting. Somehow going in reverse.

Rita Roos Seriously, what I am thinking of here is related to the concept of estrangement. Since, in Lacanian terminology, our knowledge of the world is founded on imaginary identification (via mirroring), we end up in a state of estrangement. Our self is actually based on something that exists outside ourselves. What I would claim is that your paintings avoid alienation. We can as though become assimilated into them, enter into them via the senses. They function as fixed points for a kind of surprising assimilation, completely independent of the laws of symbolic representation. I relate the spatial disorientation you work with to a removal of precisely the boundary that separates off, and at the same time creates, the self, and thereby also the Other, the place we speak from. The paintings realise a sensory utopia, the perception of being able to move about and orient oneself unhindered, because there is no outside. A making real that is impossible according to the principles of logic.

Nina Roos I understand. But that does not go against the fact that I am concerned with clarity. Not as a simplification, but as a split-second realisation of a moment in which a physically experienced clarity, a painted one, is transmuted like a nerve impulse into something else. For me this is true realism.

Narrow and Broad. Thick and Thin

Difference as the prerequisite for communication, to see both one thing and another, even though they are neither alike nor unlike each other. Jussi Niva measures and calculates sizes, distances and proportions. At Kluuvi Gallery in 1990 he showed his *Measuring Instruments*, and the viewer could take a direct step into the dynamics of procedure. Niva's colour vision also conforms to boundaries that are carefully tested. As though through the application of paint to a snowy landscape in *Snow-Clad*, or through the rainbow in *Borrowed Landscape*, we were able to participate in an extreme visuality. The eye here virtually exists for the experience of physical presence.

In Japanese culture the relationship to the unfamiliar is expressed using words like 'thick' and 'thin'. Handy words to use in a culture where relations to the stranger are dealt with through a form of assimilation instead of a drawing of boundaries. When something from outside becomes too much – too thick – the Japanese person makes it thinner, he cuts away and creates a new shape. When, in response to Nina Roos's painting, I think of the word 'materiality', I specifically associate it with the simplicity of the way, that in switching between thick and thin the paint constantly gives the painting fixed points. In Roos's way of working with paint and acrylic sheet there is a built-in guarantee that the vanishing of boundaries will not become the same as an encounter with the void. As long as we sense, sense thick and thin, we are physically present.

The Artist and the Working Method

Eva Löfdahl's artistic activity has been a directional force in Swedish art during the 80s. An intellectual approach, connections between the literary and the visual, a focus on certain strategic terms (for example 'disjunction', 'the ordinary', 'in-between spaces' and 'in-between territories'), these were characteristic features of the Swedish 80s. Groups like Wallda and ibid. now already have a legendary ring to them. The Wallda artists, comprising Max Book, Eva Löfdahl and Stig Sjölund, had a studio in common at Årsta in the early 80s and there, among other things, they staged a series of cabaret performances. Löfdahl was also one of the participants in the exhibition *ibid. II* at Münchenbryggeriet in Stockholm.

It is impossible to make a short presentation of Löfdahl's art, since it is characterised by surprises, sudden turns and constant change in terms of execution and outward appearance. The technique and the medium keep changing; Löfdahl has worked with painting, objects, sculpture etc. Still, when you follow her production through the years a totality becomes visible, or an area of coherence somewhere 'beyond' or 'beneath' the exterior. When I met with Eva Löfdahl for a conversation, it was these levels that I was most curious about. What is her artistic process and method? How does the intention look in relation to the result? And what paths do her thoughts follow?

Roos There is an interesting and exceptional feature that characterises your works throughout and makes them 'stick' immediately, so to speak. Nothing remains unclear in the relation between what we see and what we commit to memory. Can you comment on this?

Löfdahl It's incredibly important for me to be this clear, that the complication is not there. Because if there is a complication in seeing as such, in the process of perception, we often believe that we have reached the goal when we finally discover what is unclear. If the work is simple enough for us to immediately see that, and also to remember our memory of this image, then we can process it afterwards in a completely different way. And since the idea itself is a rather complex construct – formally and informally, linguistically and non-linguistically – with many mixed levels, everything would disappear if we didn't have this clarity to pin it down to. What I do would disappear in the world, it wouldn't stick anywhere at all.

Roos But how does something appear? What does this process look like?

Löfdahl This is a two-way action. Many times I have an idea about structure. Yes, perhaps structure is the best word, although it's very vague. Such a structure may, just like the structure of poetry, consist of different components. There can be a plane of meaning, a formal plane, a rhythmical plane, a dynamic plane. And when I sense what I'm interested in I look for it. I can also analyse retrospectively if I become very fascinated with something. I was touched by this thing or another, why is that? What qualities made me interested in this particular thing?

Roos So it's in an early stage that you consciously start making choices and analysing them?

Löfdahl The process is, in a way, happening all the time. It's difficult to delineate the beginning of a specific thing. In a way it's as simple as 'what am I interested in?' Nothing more complicated than that. If we take the word permeability, for example. There's something about permeability that interests me. Another quality I have been preoccupied with is acceleration, or rather the moment that appears when an airplane stops accelerating and stabilises a little instead. But I guess it's only through execution that what I'm saying becomes intelligible. If I just drop words like permeability, airplanes, acceleration, bottomless vessels or tasseled caps they will be out of context.

Roos In general, your artistic practice seems to be moving along a plane where critical moments are encountered. You catch hold of something that doesn't construct itself logically, but still visually functions like a logical construction. You make objects that we perceive as upside-down, or you evoke mirror effects that aren't based on a logically correct situation. When the construction is complicated, how far can you control the intention in relation to the result?

Löfdahl Well, I do think I can reach a decision, that I can judge whether something is right or not, without fully shifting my problems onto a verbal plane. This is part of that double-sidedness we talked about in the beginning. I'm after something but it's not until I do a self-analysis of the response to different things that I become fully aware of what that first thing was. Earlier I worked more methodically, taking lots of photographs. I noticed only afterwards, when I looked at the films, that I had taken the same picture, for example, eight times. Then it's obvious that I'm after some specific quality that exists there. Why this repetition otherwise?

Roos What we spoke about here, could you call that a kind of method you use for your artistic work?

Löfdahl Yes, I guess that's exactly what I've been describing. In addition, I collect certain objects and constellations that I know are somehow good and that I might find useful later.

Hufvudstadsbladet 5 November 1992

Sounds in White Rabbit Fur. A Theory of the Visuality of Sound

Theories of sound became particilarly current when early 20th century phoneticians tried to analyse its individual elements, thereby also shedding light on language. This led to diverging paradigms of knowledge: another kind of knowledge emerged. I refer to structuralist thought and the shock waves that continue to surge as our split knowledge is disseminated. Much of the credit falls on Jacques Lacan, who revised Freud's idea of the part-object, adding two more: the gaze and the voice.

The gaze and the voice, the voice and sound – in everyday life, scopic and vocal powers come together to create more stimulation than the senses can ever bring up to the level of meaning-creation. This blunting of the senses may well be the only real form of trance available to us, given what we are: over-stimulated receivers, mechanical senders. You need something like the drug ecstasy for aural, spatial and bodily presence to reach a devotional intensity.

The metro was shuddering along somewhere between Prince Street and 11th Street. Having spent the whole spring travelling this line, I was presumably quite advanced in my trance training, increasingly adept at blocking out the external world, at fading out mentally. The words 'I' and 'me' are shouted so frequently and so loudly that stories of mechanical self-corroboration drown each other out, creating a grotesque 'self-body'. A noise, as opposed to a voice, virtually indistinguishable, unidentifiable, broke the surface for a fraction of a second. I didn't know what it was or where it came from. In any case, the point is, my body reacted instantaneously, with rapt attention. The sound was like heavy sobbing, or a tiny sigh. My entire consciousness was struggling to locate the origin, the source of this noise. A Chinese woman was sitting in the same car, with a quantity of white rabbit fur on her arm. It was her hands, the gentleness with shich she handled the fur, that gave it away: swaddled inside the fur was a small baby.

This incident precipitated my interest in sound and in the origin of sound – its derivation from the symbiotic condition of the Chinese baby, huddled close to its mother, protected by the warmth of the rabbit fur and the mother's hands. The mother reacted to the baby's sounds with her movements, fine-tuning their shared spatial condition. With regard to the visual arts, Lacan's text of the mirror stage has had a decisive influence on psychoanalytic criticism over the past twenty years. It is the image = self that consitutes the illusory self, by means of which we more or less successfully detach ourselves from the place inside the white rabbit fur. As we know, the real is that which cannot be symbolised, or subsumed by the linguistic order. I believe this is precisely why creativity vis-à-vis visual language can be so satisfying and powerful, can genuinely fulfill the desire for wholeness, which, in contrast with the substitutive function of the part-object, need not necessarily lead back to a sense of lack.

It is the lack-transcending capacity that interests me in sound. Visual language has an in-built potential to replenish the cup of emptiness. On the other hand, sound can reawaken us by becoming an agent of the spatial condition (two bodies as one) we experienced in symbiosis. Two bodies in the closest possible interaction, the ear that listens to the sound of the heart, breathing, a single meaningful voice, the mother's. The interaction between mother and child continues even though the physical distance between them varies. This shows that the communication entails a spatial dimension, and facilitates sensations in interaction with others. This original scene, I believe, is what gives sound its visuality, and generally underpins our future relation to the world of sound.

I know a trained dancer from Helsinki who is both deaf and dumb, but who nevertheless dances to music. He says he visualises the sound, which he sees through the vibrations that his body receives from the sound waves in the room. In other words, his ability to dance rests precisely on the interactive representation-world that is experienced in symbiosis. Specific experiences from the real provide reference-points for creativity taking place outside the symbolic order. The only precondition is to do with physical space: the floor must be elastic enough for the dancer to be able to feel how his bodily movements interact with the vibrating sound.

Another example: by playing the *fort – da* game with a reel of cotton, the child acquires a symbol for the void of absence, i.e. the absence of the mother. At the same time, however, behind the symbol, the 'object' fades away: the mother's body is absent, has disappeared, yet its place is marked by a symbol, just as a headstone marks the resting-place of the deceased. According to psychoanalyst Iréne Matthis's book on Lacan, this is a nutshell-image of the process of becoming human. The subject is born in the act of naming an absence. And at the same time, the subject – like the object itself – disappears behind the symbol that emerges in its place as a supplier of meaning: the Word, a Signifier.

What I want to believe vis-à-vis sound is the opposite: that the world of sound has an inherent potential to recreate the space where the 'object' has not yet faded away – a condition that partakes of the visuality resulting from the presence of the shape of the body-in-the-*ur*-body, that is, the original *gestalt* – the First One.

Siksi 4/1996. Translated by Mike Garner

Ernst Mether-Borgström
Monograph, Otava, Helsinki 1996

Listen a Second Time, Carefully

Four years ago I wrote for the first time about Ernst Mether-Borgström's work. I recall my eagerness at the insight opened up by the works. Sometimes clarity occurs with lightning speed. Mether-Borgström's gouaches convinced me that the instance of interpretation misses the gap, those moments in a painting or an artistic career that do not fit the frames of the category (the -ism) at hand. Reading about Mether-Borgström's art within the model of 'the new image', i.e. the breakthrough of Modernism, is something other than following the visual thread Mether-Borgström has worked with, well, ever since he began his art education in the late 1930s.

This starting point is a construction too. Who can really make a final analysis of how an artistic œuvre begins and for what reason? Not to mention the impossibility of determining an artist's specific visual thinking. Mether-Borgström's laconic statement, made during a conversation this spring, seems almost ironical in relation to the accepted definition of concrete art – an art totally liberated from direct impressions and representations of nature: 'Since I was a little boy I have been interested in biology and being in nature.'

Another fragment falls into place. I recall the sketches I have seen, where Mether-Borgström draws totem poles with a symbolic language showing life as an organic, structured form, and the drawings with circus themes where the rhythm and the movements follow the circular shape of the arena. When an artist is interested in organised forms, such as the structures in nature, we may also sense that he is interested in working with different degrees and levels of visualising forms. Or, put differently, that the relation between figurative and non-figurative art is a challenge; degrees on the same scale, not an essential opposition. If we look at a piece of nature in a microscope we no longer see picturesque colour but well-ordered systems of cells. The difference concerns the way we see and how we choose to convey it.

Concerning Mether-Borgström's interest in nature I wanted to know a little more, is he attracted by something special? Again, I received a clear answer: the smells. Smell, form, movement and colour. 'I use the colours as tools, to make them live against each other and match them so they create fields of energy that affect the viewer.'

We who write have a lot to learn. To dare to leave behind the security of applying a readymade model on an artist's work and instead to turn around the problem of interpretation with the question, What model for thinking, life, reality, painting, can a specific artist's work provide us with?

Mether-Borgström's works awaken the need to adjust a favourite term, often used in connection with concrete art: form. A nuanced proposition, adequate for Mether-Borgström's practice, could possibly be a notion of form that cannot be reduced to geometrical outlines but is instead associated with a complex piecing together of visual elements in such a way that it addresses all our senses at the same time. If we think like this we come a little closer to a description of Mether-Borgström's artistic register. Among his sculptures there is a group he calls 'semaphore-mobiles'. The semaphore-mobile is powered by an engine that rotates it in one minute. During this minute it passes through four different stages where the 'colour and form pieces' shape four different constellations. We could therefore say that a semaphore-mobile produces four different dynamic interactions. Mether-Borgström, interested in exploring what is new and always prepared to leave the habitual behind, succeeds in his intentions. It is as if his works, each one of them, become permanent structures for perception and above all for how we perceive the relation between figure and ground. When Mether-Borgström fills the surface of the canvas in his larger-format paintings, for instance *Sirius*, we stand in front of a unique cosmos. The laws it obeys are unknown and at the same time highly pleasurable for our senses to explore.

For his exhibition at Galerie Artek in 1977 Mether-Borgström published *7 Theses*. In them we read, among other things, the following:

> We expect the wrong things from art, we have entered through the wrong door. Art works indirectly, it affects the source. We must start anew, from the beginning. Visual art must first of all be aware of its limits and its mission, it must protect its identity. It has its own 'niche' to live from in the intellectual ecology.
>
> We should feel our limitations, not allow ourselves to be incorporated by elements that are alien to our specific sector. Our medium is colour and form and what we can express with their help; not words, not technology, not sensation or show, not superficial decoration, to take but a few examples from the rich array of misunderstandings that art has been guilty of.

In 1995 this deserves to be re-read. An eye-opener. Above all the hidden certainty that emerges from the text fragments, that visual art is about something specific, essentially different from other expressions. Not words – Mether-Borgström is right. The relationship of images to words is an issue that has been given much attention in the theoretical discourse of recent years. The difference between them is important. Words, and particularly theoretical discourse, are intended directly for a conversational partner, another person, while visual art acts in a different way. It springs from an action, the action through which the artist has created his image. Thus the artistic medium is, at the same time, an activating passage that opens communication with the viewer. The specificity of an artwork is, therefore, not only to do with general circumstances of its medium, but very much with how the artist has used, down to the smallest detail, his chosen tools. With this I mean, for instance, the way in which Mether-Borgström's paintings are capable of holding on to the presence of the painting act. The trace can be a small gap between two colour fields, a *punctum* in the shape of a surprising, crooked line or an unexpected 'Mether-Borgströmian' choice of colour.

Mether-Borgström's œuvre is classical. Its major key is that the works are similar only to themselves, that they are the results of the way the artist has tried to resolve the challenges he has been so fascinated with addressing. Mether-Borgström is still preoccupied with getting ahead. He is busy with thoughts about solving the problems of *alla prima* painting on large canvases.

The question that preoccupies me, and that I leave open, is to do with how we could express in words what is specifically 'Mether-Borgströmian'. Every work is kept alive; when we start to look at it we become lost in Mether-Borgström's cosmos. I start to think about the real meaning of the word classic: to be independent of time, of the here-and-now of the moment, to survive the limitations of real time. Mether-Borgström's work leaves the door open for the viewer, also the future viewer.

The Golden Concept in Function

Collecting and Containing

Marko Vuokola and Pasi Karjula are two Finnish artists who turn up as a collaborative duo from time to time alongside their individual practices. Practice is the most gratifying word for characterising their artistic universe: the visual product, conceptually cultivated and intensified, carries within itself its premise, a concrete process of investigation by means of which the points of fascination and fixation are filtered and separated down to the least possible functional entity.

In the spring of 1994 Marko Vuokola summarised his puzzlement in planning a new work of art in the following terms: I need gold, or more exactly gold thread. How am I to get it? Soon after midsummer Vuokola and Karjula journeyed to Lapland with the stubborn intention of finding enough gold. The intended two-week trip grew to five weeks. They were smitten with gold fever. Travelling to Lapland for this purpose was to prove fruitful in a surprising, complex manner. A gold-digger makes his legend real for it spins a network of silent understanding among the gold-diggers.

Every year when the ice melts the season begins. The gold-diggers arrive, establish their temporary dwellings and set to work. It is hard work, digging, building a conduit in which the water washes away the earth, living more or less in the periphery of the permanent settlement, nourishing oneself with the hope that just this summer one will make a find, discovering the gold nugget that is waiting to be uncovered. Maahinen, the earth's spirit, is also involved. It is necessary to appease her, ruler of the Lappish gold territory. Karjula and Vuokola were careful to keep her in a good temper. For she was the essential condition of the whole project and they conferred on her a special cult-place complete with a wooden sculpture.

Showing, Telling and Relating

The gold-digger's place of work is revelatory. It looks like its creator, marked by his or her peculiarities. The conduits in which the earth is sieved are tailored for each gold-digger. Their function is governed by the dream of gold. One is possessed by the thought of catching such a large nugget that it will be the stuff of legends; another dreams of the finest gold dust while a third is wholly taken up by the search itself. The technical solutions bear the marks of these preoccupations.

Working, Keeping and Holding Close

Legend relates as follows. A man asks a gold-digger why he expends all this effort. Is it really worth all the trouble, for a few grammes of gold, to investigate rock after rock in extreme detail? The prospector does not answer but lays in the hand of the sceptic a tiny piece of gold. Gold gleams; gold is both light and heavy and is also malleable. A single gramme of gold can, with modern technology, be transformed into two and a half kilometres of gold thread.

Gold hides a code that cannot be deciphered and, for this reason, is absolute, perfect in itself. Throughout the ages alchemy has been characterized by a close collaboration between speculative science and the humanities, both metallurgical experiments and philosophical speculations on life's origin and nature. Karjula and Vuokola did not have experience of this. They had not felt the weightless weight of a gold nugget in the hand. When they had experienced this, the mystery took hold of them. Gold is remarkable substance which becomes even more remarkable in conception after five weeks of hard work at Palsinoja in Lapland. Thus, digging for gold is as much a task for the imagination as for the physical body. The Swedish poet Gunnar Ekelöf wrote of the alchemist:

> I seek a worthless gold
> a gold that makes worthless
> gold, all gold!
> With burnt hands I hold
> the crucible in my hand.
>
> Earth, water, air, fire!
>
> It is only when
> the dead and living meet
> that The Great Mistake
> will be apparent.

Form Function 4/1994. Translated by William Jewson

Claude Rutault
Museum of Contemporary Art, Helsinki

Definition/Method No 175 (1989–1990), Excerpts

The art-lover's encounter with contemporary art does not always go well. In the worst case there is no encounter. An eloquent example is Claude Rutault's installation at Studio N. A less-than-attentive visitor risks passing the exhibition without even noticing that there is an installation in the space at hand.

The paradox is that Rutault in his conceptual system expressly addresses the art-lover/collector. Since 1973 Rutault has been writing what he calls definitions/methods, instructions about how to realise a work. Many factors are kept open and it is left to the art-lover/collector to decide about for instance colour, size, placement, material, the number of elements. In his intention the artist is outspoken. He is interested in painting, with emphasis on the act of painting and not carrying out this act. The image Rutault aspires to is liberated from distracting factors like 'beauty', 'representation', 'emotional content' etc.

Rutault's conceptual project places the art world's set of relations (artist, artwork, art-lover/collector/viewer, exhibition institution) in a carefully elaborated system. The artist delegates a participation that can in a way be presented as a tailor-made model of art sociology. Realising the instructions of the definitions/methods may entail for instance a process that continues at regular intervals and ceases only in connection with the death of either the collector or the artist.

In *Definition/Method 69* (1978) we read, among other things, the following: 'Every year a new picture is painted in the same colour as the background wall. Every year the collector chooses the canvas to be painted. Thus the collector will in the second year have two stretched canvases of the same colour as the background wall, in the third year he will have three... For this work a yearly payment is collected. The work takes its final shape when one of the parties – the artist or the collector – dies.'

The system presupposes a problematising attitude in the collector, the exact opposite of those who are haunted by the 'Kantian spectre'. In the tradition of Kant the sole elevated objective of aesthetics was to satisfy taste and thus all other aspects were excluded. In the protocol of taste judgment of a work of art means the same as an unreflecting, natural reaction; judgment is not concerned with the meaning or content of what we see. As a consequence of this there is particular denial of referenced connections between the work and theoretical issues. In an extreme case like Rutault's conceptual installation a similar attitude may lead to the absurdity of the work of art becoming invisible to the viewer.

Rutault's work is labelled *Excerpts* (*extraits* in French). According to the instructions an excerpt must consist of at least six partial works culled from earlier definitions/methods, which in addition must have been realised at least once. The realisation of the excerpts leaves even greater space for movement than the definitions/methods. The process is halted at an early stage, which makes the viewer's responsibility for the final painting bigger; the artist's emphasis is on the unpainted painting. Only one background wall is painted in a red shade with a matching painting in the same colour. On the floor is a pile of coloured paper sheets, from a display case we can select the desired material. The white walls have been subjected to the artist's tests of format and form in pencil.

Continuity of the Elements, Sequences for Realising the Work, The Disappearing Painting are titles for the excerpts that refer to possible problems facing the viewer/creator of the painting proper. *Continuity of the Elements,* for instance, is a work consisting of a series of squares of increasing size. The last square is marked with only one corner – how long can the series continue, or must the last, unfinished square be erased? There is an almost infinite amount of possibilities for variation, serving as a support for the viewer as he begins to tackle the act of painting.

From the critic's angle there is a fascinating point to Rutault's installation. The final result, the painting extracted by the viewer from the excerpts, is inaccessible to all critical scrutiny.

Hufvudstadsbladet 28 February 1992

Silja Rantanen
Kunsthalle Helsinki

The Truth of Painting and the Painter's Contract

When a painting is good it surpasses the word and is separated from the word, it is at the same time a name and yet more than a name. Interpretation, the act of naming, is thus from the beginning condemned to occupy a more or less failed position in relation to the work. The risk of reduction is burningly close; the work is sacrificed and becomes an object of theory, which begins to predetermine it rather than the other way round.

There is a simple reason why Silja Rantanen's paintings from the 1983–1993 decade bring about this reflection. Her exhibition offers the possibility to see and understand correlations that are expressly generated by painting, in the relations between the production of the 80s and the 90s. Paintings entitled *Section and Segment of the Cupola* (1983), *Ideal Space* (1985), *Padova* (1985), *Deposizione* (1982–1983) and *Pop Braiding* (1993) are here and now associated by their mutual and interconnected complexity. And there is an element of something I wish to call 'one hundred percent', which is exactly the kind of quality that may become squeezed in the discrepancy between what is done (the painting) and the act of naming (the text).

My precarious coinage 'one hundred percent' becomes even more precarious since my aim is to connect it to a very special understanding of the notion of truth. But first back to the starting point. In her work Rantanen acts like an architect whose primary condition it is to know the foundation. In this case the foundation consists of the conventions of painting, i.e. the agreements that have determined and still determine how pictures are understood: in the Middle Ages, during the Pre-Renaissance, in Japanese art. For Rantanen the study of a Pre-Renaissance painting becomes the point of departure for a subjective contract between the artist and the painting: the space in the picture, the space in the space where the painting is situated and then spatiality turned into a few simple shapes and shining colour, as in the painting *Padova*. As we see there are many possibilities in Rantanen's study of culture, and the results acquire meanings we cannot predict. Patterns, schemes, models, originals are converted into a final point that has one significant quality: it surpasses the motif and the intention. A truth is established and its value cannot be denoted according to similarity with the motif (that which is recognisably depicted) but it is similar only to itself.

When we talk about truth in painting we thus find ourselves in an interesting circumstance: a truth can be recognised even without being similar to something else, something previously given. Its only condition is really what is included in the contract between the artist and painting, and this ideally involves a kind of moral thinking. Rantanen's paintings *Good Will* (1993) and *Good Conscience* (1992) relate to this. Both works are paintings of paintings and they comment on morals and obligations. In the middle we see a yellow field surrounded by thin 'frames' of colour: the unwritten laws. Not to mention the promise in the two works *Come più belli li sapranno fare* ('painting as beautifully as I can', as we are led to understand).

What is truth in visual art differs from the truths of other arts, it is established with other means. Even if this sounds self-evident it is precisely in this respect that a good painter is unpredictable. In Rantanen's latest *Deposizione* (Deposition from the Cross) we see two ladders, each positioned against an arm of the cross, frontally depicted. If we study the two ladders we notice how our own eye tends to impose a normalising untruth – we want to see them as objects standing straight, and we try to see them this way. It is the eye that creates this illusion. It is difficult to immediately accept the truth that the two ladders are actually moving, very slowly, towards each other, ever closer to the centre of the cross. Through minimal degrees of distance, supported by the colour outlines of the object, we arrive at the true or real significance of the work.

The latest works in the exhibition are schematic depictions of how a sweet roll is braided, or this, anyway, is what we want to believe that we are seeing. But the paintings go beyond depiction, the representation is only a means of reaching the level where the real significance is revealed. In the *Pop Braiding* diptych, the depiction of the braided sweet roll is turned into a question about the complexity of painting at one decisive moment. A sequence of the yellowish-orange dough continues on the second half of the painting where the background is violet, and precisely therefore the edges of the sweet roll are painted in a different way: different brushstrokes, a different nuance in comparison with that part of the roll which is situated against the light background. The painting obeys the conditions of painting and suddenly becomes transparent in the sense that depiction itself occupies a secondary position in relation to the thing shown by painting.

Hufvudstadsbladet 1 September 1993

Jussi Niva
Galerie Artek, Helsinki

I Spy with My Eyes

Jussi Niva's exhibition at Galerie Artek provokes sincere curiosity. I remember a moment of reflection during the Venice Biennial, in the summer of 1993, in front of Niva's installation *Borrowed Landscape*. What I speculated about was how feasible it was to try and calculate how Niva's works would develop after this, since if we compare, say, *Borrowed Landscape* with the installation at Documenta in Kassel the year before we find a consistent 'Jussi Niva'esque' attitude towards painting. I insist on talking about painting even if photography is part of Niva's installations, for the simple reason that his thinking is composed of painting's primary building blocks: colour, form, surface, space, reality and illusion.

The visual clarity that characterises the works tells us that Jussi Niva is painting's pragmatist *par excellence*. Well-directed execution helps physically articulate and embody the interesting angles, which saves his installations from pure conceptualism. Already in an early stage the word 'mechanics' featured in his work titles, and this of course refers to function and movement. In 1990 Niva wrote, as a commentary to his exhibition at Kluuvi Gallery, a dialogue between a geodetian and a builder in which the two discuss different ways of relating to the same place, based on their common task of building. In the same way that those two discussed the qualities of a place with the purpose of creating concrete and visible results Niva analyses spatiality. His artistic action testifies to conscious control and manipulation of the tools.

A short recapitulation as a guide to the present exhibition at Galerie

Artek. The Documenta work consisted of two parts: a panel painting following the wall's surface and lines and a photograph, authentically depicting this painting in space but in a smaller format. Instead of functioning as a painting the colour field panel felt rather like a palpable physical object that had occupied a corner of the room. Only the distancing effect of the photograph made the painting appear as a painting. On the other hand, the viewer standing in front of the panel was introduced to a meshwork of relations, since the colour fields opened new spaces in space.

In retrospect, Niva's installation in Venice makes me look for a possible translation of the English word 'viewing situation', an expression underlining that a situation is meant to be experienced through sight and seeing.

Niva's installations are in fact equivalent to the total situation that departs from the viewer, the very moment she appears in the room where the works are and lets her eye swing between different perceptual alternatives. Like an invisible director Niva controls the visual chain of events.

In the Venice pavilion the viewer could suddenly relate her presence to three different landscapes: the real landscape outside, the 'set' erected by Niva inside, with an atmospheric painted landscape, and finally the photographs on the wall of a snow-clad Finnish forest landscape.

What happened was that we as viewers were caught up in the middle of a landscape where levels between illusion and reality were shifted in various directions.

Hereby the text has reached its real time, i.e. Niva's exhibition at Galerie Artek. The treatment of landscape has been traded in for a scrutiny of interiors, which at the same time means a step towards a more private and intimate area. For his new works Niva has selected a group of homes, real homes, and allowed these to become the substance for the whole exhibition. Each work consists of two parts: a photograph of a room and a stack of painted canvases leaning against the wall under it. The 'formula' of the installation is very obvious and clear, and therefore the writer wishes to avoid reading complications into levels where the artist has managed to avoid them thanks to his clear-headedness and pragmatic action.

On the other hand a fruitful complication appears, touching on the basic issues of painting and spatiality, as soon as the viewer's perception begins to grasp the inbuilt mechanics. It appears that the monochrome painted canvases on the floor do not function as paintings at all, but as tools for Niva's operations in the interiors. The stacked canvases seem lifted out of the photographs, which in turn are not at all a stylish study of homes and interiors. On the contrary, Niva has 'stigmatised' the interiors with the paintings, whose formats and colours were tailored to each flat. The paintings cut through the room, forming a section that involves the given lines, colours and shapes of the room. They mark off, cover up, cut out, group together, summarise various aspects of the room and its furnishings.

This mechanics could just as well be a description of how abstract thinking functions, but the interesting thing is that Niva presents this operation with visual means only.

Here we have the core of Niva's artistic practice: an acknowledgment of the eye and perception as instances for the creation of meaning. And the result confirms how hard it is for reality to become reconciled with its fate, which is to be something else than it appears to be.

Each work title begins with the words *I Spy with My Eyes Something Being...* and then follows for instance the addition *Earth-Coloured*, which refers to the colour Niva has selected to represent the keynote of the interior.

This game, to spy with your eyes and let the eyes follow the colours was actually taken from a colouring book intended for children. Simple.

It is just as simple to judge whether Niva has succeeded as a visual director. This can be proved by the turnaround our interpretation makes. We do not interpret the flats voyeuristically, as signs of private homes, but as a site for visual events.

Hufvudstadsbladet 26 August 1994

Håkan Rehnberg
Galleri Artek, Helsinki

The Sister of Dreaming

Five of Håkan Rehnberg's otherwise unnamed paintings at Galleri Artek have been annotated. In brackets there is the word *Hérodiade*, which refers to one of Mallarmé's major poetic works *Scènes d'Hérodiade* (1871); the poem about Salome and St John the Baptist where Herodias embodies the dream of purity.

It is thus Herodias that stands out for Håkan Rehnberg at a stage where he is expressing an ever more purified interest in the painterly.

In the 80s Rehnberg's practice was moving in the area between painting and sculpture.

The *Moira* suite from 1988 became a turning point. Its yellow and grey tones are applied with a knife, at times very thickly, and the sculptural is only a reminiscence.

The vertical and horizontal partition of the colour surfaces still visible in *Moira* has now been abandoned by Rehnberg. The marking of a boundary has been relinquished for something that has instead become a condition where the act of painting is realised.

We see how the paint expands over the surface, fills it up and at the same time sustains a form of transparency. In those places where the support, the acrylic glass, is visible it is as if the movement has gone in the opposite direction; the paint has withdrawn with the aim of laying bare.

The movement is double; it skims the surface and goes right through it.

In a brief conversation Håkan Rehnberg referred to a frosty window surface when he wanted to signify a condition of bare existence that lies behind the curtain of knowing and thinking. If we erase the frost the invisible that has been drawn onto it will disappear.

If the surface were entirely covered in white we would have but one more curtain.

The hair fine balance of covering and revealing emerges in a sequence of three paintings.

In the first painting opaque yellow spreads from the centre of the surface, in the third painting there is a total break with control and calm restrained movement.

Rehnberg's painting advances ever closer towards an area that becomes problematic in relation to language, since it is expressly about what takes place outside any theme, any reduction to a concept.

Rehnberg's investigation is in fact to do with the specific ability of painting to deliver something that can only take shape through and in the act of painting.

Painting becomes the mark of a place where appearance happens – expression attains structure without the expressed being formulated or given a content.

In this sense we can say that Rehnberg has realised the dream of purity. There is room for emptiness, which however is not to do with lack but with something that is open for something else.

What we are confronted with is thus the act of painting and its rhythm linking moments together.

Looking for shapes is useless since this, for Rehnberg, is about painting that begins at the point where shape has become shapelessness, with the aim of functioning like frost on the window pane.

Regarding Mallarmé it is said that his artistic production rested on the frustrated insight that we live in a world where action is not the sister of dreaming.

Rehnberg's distinctive painting could be one of these sisters. In an orange painting the movement of colour edges in from all directions only to fizzle out in a calmer area in the middle, not immobile but rather presenting us with a silent falling.

Hufvudstadsbladet 23 October 1992

Carolus Enckell
Galerie Artek, Helsinki

Painting as Translucent Consciousness

Carolus Enckell's painting rests on and depends on its medium, light and colour, to an extreme extent. The abstract in Carolus Enckell does not belong with formal constructions, nor with expressions of ideas or emotions. It has found its own way at a crossroads of the general and the specific.

In the Kunsthalle Helsinki, where Carolus Enckell exhibited two years ago as Artist of the Year, there was an excellent opportunity to study, for example, the nuances of painting; to place one colour next to another and see the difference between them, to spot the nuance that was there, in between, invisible. This study came close, in its essence, to exercises in spirituality and it went beyond the image as materialised reality.

At Galerie Artek we notice painting of a kind that bears the marks of density and liberatedness: a combination that in itself may seem impossible. As impossible as it sounds when we speak of the painting as an intermediary between inner and outer reality. But painting is something other than philosophy, it may have properties which can only partly be grasped by thought.

By the entrance to the gallery there is a very small work, in oil on zinc, which catches the eye: *Fra Angelico Red*. The vital red is placed next to the white paint. The brush strokes are sensuous, palpable, and bear witness of the act of painting: traces of a past present that unites the painting with the living present.

Carolus Enckell's paintings become one with the possibility of painting to be an intermediary surface between inner and outer reality, where the surface has been transformed into relations of colour and light. The more I delve into the paintings, the more I tend to somewhat reverse the relation between the image, the inner and the outer. The image as intermediary surface does not, in Enckell's case, denote a boundary in space, but the opposite: the boundless, whose metaphor could be a totally translucent consciousness. The interior of the painting opens up to the exterior, and the other way round, which means that the positions never become absolute. The door and the window, which often occur as elements in Carolus Enckell's paintings, are characterised precisely by this double optics, the gaze looking both inwards and outwards. Therefore it is difficult to know if I, the viewer, receive or give out meaning.

The works *Morandi's Window* and *White Room* are in some ways connected to each other: the window as point of departure, the white room as a place we long for. Morandi, a peculiar artist who throughout his life painted the view from his window, was in this way perhaps trying to reach beyond the visible. It is an appealing thought to imagine Morandi immersing himself ever deeper into one and the same landscape, until the present became so familiar that it allowed him to see what was absent.

Density is what occurs in the central room of the gallery. Two large paintings (a diptych and a triptych) are placed one in front of the other. The work *Caput Mortuum* was named after the particular red colour which, unlike Angelico red, is the colour of coagulated blood.

The question, the question, – is in the blood,
where your eye

sees not, in the guiltless stillness
Man carries with him
(Gunnar Björling: *Resting Day)*

The painting lives, empowered by the paints and how they are applied onto the canvas. The process could be that of life's own course, and the silence afterwards. A dense surface of Caput Mortuum red is placed above an impenetrable dark blue. Approximately in the middle of the painting we find the redeeming moment; a light, sky-blue colour delicately applied so that the brush strokes leave room for air and light in-between. There is a constant repetition in the yellow, yellow intervals that provide consolation and continuity.

Hufvudstadsbladet 18 September 1992

Henry Wuorila-Stenberg
Galerie Artek, Helsinki

How It Is

Henry Wuorila Stenberg's new paintings articulate an area that is both interesting and 'difficult'. The difficulty is not painting as such or experiencing it but the succeeding step, to bring the experience to a conscious level. The title of one of the exhibited paintings, *There is no Security*, says exactly what we have to accept in our attempts at interpretation.

Four years ago it was still possible to speak of Henry Wuorila-Stenberg's works in terms of concepts like pure painting. This of course alludes to an established modernist approach comprising, among other things, the notion of an inner experience which can find its expression in pure painting. As we wander among Wuorila-Stenberg's paintings at Galerie Artek we become convinced that something decisive has occurred, a change that does not allow itself to be captured by an interpretation marked by critical distance, and with formal analysis as its main tool. The paintings simply do not have any 'look' that could serve as a foundation for formal analysis. To call these works either abstract or figurative, or to search for symbols or metaphors, leads nowhere. The paintings escape this kind of formal characterisation. Instead we should put the question differently, indeed we should face the individual work and investigate it in terms of nearness, relation or connectedness.

The paintings in the gallery's large room are prescriptive of the process-like condition that Wuorila-Stenberg has evoked. The reason that these works in particular function as the critical moment of the whole becomes obvious when we step into the room – our perception is tested in a double-sided process. At a distance the eye is struck by visionary glimpses that stand out of the paintings' delimited surface. In the work *To What Disappeared* it is a white flow that expands, corresponding to the limitlessness we associate with the sky. In the work *On the Floor* it is the strongly yellow, undulating lines that break out of the dark mass. The painting *There, from Where it Comes* is like the shroud of the peacock all washed over with a shower of signs. Yellow circular lines with an inner core of blue and black are hovering both calmly and agitatedly around the canvas. A relation to time is established, it is about the split second, the inevitable registering of perception before consciousness claims our understanding.

When the moment escapes us, when we move closer to the paintings, their relation to time changes. Punctuated time of the moment is replaced by extended time where a new dimension of the painting becomes visible. Now the visionary glimpses become secondary in relation to the dense mass of paint that gives the surface its structure. The paint is applied in thick layers that have been subjected to careful processing. The surface creates the network through which everything else in the painting comes into being; it gives the painting a place, a history, a depth. The two forms of time presuppose each other. The temporal moments give life to the dark mass that would otherwise be empty like the surface of a rusk. And the moments would not emerge without being anchored in a background, a place.

Through their attachment to time and space these paintings are ultimately about one of many possible expressions for the self. Nothing however is self-evident, nothing is secure. The self-expressive tendency is rejected in some of the paintings when the structured surface is rid of its supportive function. Instead the surface gets another function, to cover up and hide with disturbing white elements that manage to appear in places as thin films of colour. Yet this longing for light, and thereby also for a certain form of æsthetics, comes at a price. What does not fit becomes unwanted, must be denied and painted over.

Henry Wuorila-Stenberg does not make it easy for himself. The exhibition contains yet a third coherent group of works that are expressly about painting, since these paintings depart from a theme, the line of the horizon that has almost become an aesthetic convention. The viewer cannot escape all the associations that come with the theme. What the other paintings expressed without rhetoric and quotes gains ever more weight in the proximity of these expressively 'beautiful' pictures.

Hufvudstadsbladet 11 December 1992

More Representational Art
Amos Anderson Art Museum, Helsinki

Infrathin Differences

Marcel Duchamp uses the word infrathin when he talks about what an æsthetic judgment really is. According to Duchamp an æsthetic judgment is a speech act that suspends itself for instance between two statements, such as this is a painting/this is not a painting.

Between the two statements there is an infrathin passage and an indefinite difference, something that does not have a name and least of all a concept, since an æsthetic judgment is an experiment that escapes conceptual understanding. When Duchamp was then interrogated about how he defines infrathin he answered laconically that it can only be exemplified, not explained.

The observant reader probably wonders at this stage what Duchamp and his statements are to do with a review of an exhibition entitled *More Representational Art* with three young artists from Sweden, who are about to finish their studies at the Royal University College of Fine Arts, showing together with the painter Hannele Kumpulainen from Finland. And the answer?

The exhibition, which is part of the Helsinki Festival programme and is put together by artist Silja Rantanen, is a clear cut demonstration of one point of view on the problematic notion of the image, with its endless tangle of questions. What is an image? How does representation relate to what it represents? What separates a use-object from a readymade artwork?

As we know the opposition between representational and non-representational art is a construction. What is really at stake is a sliding between different aspects: what the image shows, what it captures and holds up for our observation and what makes this capture or imaging possible, i.e. the image as medium. The viewer then makes his crucial addition, what he imagines before the picture, what he gathers that he is seeing. Precisely here, in the intersection of the various aspects, the exhibition *More Representational Art* establishes an infrathin passage, so that the expressions more representational art/less representational art bite their own tails and also each other's tails.

Reconnecting to the introduction, to Duchamp's notion of the infrathin, I wish to apply his method of giving an example, not an explanation. As a curiosity some of Duchamp's examples of the infrathin can be mentioned. The heat of a seat (that someone has just left) is infrathin. When tobacco smoke even smells of the mouth that inhales it the two odours form an infrathin union.

At the Amos Anderson Art Musuem we have a neat exhibition, puzzlingly easy to look at and puzzlingly rich in notions that it sets in motion. Carl Nyström is drawing his studio in a medium other than drawing: installation. In the museum we see the framework of a room that corresponds to the outlines of the authentic studio. During the course of the exhibition, in the morning before the museum opens, Nyström rearranges the room, moving things around and adjusting furnishing details. Because the room is so painstakingly authentic we relate to it with respectful distance. We stay outside, as if the room existed as a drawing. Karin Ohlin's black, carefully lacquered wooden piano also possesses the authentic infrathin authority that makes the mute piano participate in a demonstration which Ohlin actually does not represent but creates. The piano awakens a brutal impulse to open the lid and hear sounds, to try how it sounds, to break open this amplified muteness.

Nina von Schmalensee exerts total control in her painting, which includes reality or, differently put, the relation between painting and its model. She selects a motif and makes a concrete model of it, i.e. an object that she then paints. This true-to-life model is a mute copy in relation to what it becomes when she has painted it. She does not paint from it, but paints it into something that is more than reality. She herself conditions her use of the medium, painting, and she achieves a reality whose motifs correspond to those of the model but are different and belong to another 'world of beings'.

Finnish artist Hannele Kumpulainen's painting upholds the notion of a kind of painterly tradition. When we look at her paintings in the Amos Anderson Art Museum we have the feeling that we are standing in a historical museum where variations of style and expression follow accepted art historical categories. This anachronism, the feeling of skewed temporal perspectives, is partly to do with Kumpulainen's use of compositions borrowed from Italian Rennaisance painting, but there is also another feature that makes her painting seem 'classic'. The emphasis, and the very content of this painting, is closely linked to the way the paintings are painted. Each painting seems to become a nomadic character in a landscape drawn up within the boundaries of the canvas.

Hufvudstadsbladet 24 September 1995

Gloria Patri – Pathology without a Namer

Of the lecturers at the symposium in Malmö Mary Kelly is the only one who works as an artist. I talked to Mary Kelly at the opening of *Gloria Patri* in the Malmö Art Museum. She had read her paper the day before, entitled *Miming the Master: Boy-Things, Bad Girls and Femmes Vitales*. Still strongly influenced by Kelly's powerful theoretical device, reading Lacan and Freud from the insight that these analysts became masters of/by observing female psychopatology, I addressed a question to her, a question about the relation between her different fields of practice.

Mary Kelly When I talk there is a fundamental difference if I present a theoretical argument, as in the lecture, or if I talk about my art practice. The artwork is always a visualisation that functions by way of sight, and this process helps me to think. How I visually structure the work is to do with precision, with a reduction of possibilities. The objects in the installation have to be in the right place if sight is to function, if the theoretical and abstract level I strive for is to be attained.

Rita Roos You have said that you find it hard to distinguish between text and image. Your installations *Post Partum*, *Interim* and now *Gloria Patri* all consist of objects and text, and at the same time the text is something more than just text; it is the voice of a human being, of people. In the 'Corpus' part of *Interim*, the voices were related to women's desire for pleasure, and seen from a female perspective the work induced a blessed state of recognition. At the same time the opposite pole is problematised, the male inability to hear female voice when it is not attributed to a woman's physical, real body, i.e. to the surface onto which the male psyche can inscribe its own voice, its own desires.

Kelly The development of my work is also related to the ramification of feminism in the last twenty years, from the coming into being of *Post Partum* (the work in which Mary Kelly documented, in accordance with Lacanian thinking, her son's first seven years, i.e. up to the point when he entered the symbolic order) to today's world where the everyday is filled with incidents indicating how women are in command of a kind of imitation of the master, i.e., how they fit themselves into male discourse. Just remember events like the Gulf War, when women were serving in the army. The stories in *Gloria Patri* remind us of those in 'Pecunia' (the money part of *Interim*); they are filled with objects from everyday life, as if rooted in the real world.

In *Interim*, the preceding work, the parts 'Pecunia', 'Historia' and 'Potestas' concerned the discourse of mastery, miming voices that belong to those who rule with power and money. *Gloria Patri* is different. Its psychological condition is frightening with the combination of extreme poles of the psycho-pathology of masculinity, the public one – war – as well as the private one – moments when the forbidden cracks open the psychological order which the symbolic order pretended to guarantee. Here, Kelly has changed her method; she does not articulate her observations of masculinity with a distance that will protect her female integrity. Instead her method is correlated to the pathology of her subject.

Thin, hard, shining aluminium. The top row, plates with displaced symbols of insignia taken from the American military. The next series, six trophies with bits of text which Kelly has taken from news casts where American soldiers in the Gulf War make comments: 'Kick ass', '…Busting our butts to get it right', '… Letting loose and hitting 'em with all we got'. Each trophy is crowned by a three-dimensional male figure holding up one of the letters of the word GLORIA. Below is the third series, six shields with an inscribed textual story.

As the gaze wanders along the shining objects, as it reads the heroism of war and eventually realises what this story is about it wants to avert itself, faced with all these psycho-pathological visualisations. I recall two words Kelly used in her lecture, 'display' and 'camouflage'. What Kelly is doing in her installation is to show, to display, that what the masculine pathology is ultimately camouflaging is camouflage itself, i.e. that in male discourse reality is an instrument for the self-confirmation of the male ego. Thus pathology disguises itself as normality and reality. The display is a sly one. It is not recognised as a phenomenon made for the stage. What is displayed is already inscribed in the ontological definition of being. And consequently, what is considered natural and normal in male discourse will still be something that obeys the commands of pathology.

In her article *The True-Real* Julia Kristeva asks an interesting question. How is it possible that the 'true-real', i.e. what is real in the Lacanian sense of the word, leaks through in spite of all the mechanisms set up to hold it back? Why is its occurrence a perpetual threat to reason? The enormous horror of this strange, unwanted truth that does not exclude its occurrence in the social contract. It is precisely this kind of leakage Kelly has used for her voice in the stories that make up *Gloria Patri*. The voice attains the level of the negation of the ejaculation, which instead of endorsing the basis of the phallic symbol takes it away.

Finally, we discussed the possibility that the male psyche is unable to identify with voice. It is too real, too forbidden and therefore excluded. But as the sovereign master of camouflage Kelly makes her last move. The stories end with the one about Mary Lou imitating the male voice at the gym: '… Fit in. Weigh in at the right weight and defeat her rivals. She breathed out heavily. Hard-hearted? Not at all, she told herself: It was a hard life. What she had was hard-earned and if anyone objected, well, that was, she spat on the floor, hard luck.'

Paletten 2–3/1996. Translated by Philip Landon

Rosemarie Trockel
Museum of Contemporary Art, Helsinki

Wool, Mirror and Stove

Rosemarie Trockel's exhibition in the 'Sculpture Room' at Ateneum is a fine example of how a small-scale presentation can also function as a representative introduction to an artistic practice whose foremost characteristic is a multiplicity of meanings.

When Trockel studied painting in 1974–78 at the School of Art and Crafts (*Werkkunstschule*) in Cologne the German art world was mostly dominated by Joseph Beuys and neo-Expressionist painters like Georg Baselitz and Anselm Kiefer. It was also at this time that these painters entered the American art scene, where the market was consequently dominated by men whose works sold at sky-high prices. By contrast another tendency could be glimpsed, represented by female artists like Sherrie

Levine, Cindy Sherman, Barbara Kruger and Jenny Holzer. Typical of these Americans' strategy was the confiscation of images and texts from the mass media, using them to question the ability of images to refer to reality. Images about women do not necessarily have to coincide with images of real women.

When it comes to artistic expression Trockel has taken a different route from her American colleagues, even if they are shaped by a common consciousness and *Zeitgeist*. Regarding Trockel certain influences can be traced back to Joseph Beuys and European surrealism. Beuys's heritage mediates an attitude that focuses attention on art's dependence on social structures through a practice that could be called 'multi-artistic'. One of Trockel's methods, exposing objects in display cases, reminds us for instance of how information is ordered in ethnography and anthropology. The objects Trockel puts forward vary with regard to the mode of production, they can be everything from ready-mades to objects of her own construction whose character shifts between conceptual rigour and expressivity.

Interpreting Trockel's art is a paradoxical activity, since it entails trying to affix a meaning to something consciously constructed in a mode that 'resists explanation'. What makes Trockel's work problematic and challenging is, I think, to do with how Trockel treats the feminine, always with an underlying level present that creates the gaps. In these gaps the feminine is drawn as a mental construction, invisible, elusive, written between the lines. The image for this could be ellipsis, the unfinished crooked line. 'To be a woman is to be something that cannot be delineated in a closed, legally defined text. Woman with a capital W therefore does not exist as universal determination', to quote Jacques Lacan. Symptomatically, Trockel often combines her objects with clauses whose significances usually become twisted – in addition all of this is flavoured with exquisite humour. Trockel, then, relates to her subject indirectly by presenting two different registers: that of the mental image and that of language. Rectilinear understanding is replaced by curvilinear doodling. Hidden possibilities in the form of superstitions and fantasies are evoked.

For her purposes Trockel uses the technique of surrealism, to mix the well known with the unknown. Her work can be read as a rebus, a picture puzzle where the parts do not necessarily fit together. This is particularly true of the objects in the display cases. The only way to understand a rebus is to take in the parts one by one. We cannot follow the argument, but if we are willing to concentrate on one fragment at the time much can be understood. Possibly it is our habit of reading discursively that disturbs us when we are faced with Trockel's works, but as in a dream an interpretation may be valuable even if certain parts remain obscure.

In the two display cases in the 'Sculpture Room' we find a richness of wit difficult to imagine, if we are prepared to tackle the rebus. The work *Profumo* is a small silver mirror. When we look into it we see not our own mirror-image but a life-buoy in red and white, the woollen original of which is hanging above the room's entrance. A wealth of associations comes upon us: everything from Narcissus who fell in love with his own reflection to Lacan's theory of the Other in the mirror. Has the buoy been thrown for Narcissus or for something else? Well, there is yet another story relating to the name *Profumo*. The key figure of the 'Profumo scandal', Christine Keeler, was the woman who had simultaneous affairs with the British Defence Secretary Profumo, and the Russian Naval Attaché Ivanov. The ending of that affair was predictable. Profumo sank, regardless of the life buoy that was, insidiously, made of wool.

Mundplastik ('Mouth Sculpture') consists of a small chewed chewing gum dipped in silver. Speech is silver, silence is golden, the saying has it. In this case that is reversed, the one who chews is hardly speaking although chewing may be understood as soundless speech, the activity may be just as feverish. Silence reaches its summit in the work *I'd Always Like to Be Something Special*. The grand visions have fallen flat on their face. We see an oblong object bandaged in white. One end looks like a dog's head with a mouth that is also well wrapped. The ribbon tied around the dog's neck is already waiting for its master.

Trockel's large knitted works bring associations to traditional female handicraft. But what was earlier known as handicraft Trockel has elevated into 'high art', to the same level that accommodated the male artists of the 80s. Connecting the knitted to handicraft is treacherous in Trockel's case, as the works are actually machine made and also computer programmed as regards their patterns. One woollen piece of knitting, which however is not in this exhibition, could be a prologue to the works on show. The prologue bears Descartes's fundamental thesis (knitted in wool): *Cogito ergo sum* ('I think, therefore I am'). The thesis has lately been taken up by Lacan, who thinks the clause should instead say: 'I am not, where I am the plaything of my thought. I think of what I am, where I am not thinking that I am thinking.' In other words: in the unconscious, where Trockel's woollen knits with their patterns reminiscent of Rorschach tests also exist – the patterns have the same blue colour as the famous ink stains.

In an adjacent space, which usually serves as a cleaning cupboard, Trockel has installed a small kitchen. The kitchen's attributes, the stove and the sink, are in their traditional places and also on the wall, since there Trockel has placed an artwork consisting of white metal and two hot plates, a fully fledged work in the spirit of Modernism. In the sink there is an empty plate, which however carries the promising inscription *Wurst und Fleisch* ('Sausage and Meat').

Hufvudstadsbladet 4 September 1992

Marianna Uutinen
Galerie Anhava, Helsinki

Yes and No in Bubble Plastic

Marianna Uutinen's paintings at Galerie Anhava are easy to describe this time.

Acrylic paint has been applied to bubble plastic, which results in entirely monochrome works. The earlier technique of squirting the paint over the canvas has now been abandoned by Uutinen. She does, however, continue to investigate and reveal the conditionality on which artistic enunciation rests, and she succeeds in making the foundations waver.

Uutinen's new works could be called paintings about bubble plastic, i.e. the material, look and content all coincide. Everything is about plastic.

The colours Uutinen has selected are precisely those you find in plastic toys, plastic buckets, bathroom interiors etc. The hues are ingratiating and sweetish. Uutinen's far-reaching adaptation to the conditions dictated by the material coincide with the central thesis of modernism – it is the medium that determines how artistic expression will look.

The problem of painting becomes a medium-specific problem, form depends on the specific material and vice versa. Thus Uuutinen's relation to plastic demonstrates the same logic as Modernism's relation to the canvas.

It is just that Uutinen's method leads to something 'wrong'. Through the paintings' association to plastic, above all to cheap plastic objects, she introduces a reality that is outside the realm of pure art.

It is a double tactic, that operates with the help of two concepts constantly counter-acting each other: adaptation and destruction.

This double tactic could be compared to a language where each word has two meanings that point in opposite directions. Faced with such a language we become unsure of the speaker's intention: is one meaning really a camouflage of the other or the other way round?

Uutinen manages in a supreme fashion to say both yes and no. Her paintings fulfill in format and colour the requirements of what we characterise as established painting, and at the same time they are excellent representatives of 'low' taste and aesthetics.

Hufvudstadsbladet 17 March 1993

Peter Bonde, Claus Carstensen, Erik A Frandsen
Nordic Arts Centre, Helsinki

Three Danes

On the invitation card for the exhibition at the Nordic Arts Centre there are three photographs of three wrinkly babies, Frandsen, Carstensen and Bonde. On the reverse side the word 'Painting' is printed. This makes me think; I turn the card around and become absorbed again with the three new-born. With a question mark in my rucksack I then set out for the island – later I understand that this was the first stage in the guys' frankly cynical strategy, so well conceived and carried out that it is hard to dismiss.

In the first room Bonde, Carstensen and Frandsen throw rubbish in the viewer's face. Their joint work *67 Hours of Collaboration* sprawls over the floor, i.e. the work equals all the refuse that may conceivably have been created during 67 hours of work: unwashed plates and glasses, full ashtrays, empty beer cans and not least the 'banana flies' persistently circling above the fruit hall. The irritated viewer stands in the middle of the refuse

83

without finding the tools for any kind of counter-attack, which I suspect is precisely the effect the artists wanted to achieve. They have rigged a tight moebius band between art and life, the consequence being that one functions as the legitimising of the other and vice versa. If we ask whether this may be called art we end up facing the fact that the very concept of art is fundamentally a construct or an agreement, and therefore the work *67 Hours of Collaboration* throws the ball back to the art institution – with reference to its functions of naming and legitimising art. The rubbish in the Waterfront Barrack is allowed to remain as art, otherwise the cleaning lady would have swept it away.

After the collaboration project the three artists articulate themselves on another level. However far-fetched this may sound, it is still the baby photographs and the rubbish that provide the key to the underlying attitude. The three new-born babies on the photograph are still in unity with the mother, encapsulated in the complete security of symbiosis. Trust has not yet been challenged. But later, when the child discovers that there are differences – between itself and others, and above all between itself and the mother, the encounter with the other takes place in hatred and rejection. As a red thread in the Danes' practice there is the formation of a closed circuit between these two basic emotions, trust and security versus hatred and rejection. Exhibiting rubbish becomes the introductory, absolute manifestation of the wish to drive away, to reject.

In Claus Carstensen's work rejection gains relevance on a societal level as the opposition against coercion and limits. For this purpose Carstensen uses society's symbolising mechanisms. Seventeen green flag-like canvases that hang in a row from the ceiling repeat an emblem, the circle and star. What reveals the artistic strategy is the lettering and the text written into the emblem. The abbreviation FAIAT could mean (if the exhibition catalogue is anything to go by) 'Families Against Intimidation And Terror'. At the same time the text warns against a naked evil that intimidates us. The interesting thing is that Carstensen with his use of language creates alienation. Who is speaking, who is intimidating whom? Thus language is also revealed as a representative of the symbolic, which of course is the order that the subject is initiated into, and must submit to as it begins to talk during its second year of existence. In Carstensen's work the emphasis is on submission; the reaction against coercion to submit to a social, linguistic world of legislative regulation.

Peter Bonde attacks painting, at the same time shamelessly and with humour. Most of the shamelessness is directed towards himself, since he expressly attacks the works he has created. Bonde's different versions of abstract painting have been subjected to infantile vandalising. As with Carstensen the tactic is a double one – he both exploits and ridicules the order that language represents. A brown monochrome painting has a caption with the text *Brown Flowers*, another work has the legend *Brother Dirt*. Right in the middle of the paintings two plastic bags are hanging, with all kinds of rubbish in them.

A ceaseless murmuring is heard from the rear room where Erik A Frandsen, who by the way was one of the four Nordic artists at Documenta, is installed. The monotonous humming comes from a video with a close-up of a red eye. When we connect the sound and the eye's movements a rhythm is established, almost as if the eye were doing the breathing. A contrast to this is set up by the colourless charcoal drawings on the wall that repeat the image of an androgynous woman, perhaps in pre-pubescence. The circle is closing. The raw tactic is finishing with a symbol of something innocently naïve and vulnerable. The three white neon tubes that are placed over each charcoal drawing express a necessary ambivalence. Partly they reify the body, partly they underline the insight that there are areas that are impossible to dominate or approach. 'Between me and my bed', Frandsen writes in large lettering over one of the catalogue pages, next to a picture of the charcoal drawings.

Hufvudstadsbladet 11 November 1992

Inverted Perspectives
Museum of Contemporary Art, Helsinki

The Invisible Woman

Is she ours? I don't feel that I am that person. A version of me. With three sentences Louise Lawler, Cindy Sherman and Laurie Simmons summarise their retrospectively biased exhibition at the Museum of Contemporary

Art. The backward perspective comprises a little more than ten years. All three first appeared just before the 80s, during a time that in many respects proved to be a turning point in the American art world.

How come there emerged, at that particular time, a new generation of female artists who began to investigate the place of the female in an asymmetrical and phallocentric model of both civilisation and art? If we scrutinise the spirit of the time, the shift from the 70s to the 80s, we will be able to get hold of at least some plausible leads. Europe entered into the American art scene once again; it was mostly about the three 'C' artists from Italy (Cucchi, Clemente and Chia) and the German neo-expressionists. These male painters, often jokingly called the 'Big Boys', were true children of their time and in the whirlwind of the art boom the prices of their works skyrocketed. Somewhere on the margins, however, other winds started to blow. A group of young artists stepped forward; they were born around 1950, had grown up on TV and film, had gone to college and were well-read in art history, aesthetic theory and psychoanalysis. This generation, commonly called 'the pictures generation' was gratefully acknowledged by critics influenced by post-structuralism who were trying to deconstruct, from different starting points, the aesthetic system of modernism. The term 'postmodern', covering a wide array of meanings, was launched.

In the postmodern melting pot and all the death-warrants that went with it (those of the subject, reality, the big narratives, the original etc) new insights were also launched, this time around, by theoretically informed female artists, of whom, besides Lawler, Sherman and Simmons, we could also mention Sherrie Levine, Barbara Kruger, Jenny Holzer, Dara Birnbaum, Barbara Bloom. In contrast to the biologically motivated 'Mother Earth' feminism of the 60s and 70s, which emphasised woman as nature, the focus was now on femininity as a cultural construct, under the influence of critical readings of Jacques Lacan's contradictory and obscure texts.

To avoid the over-complicated rhetorical apparatus that is now beginning to ensnare concepts like Gaze/Gender/Difference/the Other I quote an excerpt from art theoretician Kate Linker's work *Feminism and Representation* where she explains the core of her interpretation of Lacan: in his system the phallus is the centre around which subjectivity, social law and the appropriation of language revolves; human sexuality is determined, and thereby lived, in accordance with the position we take as owner or nonowner of a phallus, and therewith we have access to its symbolical structures. The phallus in this structure takes up the role as signifier, or the bearer of meanings, in relation to its absence, or lack. The latter position is taken by the girl, who can thereby be said to have a gender- specific and in itself problematic relation to language in the phallocentric order. Lacan's observations may help us to explain the abundance of 'images of women' in our society: women are by definition excluded from the linguistic order, they do not depict but they are depicted (and of course always as the image of male desire).

The most important thing in Lacan's teaching is, however, the statement that sexuality is not a 'natural' identity or something purely signified, but instead the *effect* of a signifier, derived from external social determinations.

Thus the image of woman equals woman, which is to say that woman does not exist as a subject or real woman. If we understand the significance of this we will also have an explanation why, for instance, Cindy Sherman and Laurie Simmons work with photography based on images of women we see in the visual flow of the media. Because photography carries meaning *in potentia* – meanings do not fill the image as water fills a glass but appear, rather, through the process of interpretation – the meanings can be manipulated in the direction required. Thus understood, photography can be used as a means of creating distance; a statement can be presented and at the same time undermined. In the hands of Cindy Sherman the camera becomes a double-edged weapon. She confiscates and imitates the media's images of woman and at the same time she is saying something else, that woman is not there, not present. In her early black and white series *Untitled Film Stills* (1977–80) Sherman reconstructed scenes from something reminiscent of B movies, playing the main part herself with carefully executed make-up. Thanks to the camera she can act a part and at the same time say 'I am not that person'. Thus it is the camera that lies, since it cannot capture the difference between acting (becoming an image) and being.

After *Untitled Film Stills* follow colour photographs in larger formats, in which Sherman exposes a coveted trophy of the male gaze, the young innocent girl seemingly caught unawares by the camera. The following step is a consistent reaction to the embodied dream, an abjectal rejection of the ideal via the detours of art history. Sherman now focuses on the classic art of portraiture. It is precisely against those areas of the model's body that have been subject to the highest degree of idealisation by artists that

Sherman directs her attack. Let us for instance study Sherman's version of Raphael's famous portrait of his model Fornarina. Those parts of Fornarina's body that Raphael praised the most have in Sherman's reconstruction taken on a grotesque aspect. Fornarina's breasts, for instance, have been replaced with an artificial and over-blown bosom (a prosthetic special effect) which is attached to Sherman's upper body with visible strings. The rejection of the idealised body is emphasised by the 'vomit pictures', hyper-realistic colour photographs of rotting leftovers.

When Laurie Simmons says 'one version of me' she refers in an ironic intonation to her dolls and to the little girl who identifies with her doll, unaware that the rules of the game are given and the adoption of the role is about rehearsing ready-made patterns. Like the playing child Simmons also follows a clear-cut pattern and there is no doubt about which pattern interests her. – In Simmons's world the doll has grown up and taken its given place in the confinement of the home. The plastic doll does not live in the home, she is part of the decoration, even her clothes colour-match the rest of the interior. When the woman is travelling, like in the series *Tourism*, she is a temporary guest in a foreign landscape training her gaze on its phallic monuments, the Parthenon, the Eiffel Tower and the Great Wall of China. In the latest photographs the dolls' upper bodies have developed into houses, guns, perfume bottles etc. Where Cindy Sherman heightens emotions with abject 'vomit pictures' Simmons shows the opposite, a slow death from suffocation.

The most conceptually orientated of the three, Louise Lawler, seemingly places herself and her camera at the margins to investigate what happens with the work of art after it has left the white gallery space. By peeping into art collectors' homes, into the storage rooms of museums and galleries, she discovers how context changes the artwork. It is thus not only the artist who creates aesthetic meanings but also an anonymous crowd of collectors, viewers and museum employees, and ultimately the cultural apparatus that has established the guidelines of their roles. With a discreet eye Lawler registers art as an institution, and at the same time her photographic practice just about maintains a distance from the concept of the institution. Delicately she writes *Is she ours?* above her photograph of Degas's little dancer, or she coolly observes how artworks take on the identity of market commodities in the auctioneers' back rooms. Through a very precise choice of visual angles, proportions and colours Lawler keeps up the appearance that an objective observer was standing behind the camera.

Hufvudstadsbladet 21 April 1993

Orlan
The Ateneum Auditorium, Helsinki

A Conference with Orlan

Saturday evening, it is 6 pm and the French artist Orlan inaugurates her 'conference' in the Ateneum Auditorium in Helsinki. She stands up behind the podium and begins her lecture, or 'intervention' as she herself calls it (in French the word also means operation).

After a while a video lecture starts on the screen behind Orlan's back. The video is an unedited document of her seventh operation performance that took place in New York on 21 November 1993. In the operating theatre Orlan becomes the 'actant' she claims to be. While the surgeon reshapes Orlan's face through various interventions – liposuction, restructuring the bones, inserting implants – she is in contact with her audience via satellite: answering questions, reading aloud from philosophical texts, talking.

When she was 18 years old Orlan started her artistic activities in the genre of performance. During the 70s, the golden age of body art, she handled bodily fluids and other 'impure' substances, as a premonition of the 'carnal' genre she works in today. The plastic surgery series was started in Newcastle in 1990, on her 43rd birthday. We may ask ourselves how far it is possible to go in such 'carnal' art. For Orlan the strategy is clear. As soon as there is medical threat to her life, plastic surgery will cease and another process, a legal one, will ensue. Orlan plans to obtain another identity through the legal apparatus. A new face, a new name and a body that will be donated to a museum, this is Orlan's concrete plan.

In the Ateneum hall people cringe, uncomfortably. Around 6.30 the undersigned (like many others) must get out, although the conference continues. Nausea. I see a girl stagger out. She passes out. With my gaze clouded by dizziness I think of Julia Kristeva's interest in the word cadaver (in

Latin: *cadere*, to fall) as something that has irrevocably fallen; death, putre-faction, corpses. Kristeva's verbal association is given a live illustration as I see the girl collapse and know what the video is showing inside, in the auditorium.

'My body is my art' and 'I have given my body to art' are two constantly recurring expressions in Orlan's rhetoric. When she speaks like that she provokes, at least in me, a need to get to grips with terms such as boundary and difference. There is a difference between becoming sick because you are forced to witness a bloody operation or an accident, and watching a video of the same thing in a context where you are part of an audience. Manipulation in the name of art? There is, of course, art that moves in the border zones of the abject, on the limits of primeval repression whose bodily symptoms are repulsion, disgust, i.e. abjection, but with the difference (as compared to Orlan's practice) that the medium provides a distance that moves 'disgust' to a level where other elements – laughter, catharsis, irony – can get through and be included.

When Orlan says that she gives her body to art we ask, What art? Whose art? Her own? If a work of art erases, as is the case with Orlan's operated face, its ability to be a game that precisely for that reason may handle and deal with things that are impossible in reality, where do we end up? In a lunacy that is brought about completely consciously?

The operations are carefully prepared. With the help of computer manipulated images of women from art history and mythology (such as Leonardo's *Mona Lisa*, Botticelli's *Venus*, Gérard's *Psyche*) Orlan has created a model for a self-portrait, according to which the surgeon works. Orlan claims that she is thereby subjected to rites and reborn as a woman.

During the Orlan conference in Helsinki a strange obsession emerges as the most marked symptom. Orlan is obsessed, but by what? Her verbal expounding of her own art cannot entirely answer the question. The next operation is planned to take place in Japan, with the purpose of constructing a very big nose; the biggest nose that is technically possible (in relation to her anatomy) and ethically acceptable for a surgeon to produce. Orlan is creating a mummy from what we usually, in general terms, call the western idea of freedom and the self.

Hufvudstadsbladet 20 October 1995

Art Does Not Kill

The days around the opening of *Ars 95* the weather was typical of Helsinki, a fine drizzle, wind and grey ruggedness, and we hurried to get inside. Therefore I cannot say exactly when Louis Jammes's photographs were mounted on the façade, but once I discovered them I could not turn my gaze away.

At this time I knew neither the factual background of the photographs, nor Louis Jammes's other work. I read in the exhibition guide: 'Louis Jammes is a photographer who is interested in how people outside of society live, in marginal groups and in crises that affect the whole of society. He has, among other things, photographed gypsy colonies in Madrid and the consequences of the nuclear disaster at Chernobyl. He looks for his subjects in the street and in the everyday bustle, and thereafter he reworks his images as they are being developed. His latest subjects were the Bosnian children of besieged Sarajevo.' Then follows a paragraph on how Jammes becomes morally engaged in the living conditions he depicts, how he wants his images also to have influence on the political level... And the text begins to go off in a misleading direction.

Jammes is not directing his camera in Sarajevo at the theatre of war. The photographs handle singularities, one child, one person, and the finished picture causes a stir in the 'four-part order', the connections between earth, sky, mortals and gods. What he is showing requires less attention to meaning, more observation of effect. Here the effects are not about the political level but about what is left when it is peeled off. What is a soldier other than his function as an actor in a war with the privilege of intervening into the 'four-part order' of earth, sky, mortals and gods (sacred values)?

Roos After a relatively short acquaintance with your photographs I am convinced that they are not realist in the way the guidebook insinuates. You are using a kind of æsthetics which is to do with a general understanding of beauty, for instance children as the suffering victims of war occur in a setting with angels' wings. This conscious æsthetics hits us like an obstacle and I come to think of what has been said of our time, art follows

93

us through the new diseases of the soul with the symptom (we do not know who we are) but your photographs make me add that we can still recognise the image of an angel. Therefore the æsthetics of the images becomes seemingly ambivalent: the contrast between a brutal war and the union of angel and human. This makes me grasp a third beauty; the pictures hide a secret, rebellious beauty, because in art we can disregard the established conventions according to which war, politics, nationality, independence etc get their given meaning. Therefore I want to say, even if it sounds paradoxical, that your photographs are a means of expressing actual humanist realism. In the photographs we do not think in terms of soldier or victim, winner or loser etc, but what they propose is a level where we can share our contemporary ills regardless of which category we belong to. Could you comment on these thoughts?

Jammes My photographs are nothing in the name of what can be represented, just as the title of the newly published book about my photographs says: *Sarajévo n'est en réalité le nom de rien qui puisse être représenté* ('Sarajevo is actually not the name of anything that could be represented'). I prefer to show how I see, in contrast to the mass media that pretend to show reality.

Roos But then we can take the question further to the following: what can art say that for instance science cannot? Your photographs must overcome a certain obstacle which is connected to the relation between words like political art, individual, collective – they are above such distinctions and are instead about the level where we can say, regardless of whether we are soldier or victim that we are human in the sense that our existence presupposes that some other human has done something for us, earlier. The war is a sick mockery of this, a symptom that everything has gone wrong.

Jammes War I suppose means precisely that a big machine crushes existence and there is no place for individuality, no place for man. In other words, it is about a deprivation that devours the essence of being human. In my book there is a short sequence that speaks about this: war is no destiny, it is the opposite, something that steals something from destiny, that tears men away from their destiny.

Roos In my opinion there is a kind of revolt in your pictures, but not revolt in the normal way, like in political art in the 60s and 70s. I wonder if your revolt does not occur when war as one big deprivation takes on features of universal mourning. Mourning lends a kind of secret beauty to the pictures – but at the same time it is difficult to talk about beauty because it is about war. What I mean by beauty is closer to what I relate the word to, the potential that in spite of everything exists somewhere in man.

Jammes War is death and death means all forms of death (Jammes shows the photographs of dead people that are in the book), therefore these dead faces are here.

Roos How long have they been dead?

Jammes It varies, a few hours, a few days. In Sarajevo I often went to the morgue, I took a whole lot of photographs because it took me a long time before I could get what I was looking for which I could not exactly explain. In any case I did not want to photograph blood and bloodiness. I did not touch the dead and I stopped photographing immediately when I found what I was looking for.

Roos Strange, usually you close the eyes of the dead.

Jammes Almost all of them have open eyes. In a war situation there is no time to close them. The most important thing for me was to be able to show the works in Sarajevo, to go back with the photographs. The photographs from the war in Sarajevo would for me not have the importance they have if I had not had been able to show them in Sarajevo, and the strangest thing is that the people there did not destroy them. (We look in the publication where photographs show the works in their right place on bombarded and badly damaged buildings in war-torn Sarajevo. Jammes did manage to display the pictures in Sarajevo.) Sarajevo is not only at war but it is a field of war and in this situation every building, every spot is under political control, everything can be important and in particular this systematic monitoring is important for keeping up the fighting spirit. What was rare was that I could display these photographs on different buildings and nothing happened, no one attacked them – in a context where every text, information, action is the target for political reaction.

Roos In your life, then, do words like joy, happiness have any meaning after visiting, as you have done, places like Chernobyl, Sarajevo?

Jammes There is not much difference between my life and my work. I do not see myself as an intellectual, but I live, work and act instinctively and my obsession is about what I do.

Roos You often use children in these images, was that an instinctive choice?

Jammes It was not only children I photographed, but one reason is that when I wanted to bring the photographs back to Sarajevo that required a certain symbolic level in the pictures. The people in Sarajevo are very sensitive to symbols, for instance the Serbs use incredible amounts of time to destroy symbols like libraries, monuments etc and a picture with an angel of a child does symbolically speaking seem to be above the level that separates allies from enemies. In Sarajevo very many rapes are committed, women are raped, children are raped. An angel cannot be raped or violate anyone.

Roos So, the way in which you use the concept of the symbol is adapted to the reality that exists in Sarajevo.

Jammes An angel does not react with revenge. So therefore I think it is possible to show the pictures on each side, and people in Sarajevo understood this. There is a producer and director in Sarajevo who has made a short film about a soldier. The soldier is a monster only if you know what he has done. He kills hundreds with his bare hands, he rapes young women and kills them afterwards. But in another way, and therefore this film is very interesting, you understand that this man could also be on the other side. The film shows how he became a monster in a few weeks by becoming a soldier. It is war that is the machine that creates such monsters. War can devour almost anyone and create a monster out of this human. It is difficult to understand cruelty like Nazism, the concentration camps etc, but in this film we understand the logic according to which a young man who could have had a completely different future begins to do monstrous things. I learned a lot from this film. War gives no one any chance to be human.

Siksi 1/1995

Death Angels on the Catwalk

'Yesterday I was what you are, tomorrow you will be what I am.'
(Roland Barthes: *The Fashion System*)

Rush hour in Helsinki, rapidly flicking through fashion magazines in the Stockmann department store before leaving, stimulate my eye to the point of chaos by allowing visual material to flow in at a tempo that is almost reminiscent of jogging uphill without slowing down. Unexpected signals from the cerebral cortex. I want to take the *Prêt-à-Porter Collections* catalogue (vol. 7, Autumn & Winter 96–97) home with me. Something in the pictures of the catwalks in Paris and Milan breaks through and excites an intellectual need to stop.

At the beginning of the catalogue is Vivienne Westwood's spread, of models with their eyes shaded in the way that people in bad films camouflage diseases, tuberculosis, for example. The headline is: 'Avant-garde goddess made the asymmetrical glamorous look.' Eye focus totally eliminated in Martin Margiela's models with greyish-black gauze (painted directly onto the skin), like a mask, covering half the face with a line that ends where the tip of the model's nose begins. Glamorous? If it is, it's glamorously deathly, an avant-garde look that presents a borderline case where the next step could involve illustrating the very face of death. 'Yesterday I was what you are, tomorrow you will be what I am.' And so, what will I be tomorrow (in the future tense)?

With regard to the distinctions in *The Fashion System*; what I am interested in here is what Barthes calls 'image-clothing', which equals what fashion photography represents, as distinct from 'written clothing' and 'real clothing'. Pictures of a catwalk comply with a certain standard: the models are usually pictured frontally and the spatial relations between forms, lines, surfaces and colours are extremely controlled so that the connotation of the pictures will conform with the look that the designer was trying to create. In a way, the formula is very simple, for if, in its eloquence, the rhetoric loses focus this is not just a matter of a crass creation, but also of diminished economic value for a product which has to sell.

Without going any further into all three systems that Barthes links with the rhetoric of fashion, in what follows I will focus on one of them – the rhetoric of how the wordly (reality) is designated, i.e. the representation that fashion gives to 'the world'.

97

Through the driving force in fashion being the dream of identity and play with this (to be oneself, and through this self to be noticed by others) it becomes what I seem to see as problematical in the *Prêt-à-Porter Catalogue*: pathological appearances, photographs that launch a look that most resembles illustrations of women in various stages of disease.

Barbara Bui's women who wear wigs with pale, eyebrowless faces make me think of patients undergoing chemotherapy. Comme des Garcons' doll-like creatures are like frail girls taken from the anorexia clinic; disproportionately large hairdos, over-large, heavy lengths of cloth that the bodies seem to manage to support only with effort. And so on; well aware that my associations come from the real world, from that which fashion simultaneously fills with representations. Recognise here that even if reality is problematic, fashion is so only on a theoretical level. Nobody wants to buy problems without possible substitutes, dreams, parallel realities, and accordingly, these Death Angels should also be welcome.

Times change. In 1967 Barthes writes:

Such is the Woman ordinarily signified by the rhetoric of Fashion; imperatively feminine, absolutely young, endowed with a strong identity and yet with a contradictory personality, she is named Daisy or Barbara; she is often seen with the Countess de Mun and Miss Phips… and she likes everything, from Pascal to cool jazz.

Barthes goes on to say that we clearly recognise in this monster the permanent compromise that marks the relationship between mass culture and its consumers: dreams and reality, ideal and reality are combined into a fiction that is intended to be consumed.

Today Daisy and Barbara try to learn about Safe Sex, occasionally fail, and are periodically made anxious by the thought of the tiny virus that could slowly eat up their bodies. In between, the body is kept in trim and weighed, as little flesh as possible on the legs. Tormenting bulimia or noble refusal of food are familiar phenomena to today's Daisy and Barbara. It is specifically into this syndrome that the rhetoric of fashion enters, arriving with euphoric images that give the rejected, constricted, abject, the 'sick', an appearance that can be transformed into something as banal as an article of clothing.

Glamorous Death Angels sweep past on the catwalk.

Siksi 3/1996. Translated by Mike Garner

Damien Hirst
Gagosian Gallery, New York

Halali from La-La-Land

When the means of going forwards are lacking, we turn to something else. The pain is directed at our own body; the phantom pain throbs, signalling danger. Something has become impossible to talk about, and our position is that of a neurotic, with any attempt to act undermined before it even gets halfway. If a voice from outside, with a word as its spearhead, manages to penetrate the flesh, with questions like how, where, when, why; if it succeeds with its retroactive method of supplying the destructive transgression with a resolution, a meeting point is established outside, in the word, and the narratives can flow forth.

In fact, there are not one but two boundaries that have to be crossed; the smashing of locks and security chains, and the setting up of new boundaries that have to be crossed so as to tease out the joyous potential of transgression. Precisely this is the significance of the starting hue or cry, an expectation we wish art could satisfy. I am reminded of the words of the philosopher Cecilia Sjöholm at the *Beyond the Rule* symposium in Malmö: 'If art is transgressive it is so specifically because it does not intend to be so. The experience of transgression arises outside of every existing discourse.' A mentally undisturbed place where the contours are so diffuse that they do not permit themselves to be controlled either by the art world or by some other institution with a legitimising function.

Just before the symposium I had seen Damien Hirst's conquest of the American art world at Gagosian Gallery in New York. A smart mega rampage – woe betide the unhappy writer who leaves the gallery without any buzz. So much energy (and money) being mobilised, and so little in mental terms being passed on and propagated. Nothing – like visiting a progressive funfair where all the rides work to calculated effect. No diffuse linkages, no ambivalent feelings indicating that a latent interest, despite everything, is pressing forward towards the light. Instead, just nothing.

I suspect that Hirst has learned far too well where American pragmatism comes from. To say that the biggest is more visible than the bigger, and the big more visible than the smaller is not practised irony, but a fact to be reckoned with in a society where action and function constitute the primary requisites for existence. Thus, Hirst has stepped up his format. In the centre, an enormous ashtray filled with stubs (smoking is prohibited in restaurants and bars in New York). On the wall, mechanical paint-splashing brush machines (a vulgarisation of the Pollockian method). And cut-up animals in bits, preserved in separate glass cases.

For sure, a crime has been committed, a rule of life and death has been broken. But the root-cause of the symptoms of masculine psyhopathology is not the crime itself, but rather the horror of it. And as long as the crime lives on as an unbounded mental representation, the madness will find sustenance. In brief, without going further into psychoanalytical theory, what could be more interesting from a feminine position than specifically this insight into the madness that exists on the other side of the gender boundary? A communication between hysteria and terror, somewhere in La-La-Land.

Where the stores are empty, when we stare at the stubs in the ashtray, and see that there is not so much more to add, it is the spearhead that we miss, words and pictures that brutally violate the inability to cross precisely this, the boundaries.

Siksi 2/1996. Translated by Mike Garner

Jan Hietala
Museum of Natural History, Observatory Museum, Gallery TRE, Stockholm

Virgin ground

In the summer of 1994 Jan Hietala took part in the Swedish-Russian tundra ecology expedition that followed in the wake of Nordenskiöld's Vega Expedition (1878–80), which was intended to investigate the Northeast Passage. Hietala's account of the journey became the installation *Terra Incognita* – untrodden ground – divided into three sections in three different places in Stockholm. Saved for a night long after my visit to Stockholm, I read Hietala's notebook of journal entries from the trip, plus the accompanying photographs. The Swedish-Russian group passed 180 degrees, giving a divine, shadowless night. Maybe it is this that gave the photographs their strange intimation of another air, another colour?

> The journey has begun: Meaninglessness. 07/10/94
> …standing there on the stern… experiencing inner meaninglessness… what am I doing here… like a convergence of my entire previous life… transparent and without permanent utility… value… something which is true and probably the only truth around me… sailing over an odourless open sea… endless… limited only by the convex horizon… pale sun… a similarly pale sky… the wake gurgles and bubbles… leaves a trail over the otherwise calm sea… what am I leaving… what is it that I no longer want to see…

The expedition takes place in the name of science. While the researchers carry out their tasks Hietala goes his own way, as his concerns arise in the moment, on site. His presence on the expedition is raising questions. Science. Who is speaking, who asks the questions? When? Where? And, finally, how? An expedition is a series of events with equipment, boats, helicopters, flesh, blood, skin, damp, heat, cold, people. Dropping a scientific discourse into concrete reality, into being in the world, does not actually function at all, which is what *Terra Incognita* makes us suspect. The constellation that can be read from this is as follows: the researchers on the tundra expedition worked, according to their contracts, with the scientific norm, as distinct from Hietala, who played with the terms of reality; the relationship between *vrai* (true) and *semblant* (apparent). With Hietala this gives rise to a delicate variant on *le vraisemblant* (the probable), which specifically presupposes the presence of someone who gives meaning to what is felt, learned and experienced.

I think about the two earlier works I have seen by Hietala, the installations, *Whom the Gods Love Die Young* and *Deixis*, compare with *Terra Incognita*, and believe I understand. In *Whom The Gods Love Die Young* the walls of the room are red, and small video screens hang in the air. Feel a little uncomfortable. Almost like in pornographic literature, where the text is reduced to a few elements, do this, do that, plus the accompanying obscene descriptions. I go back. And I see. Hietala has succeeded in stripping off a kind of imaginary level, and instead he lets the course of events oscillate between the real (not seen, intimated) and the symbolic: There are props, there are actors, two men on a sofa, a woman in the middle, and the

101

absence that exists in the work is a real absence, not a present symbol for absence. Absence and emptiness are as though nothing, intangible, and the symbol (what we see on the video) is an excerpt from something that could have been Leopard von Sacher-Masoch's daily life. Cold, cruel, and the people on the sofa are specifically actors in someone's private drama. The voice that is not present in the work, but which a sensitive viewer can sense, is gradually heard thanks to the video, which shows a monotonous repetition of a close-up of the male sexual organ in the autoerotic act.

Deixis works analogously. A paradox: It is said that artistic creativity is rooted in the experience of emptiness, and that emptiness is its driving force, it is emptiness that demands a shape. But Hietala's product contains this emptiness. It is contained without showing anything of the cycle of emptiness – the *Deixis* installation, in which the body is HIV-infected, acts like a hypodermic needle that hits the right vein. We feel the pulse beat. Hear it.

From sexuality and interiors to tundra and science. In the tundra, presence nevertheless becomes absent, albeit in a different way.

> …hit by the feeling here like at the other points on the trip… that I am being watched… as if someone follows me on my walk… moves… just behind me or beside me… maybe an animal… a number of different ones… experience the feeling of being under examination… dissection… instead of me being the one to watch…

Thus the sequence of events is linked once again to the question: Who is speaking? Who is seeing? At the Museum of Natural History with Hietala's section *Neshkan – on the Scientific Journey*, there is a photographic portrait of the leader of the expedition.

> …looking like a man who is conscious of his own importance… that he is the centre and for those around him a motivating force… and around him there is a strong magnetism which only exists in those who have succeeded…

The other thing that Hietala shows in *Neshkan* is something the expedition's Russian researchers would prefer to pass by: oil drums, pollution, glass splinters, "natives".

Pevek – on Collecting at the Observatory Museum is the installation's most difficult component. Hietala, who in this work deals with time transversally, sets out objects and microscopes. Occasionally he has gone about this so delicately as regards the museum that one almost passes by his additions. Hietala as though goes all the way, by using the principle of the museum-educational reconstruction, a starting point which in itself sounds hollow. Despite all the reconstructions, real time is still absent.

In the Vega Room, where there is a stand depicting Nordenskiöld, we get a surprising view of two photographs, discretely placed by the door: a male genital organ, beautiful and self-evident, and another photograph that shows a veined, sort of rusted surface. In the middle of this stands Nordenskiöld with his self-satisfied discoverer's ego, he who has surpassed all other men, who has devoted his life to the exploration of virgin ground. But no such land exists, and it is perhaps precisely for that reason it was so important for Nordenskiöld to take possession of the virginal.

> He has understood nothing of truth, nor anything of woman. Because, indeed, if woman is truth, she at least knows that there is no truth, that truth has no place here and that no one has a place for truth. And she is a woman precisely because she does not believe in what she is, in what she is believed to be, in what she thus is not. (Derrida, *Spurs*)

Is this the node that can be discovered within both science and sexuality? The node that makes the truth into a disguise for an unacceptable concept of lack; layer upon layer of transformations and distortions. Who was Nordenskiöld, why was it specifically he who wanted to live out the metaphor, to set foot on *Terra Incognita*? In the innermost room there is an arrangement, *Forget-me-not*: the microscope is placed on a base with a photograph of a young, tundra woman's face, above this is a dried forget-me-not flower. In the microscope your eye goes straight, frontally to a photograph of the female sexual organ.

The meaninglessness finds its redress, the right word does not come when you need it, it comes unasked, later. The sensory organs take things in, smell, see, investigate in the installation at Galleri TRE. The desiring individual finds peace for a moment. For this work Hietala has painted on acrylic glass colours I see as those of the tundra. The ground is a photographic reproduction of Wrangel's island seen from the air. In contrast to the shapes of the superstructure, the structure of nature is actually unproblematic, it follows a rhythm parallel to the correspondence Hietala has set up between the format, colours and sequences of paintings.

Siksi 2/1995. Translated by Mike Garner

A Conversation about Private at Alby

Gallery F15, celebrating its 25 years' jubilee this year, is something of an eccentric among Nordic art institutions. The gallery is a little out of the way, situated in beautiful natural scenery outside Oslo, in the manor house at Alby which was home to a shipping family. When you add the fact that the gallery's task is to show significant Nordic and international contemporary art the reason for thinking in terms of centre and periphery, provinciality and urbanity vanishes almost by itself.

Gertrud Sandqvist inaugurates her directorship at Gallery F15 with the exhibition *Private*. The six artists who participate in *Private* each have a space at their disposal in the freshly renovated building and every installation is made with that specific place in mind. Video artist Tony Oursler's speaking, dream-like phantom dolls populate the stairwell like an organic network. On the ground floor Olav Christopher Jensen's wax figurines *Sleeping Poets* are resting, undisturbed by Marianna Uutinen's uncensored drawings on the subject of Napoleon. On the top floor where the view opens towards the sea Lawrence Carroll has left his nomadic traces: a pile of folded tarpaulins, a wooden box, some canvas. Nina Roos's series of paintings take the opposite route, anchoring the room, following the wall like panelling. The *enfant terrible* of the exhibition, Anders Widoff, represents private disorder with his installation.

The word private makes you pay attention, it is a word there was hardly ever reason to use during the 80s in an art context. With feelers stretched towards the 90s I met with Gertrud Sandqvist for a conversation.

Roos Let us begin with the simplest of questions: What does *Private* mean and how have this special building, the concept and the artists found each other?

Sandqvist When you get to know certain artists and their works you begin to see the enormous discrepancy between what is officially stated and the actual thoughts behind a work. You see that an incredible amount of things are really to do with a private sphere and it is then, when this sphere is there, that something starts happening also in the work. In general you can see how artists in their ways of working with art are increasingly making use of these ruptures in everyday life.

Roos I suppose the ruptures in everyday life are also stressed in the relation between the work and the viewer, because this is an area where the viewer has experience?

Sandqvist Yes, it's almost impossible to understand the works by artists who are interesting now without using your whole register as a viewer, also the most ridiculous or officially wrong or absurd ways of thinking. This openness, I thought, would of course be very interesting to show in an exhibition. Another possible reconstruction would be about something private. I really wanted to open the first exhibition of my own with artists whose works have meant a lot to me. The concept was gradually deepened because the building is so specific. Since this is a home converted into a gallery, and since it was also run as a family business for many years, there are many little flaws, so to speak, and special memories associated with this very place.

The interesting thing then is that you're not working with a neutral institution but on the contrary an institution almost soiled with different expectations. Breaking with that wouldn't be possible, I think, by inserting a totally clean exhibition but the other way round, working against it but on exactly the same terms.

Roos It seems as if *Private* were enhancing an attitude that is in the air or at least upcoming. Could you comment on this?

Sandqvist I think it's partly about trying to find ways of moving on from what happened during the past ten years. To avoid being trapped in a very theoretical discussion about language games or in the world of clichés where the neo-expressionists were working, many interesting artists are shifting their perspective a little and you notice whole new parts, things that have been uninteresting or were considered too private for bringing out. And that's always the case with art, that these shifts are the real points of interest.

Roos Working with shifts puts quite a demand on the artist, most of all a delicate handling of the means, the process and the expression, which I think is apparent in *Private*.

Sandqvist All six artists work with great precision and exactitude and this is an exactitude that is not to do with belief in a certain theory or a certain analysis but it is about something that is happening in the gaps between this or independently of it. And then it becomes extremely exciting to follow the process as the artists were making their installations and see how the rooms become nodes for associative fields of a certain kind and how these fields hook up with one another.

But what this demands from the viewers is that they leave behind some of the passive and distanced attitude they have been taught to adopt when it comes to art, that they let go of some defensive positions and give the exhibition the time it must get. It is interesting to see how many of the artists are more or less consciously forcing the viewers to spend a certain amount of time in the room, which is very important for noticing these shifts. Anders Widoff, for example, does this with his text on the wall. Marianna Uutinen has worked with a more brutal kind of shift since she simply lowers the ceiling in her room, thereby forcing the viewer into an unusual position. Olav Christopher Jenssen is closing the space around his wax figurines, to the extent that you become fully isolated. Once you're inside you won't immediately run out again.

These installations rediscover a presence that actually makes it possible to see what surrounds us, also what is unexpected. The unexpected is perhaps a little roughness in the work that doesn't appear where we imagined it should appear. Provided we remain attentive we become present, and then of course we let go of all thoughts of who we are, who the artists are, how this ought to look.

Another characteristic of *Private* is that it lacks references. *Private* is not a language-based exhibition, it's difficult to grasp in a few precise formulations. And just because it is only partly accessible on the level of language it becomes elusive.

Roos This obviously irritates those who work with neat categories?

Sandqvist Sometimes you could even ask yourself when you saw some works from the 80s whether they were at all interesting to make, since what they were supposed to show was so very controlled. The works were to be interpreted exactly, according to a certain context, and all other interpretations were wrong. And then you have actually killed visual art, there is no longer any point in dealing with the image.

Another aspect of the private is to do with the relation to other kinds of visual media, both advertising films, television films and ordinary feature film – that is, visual means used to address as many as possible and based on units that are calculated to provoke emotion in the largest possible group of people. The artists who participate in *Private* work in a totally opposite way, not at all with what is commonly shared but the other way round. Yet if visual art is not to be sucked into a general mudslide of cinematic expression I think we have to say something different, that visual art is perhaps not for all, at all occasions, always, everywhere. It's important to remember that what I'm saying doesn't represent some kind of elitism, but it's about a wholly different level, another quality of experience.

Hufvudstadsbladet 3 May 1993

Museum moderner Kunst, Frankfurt

Visionary, Dramatic Museum Thinking

A typical tendency for the larger German cities has been the insight that they need to make conscious cultural policy commitments in order to stand out in a European and international context. New, modern museum buildings have emerged rapidly, with the result that Germany in particular has become the functioning model and object of study for this kind of architecture.

The Museum of Modern Art in Frankfurt was finished in the summer of 1990. The building, located at walking distance from the railway station, is exceptionally placed on a wedge-shaped plot between two lively streets. In this completely urban environment the architect Hans Hollein has designed a triangular building that fills the plot with maximum efficiency. When we study the monolithic façade it is hard to believe that the three-storey building actually comprises 50,530 square metres. Hollein's architectural solution that uses the street level is specially tailored for such an urban environment. It is as convenient to step into the museum as into any shop. The emphasis is thus on what the building conceals, a number of variously sized rooms that are expressly designed for exhibitions, bearing in mind the requirements of contemporary art.

The expectations that the city of Frankfurt has of its museum are interesting from the point of view of cultural policy. The museum is allowed to go straight to the point, so to speak, to expand its collection, containing works from 1945 onwards, with topical contemporary art that highlights the current pluralist attitudes. The level of ambition is high, what the museum acquires must be interesting also in an international perspective.

This declared programme differs considerably from the usual responsibilities of a state-run museum: mapping national tendencies and presenting contemporary art starting from its historical connections. It is symptomatic that there was not a single mention of the notion of German art when the museum's direction was decided.

Another issue is how a museum presents its collection. The exhibition currently on show in the Frankfurt museum receives the highest marks, a professional and uncompromising juxtaposition that functions as one of many possible introductions to contemporary art. The museum director Jean-Christophe Amman, well known for his earlier activities at the Kunsthalle Basel, has delivered on one of his stated intentions, to try and show a representative selection of individual artists' œuvres instead of concentrating on separate artworks. Each room has been given its own dramatic charge, it is hardly possible to achieve a higher intensity in an exhibition that is essentially based on a collection.

The collection's artworks from the 60s were, according to Amman, particularly problematic – how to find connections to the 90s that would justify their presence? A fine example is the room with the 'date works' by Japanese artist On Kawara. Kawara made his first date work in New York in the 1960s. Thereafter he has continued to paint a certain number of them every year. The painting thus equals a date where the writing is always white and where the colour of the background varies. For his exhibition Amman has brought Kawara's older date works from the collection together with fresh ones, which he has borrowed directly from the artist. A reversed relation becomes apparent in front of the date series. Usually when we see the works of an artist stretching over several decades we learn something about the artist's development; in this case the paintings are repetitions through which we can refer to our own development.

Another example of how an artist's older works are followed up by newer ones is Gerhard Richter's series *18 October 1977*, which the museum has borrowed for ten years. The series is about Baader, Ensslin and Raspe's deaths, that is about the leaders of the Red Army Faction (RAF). Richter has based the black and grey, photo-realist works on the police's archive photographs. It is difficult to untangle the reactions to the series. One sequence for instance renders Gudrun Ensslin with a smile on her lips, obviously surprised by the camera. At the same time, like an inevitable fact, we are reminded that precisely these people became key figures in the trauma that not only *was* an episode in German history but very much still *is* part of it. As we know it was on 18 October 1977 that Baader, Ensslin and Raspe were found dead in their cells. Richter's controversial series has only been shown in public twice before.

The Korean Nam June Paik, who is considered one of the pioneers of video art, fills one of the rooms with his installation *A Candle* from 1988. The interesting thing is that this work shows Paik moving in the more minimalist direction that characterised his earliest works. In the room there is one single burning candle, captured by the video camera in countless coloured projections. Paik himself thinks that the work is an expression of 'anti-technological technology', a subject that currently fascinates him.

The rooms with Pop Art provoke nostalgia, here Andy Warhol's *Brillo Boxes* are neatly lined up on a shelf next to a young Marlon Brando. During these thirty intervening years, did anything pioneering really happen in art? This is how fresh Warhol's works feel. The same can be said about the work from the 60s by Claes Oldenburg that we find in a nearby room. During this time Oldenburg was dealing with the aesthetics of American everyday life – the bedroom interior reconstructed by Oldenburg is a typical example of a style that could be characterised as American Dream.

Among the younger artists two interesting women are represented, Katharina Fritsch and Rosemarie Trockel. Fritsch's installation is a nightmarish scene where 32 precisely identical men dressed in black sit lined up at a table in exactly the same pose. The uniformed figures continue like an endless image when we think of the countless models in real life, male groups at meeting tables. Trockel, who works with the most varied means, contributes a piece consisting of woven wool with a woven text: 'Do nothing to me / But fast.' A simple effect of 'female logic'?

Hufvudstadsbladet 12 June 1992

Glamorous Cultural Nomadism

The flight from Helsinki to Venice is a painful reminder that the journey leads to the heart of a European continent where political and social unrest, disintegration and warfare are realities. During touch-down in Germany it is impossible to overlook what is happening outside of the protected no-man's land of the airport. And Italy itself, so terribly close to the fighting in ex-Yugoslavia.

The journey's actual destination, Venice, which is hosting the international art Biennale for the 45th time, is with its exceptional combination of fragmentation and wholeness almost a symbolic apparition – built on a group of islands in the Lagoon and kept together by a unified architecture whose damp-infested buildings in themselves represent a kind of æsthetics of collapse. Without any doubt we may claim that this year's Biennale has grown to become a mammoth event that, at least during the opening days, almost threatened to explode the city's measure.

And we ask ourselves if the Biennale is not this year approaching the limit of its own disintegration, which, ironically enough, reminds us of how closely linked concepts such as fragmentation and wholeness actually are. It is obvious that the man behind this year's project, the Italian art critic Achille Bonito Oliva, has created a whole that seems to safeguard the Biennale's position as a prestigious institution; the exhibitions in the national pavilions in the Giardini are surrounded by a whole array of others throughout the city.

Achille Bonito Oliva has called his Biennale *Cardinal Points cf Art*, originally as a reference to the four quarters of the compass and how they affect each other. Instead of presenting a limited, critical viewpcint, Oliva claims that his theme starts from an acknowledgement of cultural nomadism and the coexistence of the languages that have created contemporary art – an acceptance of the 'idea of travelling' with a self-evident reference to 'other' cultures.

The best expression of this idea is on the institutional level where Oliva's tendency towards 'denationalisation' is most visible; the cards that denote national belonging and borders have been reshuffled in various ways, and among other things Oliva has urged the commissioners of the national pavilions to invite artists of other nationalities.

Thus we find for example the American Joseph Kossuth (of Hungarian descent) in Hungary's pavilion and Hans Haacke (residing in the US) invited by the German pavilion, and in the section of the Italian pavilion called *Punti dell'arte* there are names such as Beuys, Baselitz, Buren and Kirkeby. In this respect Oliva's effort contains a moral quality which is undeniable in a political climate where national origin is one of the contested issues.

Otherwise it is unclear what Oliva really has in mind with the cardinal points of art, i.e. whether the theme is of any relevance to the content, to art. The question arises in particular since a certain retrospective tendency is obvious in the selection of artists. Also the unchallenged cardinal point of art Marcel Duchamp is honoured with a separate exhibition at Palazzo Grassi (which is not part of the Biennale).

The issue appears even more obscure when we relate it to Oliva's intention of presenting a Biennale based on the idea of the mosaic which in itself is at odds with the super-structure of order, division and systematic organisation that strongly marks the Biennale as an institution.

After several days of wandering about through the different exhibitions the mosaic idea seems more and more problematic. We encounter many separate parts that are impossible to piece together since every single part is of a different material or structure and precisely therefore would need individual attention. Thus Oliva's commendable thought about 'denationalisation' should not have left unnoticed the fact that the individual work is often anchored in a specific place and belonging that shapes its context.

In this mammoth project it is as if the contextual aspect were either forgotten or drowned in the overwhelming range and thereby one of the conditions for communication between the work and the viewer is absent.

The consequence is what we could foresee; those who manage to stand out best are the well known American and European names, since we are familiar with their backgrounds. Attempts at making trips in other directions (ethnic, peripheral, marginal) become an impossible undertaking at least under these conditions.

The two artists that rule supremely over the Giardini area are Hans Haacke and Ilya Kabakov. Each have on the artistic level managed to deepen the implications of the Biennale's theme. The pavilion is problematised with the idea of nationality as a starting point, and in addition criticism is levelled at what this institution represents. In addition, both artists demonstrate that art with a mission in 1993 is more about conversation than about answers and solutions.

Hans Haacke's installation in the German pavilion (with the text *Germania* above its entrance) hits directly at the sore points of the country's history. When we step into the building we encounter an enlarged photograph of Benito Mussolini and Adolf Hitler taken in June 1934 when Hitler visited the Biennale and was received by a whole crowd of young Fascists.

Inside the pavilion Haacke has carried out a simple, aggressive operation. The marble floor has been hacked to pieces and now consists of thousands of shards. On the rear wall the word Germania is printed in big letters. In its simplicity Haacke's installation refers to a context that hides complex problems with uninvestigated issues – Haacke's action equals a refusal to accept.

Ilya Kabakov, born in the Ukraine, nowadays living in New York, has occupied the former Soviet pavilion in characteristically Kabakovian fashion, tenderly and clear-sightedly. The building is encircled by an unpainted wooden fence that robs it of every expression of grandeur (the adjacent German building represents the neo-classicist style).

Kabakov shows no more and no less than real trash, the building's interior looks like a gathering point for all the rubbish in the world. As we walk through the narrow corridor we approach the sound of Soviet marching music which can be traced to a blaring loudspeaker placed in a reddish-pink guardian's hut in the back yard. Also, now, liberating laughter is present in Kabakov's work.

The other intelligent reflection over current political issues through the history of the Biennale is carried out by the Frenchman Christian Boltanski in the Italian pavilion. Boltanski's black and white photographic installation consists of documents about works from the Biennale in 1938. In a comment on his installation Boltanski points out the following: in 1938 none of the visitors seemed to be occupied with anything other than the question of which of the artists would be awarded the Golden Prize. 1938 was the year when Hitler invaded Czechoslovakia, when the Sino-Japanese war was going on, and the Spanish Republic collapsed under murderous conditions.

How was it this year at the Biennale, how many had the energy, in the heat during the glamorous opening functions, to talk about for instance the butchery in former Yugoslavia?

Hufvudstadsbladet 28 June 1993

Ars 95, Museum of Contemporary Art, Helsinki
Interview with Maaretta Jaukkuri

What Is the Thinking?

The Finn has reason to feel a little proud. When the world at large cuts back on exhibition projects the Finn – who else? – starts carrying out a comprehensive international exhibition of contemporary art. Without doubt the series of *Ars* exhibitions (1961, 1969, 1974, 1983) has created an important institution for contemporary art. For instance the *Ars* exhibition of 1983 has repeatedly resurfaced in discussions during the years, one person remembering one thing, the other something else, the point being that we share a key to a 'generational event'.

Ars 83 showed different parts of the field of art, from land art via Neo-Expressionism to the Trans-Avantgarde. And now, in 1995, when art is characterised by its being in-between, when contemporary art at its best succeeds in shaking off definitions that have become too narrow – what is the thinking at the Museum of Contemporary Art where the task has been to elaborate the much-anticipated *Ars* exhibition? We could add: much-contested. It is in the nature of things that such a venture shakes up the art world.

For my part I hope that the eternal harping about phenomena inside 'our art world' could be put aside when there is, for once, a unique possibility to experience, discuss and analyse works of art. The significance of the *Ars* exhibition is in something very primary: an occasion to look around, to see art.

Museum director Tuula Arkio, curator Maaretta Jaukkuri and assistant curator Asko Mäkelä (responsible for the part of Ars entitled *Artificial*

Reality) are the persons behind Ars. I meet with Maaretta Jaukkuri to get answers to my curious questions during the intensive stage when the exhibition is taking shape in the Ateneum building.

We talk about *Ars* as an institution and Maaretta Jaukkuri offers a clarification:

Jaukkuri If anyone questions *Ars 95* there is a simple defence. We must not forget that the objective of *Ars 95* is to give basic information about contemporary art in particular to those viewers who do not work with art and who therefore do not have an expert's view on the state of affairs in art today. *Ars 83* had a different function, since the times were different. It became a kind of introduction to what was new, but today, when artists and writers are relatively well acquainted with contemporary art through travelling and journals, our thinking has been different.

We hope that the exhibition functions as a small-scale model of the 'current' state of art, that the viewers are able, through the individual works, to create an overall picture that reflects the situation in contemporary art, that the works clarify and complete each other so that a possible context emerges for the viewers. If we depart from such thinking we can claim that Ars 95 is not a mega-exhibition but the opposite, a small-scale model of the situation and the art we are living right in the middle of.

Roos In the preliminary information about *Ars 95* a kind of concept is presented with a thematic division: *Individual, Society, Image/Language* and *Artificial Reality*. How did you arrive at this and how does the division function?

Jaukkuri At the beginning, as a thinking tool to spark ourselves off, we discussed the concept of identity, which of course has been a keyword in recent years in both art and theory. Gradually our thoughts became more coherent as we travelled around with the purpose of selecting works for the exhibition. We realised we wanted to relate the concept to something, since the ability to relate is so specific to art as expression – and identity is nothing if it does not exist anywhere, does not have a place.

Thus it dawned on us that the relation between the private (the individual) and the public (society) is the relevant axis around which identity and other topical notions are circling. I can give one example. Through art what is most privately experienced can be stated in public and the visual presentation can make the viewer, as a representative of both privacy and

115

collectivity, take part in and communicate with the reality of another individual. Freud had already realised that when the private or personal is articulated guilt is reduced since the topic is introduced at a public level.

Roos What you say leads to an interesting about-turn for the idea of the theme. A concept like this for *Ars 95* comprises a problematising of 'compartmentalised' thinking as such, it presupposes flexible thinking and creative transitions between different concepts. The third section, which received the working title *Image/Language*, what does it relate to?

Jaukkuri The title *Image/Language* refers, among other things, to an interesting observation. Today the artist is no longer the heroic figure who tells about his inner life and his feelings in his own language, but quite the opposite; he uses and develops his language starting from the visual language that already exists. I think this opens the work up to communication.

It is actually true that art implies a permissiveness, that the work with its special means can express things that are impossible to make public in real life. And this transgression of the boundaries between private and public, from each side, is a contemporary issue. Kieslowski's *Blue Film*, for instance, touches upon the subject and Jonathan Friedman among others deals with precisely the distinction between the private and the public in his anthropological research. One important thing to note concerning the themes of the exhibition is that they are not intended to offer ready-made answers. The answer you yourself have to provide, as the viewer.

Roos What you are talking about makes me think of the Documenta exhibition, which was a gigantic manifestation of the 'collapse of hierarchies'. It was launched as an exhibition without concept, without theme, and the critique of the exhibition went in either direction. Perhaps the exhibition would still have benefited from presenting a simple basic concept as a preliminary working tool, at least for the viewer. Instead a new prohibition was created, a new denial.

Jaukkuri This type of international exhibition reveals the problematic concept of 'the public'. My opinion is that we cannot speak of the public as a homogenous mass, that this is ultimately to do with a very heterogeneous group. Each and everyone who comes to the *Ars* exhibition does so in his capacity as an individual, and it is only at the individual level that real communication with the work takes place, an interaction between giving and receiving. I think the 90s in general is the decade that relates, for instance, the notion of responsibility to the individual level.

One more thing about the theme *Image/Language*. Formal innovations that concern art are, in my opinion, almost impossible to find. Therefore it becomes ever more important to listen to what the work is saying, how it is being said and what expression is being used. It is around this aspect that the most radical things in today's visual art are happening and the artists in the *Image/Language* section represent this ambition. They use an existing visual language, but they use it in such a way that the work becomes a synthesis with something new that transcends the formal elements.

Roos One last question, I know that those who are interested in the practice of 'name dropping' are sitting with the list of participating artists and speculating. Are there any safe bets, too many or too few? Or has there been too much or too little risk in the selection of artists?

(Maaretta Jaukkuri smiles discreetly – that question is part of the game that is being played in the art world.)

Jaukkuri For me personally that social game is totally irrelevant. If we look at *Ars 95* from the perspective of the selection of artists we must remember that the Ateneum building sets a physical limit on the amount of participants, though of course we would have liked to show more artists. We are, however, pleased that practically everyone we invited agreed to participate. In addition there is a number of artists in the exhibition who have actually not showed internationally before, for instance representatives of the Baltic countries, and in comparison with the most recent *Ars* without a single participant from our own country the situation is more positive for Finland; we participate with six artists.

The interview is closed with pleasant laughter. Maaretta Jaukkuri says, with a humorous glance:

Or actually you can write that we have taken no risks whatsover, since here at the museum we can vouch for the fact that the exhibited artworks are of guaranteed quality – contemporary art of the most exquisite kind.

Hufvudstadsbladet 5 February 1995

Smart Show
Wasahallen, Stockholm

'Smart' for the second time

Smart Show had its debut last year, and this year worry was already voiced:
is the event becoming too established? Has the freshness turned into smart
mannerism?

This is how the initiators (an independent group of Swedish gallerists
and exhibition makers) express themselves: 'Just as last year Smart Show
wishes to function as a catalyst for Swedish and international contemporary art. We are convinced that the best way to vitalise the Swedish art life
is to broaden the areas of contact between different participants; we want
to invest contemporary art with new life by creating an honest, unpreten-
tious and suitably sized meeting point where artists and the public, collectors and gallerists, curators and critics can meet with art and with each
other.' And the show went on in the Wasa Hall for four days. At times there
was not enough space.

It becomes trickier to address the criticism that was directed at *Smart
Show*, that it now as a two-year-old risks becoming 'institutionalised', that
it might become predictable and mechanically confirm what is expected
from the category in question, the younger generation. We must wait for
the decisive third year. Still this year *Smart Show* managed to position itself
as an alternative to the suave Stockholm Art Fair that opened one week
later – one sign of this is the diagnosis an 'established' gallerist gave *Smart
Show*: teething trouble.

What is topical about Smart Show is, in my opinion, the art shown by
the fair's 40 exhibitors (over half of whom were foreign). Little painting,
much media art; sex, violence, brutality dominated the imagery. The whole
unruly mix has been called the fast food of visual art by some critics, and
by others a sign of the tendency that goes under the name of 'New Reality'.
Although we know that the gallerist who is on his way to an alternative
fair tends to showcase work of the trendier kind, and although we know
that art exhibited under the label 'younger' favours a pungent expression
we cannot disregard the fact that the works shown at *Smart Show* exist *de
facto*, have an impact on the public and thus function as a symptom of

what is typical of our time.

But when you wonder how this typicality is being defined in this kind of context, then you do become a little worried. I am not referring to the works displaying sexuality, violence and 'offensive material', but instead to the way in which imagery is being used and how this usage in turn functions as a symptom of something typical of our time – what are we like, what does our reality look like, what is our world like? The questions become relevant particularly if we connect them to Julia Kristeva's simple thesis that art (like many other things) shares the sickness of our time.

The insight for which I am grateful to *Smart Show* is to do with how a misunderstanding is revealed. Until now I believed that the expression New Reality means roughly the same as a newly awakened interest in realities, that the focus was on the real (even if this can, of course, be expressed through abstract means). The amplification of this dimension at *Smart Show* makes you suspicious; imagery is being used so effectively that the intention can hardly have been to show 'reality'. Instead I believe that the material aims at another effect, to create as fast and skillfully as possible an art that seduces. This would explain the impression that art is feverishly hunting for visual material that competes for our attention by means of excess. With this use of images death, for instance, has lost its anchorage in any real experience of death, it has become a visual sensation among others – one ingredient on the menu of New Reality.

To describe what is mentioned above with an instructive example from *Smart Show*. I studied with fascination the photographs by Wolfgang Tillmans that were exhibited by Daniel Buchholz, Cologne. Afterwards these superb photographs with intimate fragments of urban reality stuck in my memory in a disturbing way. Tillmans's way of photographing a person or a situation varies according to the subject and therefore each picture is photographed in a specific, tailored way. At the same time I was wondering why I felt that I had seen everything before even if I could not possibly have witnessed for instance the erotic scene that Tillmans had photographed in a close-up.

There is a possible explanation. Tillmans's photographic strategy can be compared to the way in which journals like Vogue or Elle manipulate photography – every photograph aspires to a maximum of seduction, an advertising shot for a perfume has the same aim as the zoom-in on Kate Moss's pelvis (a supermodel). This is the photographic language that

119

Tillmans has such sovereign mastery of, and the reason is possibly that he started his career as a photographer for fashion magazines.

A depressing insight, because then we are back in the art of quoting from the 80s, only the difference is that the quoting is now performed more smartly. At *Smart Show* there were, however, good exceptions. A new acquaintance for me was for instance Tracey Emin's little installation at Galleri Andreas Brändström. Emin, born 1961 and living in London, is working at the boundary where visual possibilities of expression are challenged by a rare combination of personal frailty and strength.

Hufvudstadsbladet, 19 March 1995

Taidetta
Contemporary Finnish Art in Stockholm, 1995

Helsinki Today – an International Remark

The other day when I was walking along Arkadia Street in Helsinki, distracted by my thoughts, I almost collided with ironing boards. A man, a Russian, was lugging along a number of brand-new ironing boards wrapped in transparent plastic, seven of them. Even more ironing boards, this was just the beginning of the parade. One Russian woman could only carry three, her stronger woman friend was carrying six, the daughter one. Ironing boards. I decided to trace the source and yes, I was right, the Russians were emptying the nearby cut-price department store of ironing boards.

General downscaling and specific background – the expression occurred to me as I was pondering various phenomena of our time. Helsinki is, with regard to ironing boards, an international city. The Russians, that is, who bring the boards to St Petersburg. And the Finns, the elderly ladies who go over to Tallinn to replenish their reserves of butter and weak beer, what should we call them if not provincials of the first degree?

These phenomena feel neither new nor old. They are natural, rather. In the Finns' register of experience there is a separate chapter for relations

120

with the eastern neighbours, whether they have been articulated during decades of silence or by trade and consumption as now, in this early stage. Therefore, if you think international in the eastward direction, Finland is more active than the other Nordic countries. Roles being exchanged, positions shifted, rates soaring so high that they must fall once more. We live through one decade, only to reinterpret it when the following decade begins, and then once again when the century is over. Relations, interpretations and evaluations, in reality and in present moments.

What Euphoria

In 1991 the book *Koko hajanainen kuva* (The Whole Fragmented Picture) was published, where Marja-Terttu Kivirinta and Leena-Maija Rossi go through Finnish art of the 80s. Expectation was in the air, as if art was placed under a great bubble, in which all the things destined to become new and interesting were being cultivated. Since the picture was now fragmented once and for all, something decisive was bound to happen to Finnish art. And with great eagerness people started to orient themselves among the 'discourses'. In 1995 the need is quite the opposite. If we want to orient ourselves in Finnish contemporary art, and discover the topical, we have every reason to downscale general expectations and instead sharpen our instrument for scrutinising the specific. I remember an interview that I recently did, and a statement by Maaretta Jaukkuri, chief curator at the Museum of Contemporary Art. She quoted a philosopher who thought the most interesting thing right now is returning to first questions, not in terms of the answers but in terms of the operational modes that produced the answers.

That signals something important. Confronted with the bulimia of the 80s – the art of quotes, manipulated images, staged images, mass media images – you wonder if the expression is a symptom of a common stand experienced in relation to reality, or if general/international visual expression is actually a relief for both artists and critics. The artist's creativity is about manipulating coded material, not thinking beyond that, not thinking *as such*. The critic's activity is about repeating. When he sees an aberration, an innovation, a stranger that he cannot 'unpack' with repetition, then he falls silent.

About and around the Unsaid

Many of the artists who are topical now in the mid-90s finished their education in the late 80s. And as a Finnish specialty, there are important artistic oeuvres that had already begun in the 70s. In the autumn of 1995 the Museum of Contemporary Art showed a retrospective by Pekka Nevalainen. The oldest work in the exhibition was from 1976, a photograph of a performance where Nevalainen walks through a snowy landscape, leaving behind a trail of primary colours. 'I was interested in painting but I used another medium, performance, to express my idea of painting.' Laconic and simple. Nevalainen's exhibition said important things about Finnish art. A mentality and a culture characterised by the unsaid has yielded positive harvests for visual art. At his best, a Finnish artist makes himself master of his medium, whether it is painting, sculpture, installation or photography. This precision helps make the big theoretical issues of contemporary art less dramatic. For instance the (international) tendency that strives for direct anchorage in concrete reality (as a reaction against the art of quotes in the 80s) becomes almost in-built with an artist like Nevalainen. When the medium is refined it is put into direct contact with the rest of the content – the work becomes real, regardless of whether it refers to concrete or imagined reality.

Another example, Martti Aiha, who since the 80s has sculpted in wood with generous ornaments reminiscent of northern Finnish woodcarving. In his book about Aiha, entitled *Kotiinkaupuun kuva* (The Image of Homesickness) Tom Sandqvist writes, among other things, the following: 'White stands for life, red for blood and ubiquitous violence, black for death and sorrow, gold for the alchemical hope – it is as if the winding, mind-boggling ornament tried to encompass them all, to cover them all together with their final origin in what can only be shown, never said, never said in words on the discursive level where language plays with its different meanings, significances and references to what cannot be said.'

Provocation

Quagmires are approaching, the quote above leads over into the feminine, in the sense of mentality, state of mind. Going further than you were instructed by the framework, representing and expressing what transcends the hierarchy of orders that in turn rests on the first, symbolic order given in language. The sculptor Reijo Hukkanen works in Oulu. His sculptural objects are almost impossible to look at. You lose yourself in them. Organised jumbles of various objects, shapes, materials; repulsive and therefore so alluring. Hukkanen seems to be scraping his way through the varnish and holding up unfinished lumps of matter. This is me thinking aloud according to Julia Kristeva's terminology: such abjection, such holiness. What Hukkanen does is to crush sculptural blocks of Finnish natural stone, making a beautiful sound.

And painting? After the Finnish wars recovery was slow and the Modernist breakthrough happened relatively late. Things were slow indeed. Concrete art (and Modernism in general) is still a ghostly presence, thanks to its position as *éminence grise*. When the norm is strong, this can have positive effects and turn into an advantage. Artists like Silja Rantanen and Jussi Niva work rationally, they think in terms of construction, architecture, colour, surface, primary perception. At her exhibition in the Kunsthalle Helsinki in the autumn of 1993 Rantanen showed one of her highlights. She showed sweet rolls in various stages of becoming plaited. It is not the motif as such that makes the painting, when the medium floats supremely to the fore.

And the sanctity of painting? In Finnish contemporary painting something I wish to call 'real provocation' has just been launched at the formal and expressive restraint and predictability that used to characterise the field. In the 80s even the very wildest, most expressive painting began to acquire, both here and in Europe, a characteristic look. The language was repeated, became repetitive. Among the painters Marianna Uutinen has been the hardest hitter. Uutinen does it with a gesture, an action that may be the concrete act of squirting paint at the canvas or contemptuous laughter at the kind of painting that fiddled with gridded systems or tried to make the 'interior' stick onto the canvas. Others do something else, a realism of the real (in the Lacanian sense). Time in these paintings can be infinitely fast, it is about the split second during which a condition belonging outside language can acquire mass and substance. The break becomes brutal, when you paint what was never supposed to be painted; the precondition of practice is the total refusal of well-known operational modes.

While we are on the topic of provocation, Teemu Mäki is most frequently mentioned as the *enfant terrible* of Finnish 90s art. I myself would rather call him a true existentialist. Life and death are explored through sexuality. His own body serves as a sounding board for anxiety, torment, meaninglessness and pleasure; precisely the kind of projection screen nature had become in early Finnish painting.

To Be Continued

After the cut-price department store, the Russians and the ironing boards, I pull myself together and continue towards my actual goal. Which is visiting the museums in the peripheral area around Arkadia Street where Swedish artists exhibited in the autumn of 1995 under the title *Strange Phenomena*. I freeze for the second time – which phenomena do they have in mind?

what is officially stated

Pekka Nevalainen

Ah, but the sky was blue. Ah, but the leaves were green then, when we first began learning to subsume the outside world into words. Tentative efforts to understand that green is green, that the sky is high, that I exist in a body that is small, in a world that is large. The experience of differences, nuances, proportions is real for the child as long as the enthusiasm for ordering the surrounding world is still functioning, before re-ordering and subordination have become life with a compulsion.

The Finnish title of Pekka Nevalainen's retrospective exhibition in Helsinki is *Piiri*. On hearing the word *piiri*, every Finn starts to chant a Finnish nursery rhyme, *Pieni piiri pyörii lapset siinä hyörii*. It describes a ring game in which the children go round in a circle, a merry-go-round game. On the cover of the catalogue for *Piiri* is a photograph of Nevalainen sitting in the middle of a circle that he has drawn in white chalk on the ground. This is actually the only statement that I have seen by the artist and an important one. I think here of a fragment from Roland Barthes' *A Lover's Discrourse: Fragments*. "I want to change systems: no longer to unmask, no longer to interpret, but to make consciousness itself a drug, and thereby to accede to the perfect vision of reality, to the great bright dream, to prophetic love."

In one of his earliest works, a black-and-white photograph, Nevalainen is squatting, naked, filtering sand through his fingers, and he considers every grain of sand an important part of the work, together they form a whole, a little mountain of sand (Nevalainen, quoted in the catalogue). A slow, painstaking process as a marker for the change of systems on which Nevalainen's art is founded. As that art is a waking dream, everything is permitted, the requirements of coherence have already been met, since the person who is in that waking dream is the protagonist, the artist, in the place where the process is to be (re)established, turned into a waking reality. The first room in the museum contains a pile of material entitled *Nature Document*. Here is the large green leaf that sticks up from the floor like a sculpture. Trunks of Finnish varieties of tree, sculptures of forest animals made out of bits of wood, targets for sharpshooters, nature documentaries on video. In relation to the document, the scale of the human body becomes like an elastic band that is adjusted, depending on where in the room we are standing.

The grains of sand that Nevalainen allowed to run through his fingers in 1976 took on a further significance in his work with the Indian mandala, in which the triangles are filled with various pigments. In the retrospective exhibition, the 'mandala space' with the mysterious, orange tent from 1982 is the space of the sun, flowers and eternity. What is interesting is that we can make pronouncements on Nevalainen's art in this way, and view the sun, the flowers and eternity without a trace of cliché or routine. Generously painted flowers on glass (*Leaves*) lined up along one of the walls, ready for the biblical exhortation: go forth and multiply. The flowers do this with an amused smile, not so that there is an obligation or compulsion, but out of enjoyment. Nevalainen's mandala space looks as self-evident as any kitchen.

The key image in Nevalainen's installations is a beautiful one, beautiful because it is ingenuous. Perhaps that is why I constantly think of Barthes and an excerpt from *A Lover's Discourse*. The fragment *I want to understand* ends with a parenthesis:

(And if consciousness – such consciousness – were our human future? If, by an additional turn of the spiral, some day, most dazzling of all, once every reactive ideology had disappeared, consciousness were finally to become this: the abolition of the manifest and the latent, of the appearance and the hidden? If it were asked on analysis not to destroy power (not even to correct or to direct it), but only for decorate it, as an artist? Let us imagine that the science of our lapsi were to discover, one day, its own lapsus, and that this lapsus should turn out to be: a new, unheard-of form of consciousness?)

In the installation from 1991, *In the Picture Anton is so Brave and Energetic*, the child Anton is running from his mother's embrace towards the camera. This is what the photograph is about, about the moment that proves that the intensity is still there, nothing has yet been shattered. Nevalainen's confidence that his own art can continue from this point, from Anton's position, gives us faith. The strength this gives us is light and yet serious, like that of play.

Siksi 4/1995. Translated by Mike Garner

Tomorrow Is a New Day

What I had intended to ask about and had prepared for lost its significance. Jaan Toomik, born in 1961 and working out of Tallinn, is tired of talking about and explaining his works. He says this straight out, and I believe him. Perhaps he has faced too many uninformed questions about his project outside of Estonia: the São Paulo biennale in 1994; *Ars 95* in Helsinki; the Container 96 project in Copenhagen this summer; along with installations in England and Germany.

The Way to São Paulo – a project lasting from April to October 1994 that was carried out on the geographical axis Tartu, Prague and São Paulo – sites of significance that surprisingly enough can be seen to form a straight line on the map (Tartu, Toomik's home city and the intellectual capital of Estonia; Prague, the midpoint of central Europe; and São Paulo, legendary goal of many travellers). For the destination São Paulo, Toomik made a mirror-glass cube that was left to float free on the river that runs through the city. He writes: 'Object in motion, representing the illusory matter. On the one hand being all that is reflecting, absolutely free simultaneously, independent, having no memory, which transforms it ungrasping from reality. Through free motion, constantly eliminating time and space in its essence.'

To have no memory, to do away with it. Memory is meant to fade. To commemorate his brother's death in 1992 Toomik made *Windows*. A kilometre of documentary film had been thrown out of the window after the strips had been set alight. At the Kunsthalle in Tallinn Toomik installed the strips alongside the window, like a roller blind that also let the light filter through.

He does not sit still in one place for long. I remember reading that he practised karate: 'I need the physical, it is one of the simplest ways for me to achieve some kind of spontaneous calm. My memory, my own history is disturbing, I want to do away with it.'

By his bed Toomik has a world atlas, which he likes to leaf through. We look at the atlas. Toomik locates Nepal, a country he would like to go to. He tells me about his trip to Albania. The little country was covered with concrete bunkers sticking out of the ground; for their defence, the Albanians build one bunker the size of a person per inhabitant, for them to hide in if the need arises. The country is thus clad in a functional installation; Toomik likes the idea of this, having staged many of his works and performances out of doors, studied old castles, dug into the earth and, like a shaman, initiated ritual acts with fire, drumbeats and cries. For instance, at Güstrow in Germany he dug a series of holes in the ground in an East-West direction, at the bottom of which he installed mirrors that made depth into sky.

Now, as I write, I curse myself for forgetting to ask him what he did with the bits of human bone he found in the earth.

Roos Jaan, you started off as a painter of expressive, almost hallucinatory visions, what was the situation like then, I mean, just now you said that you are constantly trying to find motivations for making art at all?

Toomik My life at that point in time was like finding yourself in a completely enclosed space, and it was an insane life, that is why I started to paint.

Roos What is an insane life?

Toomik I was dependent on other people's feelings, far too much, and in the long run that became messy.

A documentary about Toomik has just been completed, produced by Tallinn TV. We watch it on video. What one notices is that Toomik's attitude has become increasingly minimalist, he refines, peels away. Refining, making the memories fade: is this a way of defining a position in which freedom can be experienced, is it the place that correlates with the impulses that Toomik worked with in his latest pieces?

After the conversation with Toomik, it occurs to me that he did not say a single word about his experiences of the upheavals that Estonia has been through, with the word freedom as their political goal – for the present, talking about things is not his way of expressing himself.

Without knowing that, Toomik's passion for travel would almost sound like a cliché. Each work has to be a journey, he rarely repeats what he does. He changes register, and is afraid of getting stuck in the stereotype. The unease lives in his body. After his brother's death, Toomik went to Germany on a grant, and cut himself off completely in the wine-producing area of Speyer. What he did was to photograph sunsets over the vineyards, drink wine, and install the photographs of the setting sun as labels on empty wine bottles lined up in rows.

Joy. At *Ars 95*, Toomik showed a video that immediately imprints itself on the viewer's retina. Here, visual joy is the same as a rare moment of experienced joy. On the afterdeck of a ship in forward motion, surrounded by cresting waves, Toomik jumps up and down. Weightlessness.

Suddenly he asks me a surprising question: 'Are you happy with your life?' And then immediately starts telling me with evident glee about his own morning. Early each morning and late in the evening, he cycles to places where he studies sunrises and sunsets. His next work will be a video installation based on what he has photographed during his panorama trips. This is an old passion, he and his brother were in the habit of making just such studies together. This particular morning, something very special has happened. A strange tale. At the usual panorama site before sunrise he had met an old lady who he had seen ten years before while standing on the exact same spot with his brother.

Toomik She laughed beautifully at him, and she was right. Just before the sun comes up you feel clear, empty and fresh, and you can feel the way the beneficial emptiness slowly vanishes and turns into bright daylight. Sunset is different, it is more weighed down, and thus more human. Nostalgia is aroused when the sun goes down over the horizon. What I want to remember is the woman's smile, still just as beautiful as it was ten years ago.

Siksi 3/1996. Translated by Mike Garner

Marjatta Oja
Gallery Pieni Agora, Helsinki

Mother and Daughter

What is a video installation? If we look for an objective definition it could be described as a work that is based on the interaction between a video image and an environment constructed by the artist. It is considerably more interesting to view the installation as a meeting place for opposite aspects of one medium – for instance a union of art and technology, the visual space of the video monitor and physical space, subjective vision and the concrete volume of the machine.

Marjatta Oja is working with this medium in an unusually productive way. The preconditions are topicalised and exploited only to the degree necessary for visualising content. Thus the technical aspect is played down as it becomes integrated with content.

The video installation *Mami* studies the relation between mother and daughter starting from the concepts of near and far, which are related to time and space. These four concepts are almost concretely present, as they also correlate to the technical construction of the installation. In the gallery a small square room has been delimitated with the help of linen sheets. In the room a kitchen video is projected. The daughter (life-size) moves around in her kitchen. In the exhibition space a monitor has also been added, which shows her mother. She sits in an armchair and talks about her childhood. The same monitor is also seen in the kitchen video. This means that the daughter sitting in her kitchen can synchronously watch the video where her mother is speaking.

The ever-present mother is the theme that is effectively staged. The pictures become documentary, real in the same way that a photograph can always be described as being in unity with its referent. This authenticity is interesting in combination with how the problematic itself is happening on the psychological level and in addition is being expressed through techni-cal maneouverings of time and space. The mother in her armchair is in the daughter's kitchen, and simultaneously actual time produces an ever greater distance in time between them. Herein lies the difference between the images of memory and the images in the monitor. The images of me-mory exist outside the present, in contrast to the video, which brutally deteriorates with time.

After a while we start noticing the sound effects. What is the mother saying? We hardly hear anything, because her voice is being drowned by kitchen sounds from the daughter's kitchen. Irreconcilable things are being hinted at: the dilemma of the present mother? What is the daughter saying? Is she the daughter who, according to Kristeva's terms, has two alternatives: either identifying with the mother's body without voice or language, or with a voice but without a body, a 'virgin of words', in a position from which it is impossible to transcend the given boundaries of speech, impossible to oppose authorities.

It feels like a relief to enter into the second room of the gallery, because there we find an installation with the same woman (the daughter), but now she is sitting and painting in front of a window. The psychological and concrete levels are united in something that could be summed up under the heading: a room of one's own.

Hufvudstadsbladet 25 October 1991

Artist Anna Ghéczy, researchers Marja-Liisa Honkasalo and Terhi Utriainen
Porthania, Helsinki University

The Last Words

Women committing suicide: time dragging itself ever closer to the decisive act, which becomes an absolute limit separating before from after. On each side there is the suicide note, before the act and after it, meant to be read by the closest circle.

The exhibition at Porthania serves another intention than artistic ambition. It wants to give voice to women who have committed suicide. White fabric is installed like the walls of narrow corridors. On the fabric there are simulations, in black printed letters, of farewell messages left behind by women. The immediate trivial association is to sheets hung out to dry.

Conceptual art's preference for using text, most of all truisms, has somehow made us accustomed to dealing with verbal content in art. It could be said that today's art is turning the documentary into a staging of fiction. In this connection the impact of the installation at Porthania is redoubled. What we are seeing is real, it is true in the original sense of the words used. And we are wondering what reality is hidden behind the texts.

Unfortunately the researchers Honkasalo and Utriainen have at this stage not yet finished their comparison between men's and women's suicide notes. Half of the riddle is thus left unresolved. Yet they are right to point

out that researchers in Finland have mostly been interested in men committing suicide. Also, the ratio of men to women regarding suicide is 4:1.
So what are they like, the suicide notes left by Finnish women? Usually
they are short, and they contain combinations of various conflicting elements: comments about life, about taking leave, departing, concern for the
loved ones. Direct references to imminent death are unusual. Departure is
expressed indirectly: greetings, goodbye, I have to go. On the other hand
the messages tell about the woman's life, and most of all about family life.
It is as if her world was reduced to everyday triviality marked by an angst-
ridden atmosphere. Until the very end her whole being is immersed in
everyday concerns.

Honkasalo and Utriainen have discovered a recurrent element in the
content of those messages, which they call last wills. The term refers to the
concrete distribution of property as well as directions concerning internal
relations between the survivors. In the latter sense a last will may impose
limitations on other people's lives, or create feelings of guilt. The last will
takes on an interesting aspect if it is compared to the message that was
often communicated at the same time, of not being able to stand anything
anymore. With her last will the woman leaves behind her absolutely last
words, which means that she will emerge as an active subject after her
death. However, not being able to stand anything anymore is quite the
opposite. It means being powerless, being subject to circumstances. Could
death for the woman be something that exorcises what she experiences as
a lack of self, thereby becoming a rite of initiation that makes representations around a self possible: a journey towards being a subject?

Anthropological studies of female mystics and their experiences have
proved fruitful for the interpretation of women's suicide notes as well. The
decisive observation is the way in which the female mystics crossed over
into life at the nunnery. They did not change roles as radically as their male
colleagues did when they left one life for another, which can be sensed,
among other things, from the language these women used to interpret and
articulate their liminal experiences (their visions of the sufferings of Christ
and Mary). Unlike the men they kept their everyday language, anchored
in their own world of corporeal experience. The women's religious liminal
was, in fact, the utmost deepening of everyday basic experiences. They
moved effortlessly from one context to another. This coincides with the
observations about women writers who committed suicide. Virgina Woolf

sank herself wordlessly into the river with the stone in her pocket. When Kirilov, a man, commits suicide in Dostoyevsky's novel, it is to show that his will is stronger than God's. The Russian poet Marina Tsvetaeva writes something very different before her suicide: I don't want to die. I just don't want to be.

Women can commit suicide without tragedy, even without drama, without giving the impression of escaping from a heavily-policed border. As if suicide were a natural, inevitable, irresistible transition.

Hufvudstadsbladet 8 November 1991

Olav Christopher Jenssen
Museum of Contemporary Art and Nordic Arts Centre, Helsinki

Lack of Memory

Olav Christopher Jenssen, a Norwegian painter who since the beginning of the 80s has been living in Berlin, showed a widely-noticed exhibition last year at Kunstnernes Hus in Oslo entitled *Lack of Memory* and consisting of 41 paintings. In the Museum of Contemporary Art fourteen of the paintings are now exhibited and form a kind of old-fashioned picture cabinet; three of the walls in the room are covered from floor to ceiling with the large canvases that measure 275 x 255 cm.

Earlier Jenssen painted in layers upon layers of paint that more or less covered each other. The secretive and hidden was an important part of the content, and this was possibly one reason for the critics' tendency to treat Jenssen's work as confirmation of everything they wanted to read into and out of 'Nordicness'. The paintings in *Lack of Memory* have a different approach which is not necessarily explained only through a comparison with the earlier works. The direction can also be the opposite, the new throws light over what precedes it.

The *Lack of Memory* series is about individuality, it discovers and presents the complexity of the individual statement with immense respect for its integrity. Much is allowed, variations from tender clumsiness to ele-

135

gant refinement. Through the paintings' refusal to submit to a pre-arranged harmony, variation and difference are converted into amazing strength. 'I intend to work against speculativeness with all honest weapons that exist. Life cannot be solved as a tactical problem' says Jenssen himself in an interview in the journal *F15 Kontakt*.

Many reviewers have talked about the enigmatic presence of these works. The enigmatic is rather to do with the issue of how an artist has managed to create a presence that opens towards the viewer so complete-ly that the experience can be shared without hidden secrets and references. The presence in itself is not enigmatic but generous and open. Every pain-ting speaks from its own conditions, anchored in the obvious skill with which Jenssen handles the image's formal means of impact. And it is precisely here that the critic's problems begin. Attempts at placing the paintings in cate-gories falter; figuration, abstraction, symbol, metaphor are concepts that in this case lead to limitations instead of providing explanations.

The title *Lack of Memory* contains meanings that we can hardly avoid relating to the paintings, their presence, openness and mobility. The oppo-site, clinging to memory, means painting like we have learned that we ought to paint, starting from a defined place with an overriding array of structures that painting must then try to hold on to. The openness in Jenssen's work is, I think, to do with the artist's modification of the concept of place through a kind of mobile fragmentation. The place is no longer a uniquely designated spot, but it shifts so that its superstructures become shattered.

Yet in *Lack of Memory* there is a given place, the place where painting begins. And beginning is here the same as submitting oneself to an empti-ness while giving it limits that fill it with possibilities. These possibilities are what we encounter in Jenssen's painting.

The lack of memory can be compared to a forgetfulness that does not remove but preserves incidents that can neither be remembered nor fully rejected; the indescribable that lends surprising intonations, voices, atmos-pheres, colourings and levels to what we consciously understand and grasp. The fourteen paintings describe such indescribable things.

If we travel out to Suomenlinna, to the Nordic Arts Centre, the context becomes more intimate. The gallery room has been condensed and dimin-ished with dry walls where Olav Christopher Jenssen's exquisite drawings are placed close to one another. The hanging and the atmosphere make me think of family photographs in which the links between the persons who pose tell us something important concerning relations between them.

The world housed in the gallery exists for itself but it is still possible to share it thanks to the drawings being authentic, they are true to their medium. They are not sketches for the paintings but their expression lives in the vicinity of life that has been lived and is still being lived. Since the drawings cover rather a long period of time it is precisely their instability that testifies to this anchorage. A photograph that is looked at later can feel like a ghost image, while the here and now of the drawing is unmissable thanks to the presence of the hand that creates form.

When Jenssen draws he does not copy anything but gives something character. We can write letters by drawing, or marvel at the food in New York or investigate how a small blot on the paper can grow into an organic shape. Jenssen manages, much like a virtuoso writer such as Roland Barthes, to start from the personal and then bring it to a level where a coherence is created that surpasses the first impulse or intention, for a drawing may be created in a moment of sudden distraction.

An angular line or a softly shaped loop in Jenssen's drawings may be exactly the smallest possible expression of qualities that are larger than words can describe.

Hufvudstadsbladet 1 June 1993

Georg Gudni
Galerie Artek, Helsinki

Cloud, Sky or Air

Faced with grandiose landscapes that touch me body and soul, I have often wondered what I am really seeing. In any case it is not the landscape the postcard depicts. The reproduction lacks something significant, it causes no picture to appear on the retina when I close my eyes – a picture that can even recall the smell of damp air in a hazy landscape.

The Icelander Georg Gudni (b 1961) has been painting the Icelandic landscape since the beginning of the 80s, above all the mountains around Reykjavik. In the beginning the paintings portrayed the well-known silhouettes surrounding the city. Traces of this phase are also present in the exhibition at Artek. A series of small works on paper denote how the artist works with the landscape that literally develops in front of his eyes. Gradually the paintings changed, and Gudni took to signifying the summits with soft curves. With this new signifier, the paintings' relation to outer reality also changed. The abstraction became ever more visible. Only a few of the exhibited works have a line to denote the horizon, otherwise they are wholly abstract, like the picture generated on our retina.

Three paintings, at the same time monumental and transparent, on separate walls in one of the gallery rooms, are mirroring each other. The shining surface makes the blue paint look almost transparent – a substance like air and water that flies and flows without resistance and without specific gestures.

Gudni's paintings exist in regions that are difficult to reconnoitre, where the picture looms in a condition that predates depiction. It still contains possibilities in the same way as our imaginations, it surpasses the faculty of sight.

Yves Bonnefoy lists words in one of his prose poems: The first word was 'cloud', the second word was also 'cloud', the third, fourth word etc was 'cloud', 'sky' or 'air', no one knew for certain. But already the seventh word burst asunder and was erased, it no longer differed from others that had burst and were erased further below, no longer differed from others infinitely, others that were ashes... If we may also allow the cloud, the sky and the air as metaphors for the picture we could say, in a paraphrase of Bonnefoy, that Gudni's painting is about the six first words.

Hufvudstadsbladet 15 March 1992

Waves, Breathing, Kiss

Ange Leccia works are circular. The most concise characterisation I can think of for his works is as follows: they situate themselves as the point in the centre of the circle. It is only when they have noticed that point that viewers see what lies between it and the circumference – for example, that Leccia's work can be a video projection or two excavator buckets, their mouths facing each other in front of an art museum. How carefully we then try to figure out the realisation of Leccia's practice, this becomes secondary in relation to, well, to what?

When Leccia was invited to show in Japan, the curators wanted him to make an exhibition inspired by the country's technology. But, when he was in Japan it was the opposite, the people, that began to interest him, and instead the outcome was a work (a photograph) with a boy and a girl. Their faces meet, and their lips almost meet, in the second before the kiss. The link between the second and repetition – in another work Leccia has the camera repeat again and again the last breath of a performance by Maria Callas.

Leccia's work at *Ars 95* is situated high on the inside wall over the main entrance, which makes it possible for viewers to alter the height from which they want to see the video projection, which is extremely enjoyable in its simplicity, we lose ourselves in the endless surge of the waves. In my thoughts, I call the work *The Waves*. But note that the title is *Sea*.

Roos Is there any difference between these two titles?

Leccia I prefer to call the work *Sea*, because it is about the contact between a piece of land and the sea, and about the motion that is constantly going on between them. In the contact zone where the sea meets the landscape, there is this activity, this motion I am interested in. For me, it involves a concrete act with far-reaching implications; the artist tries to stir up the system, and he makes waves, creations. Constant fluctuation, motion equals energy. (Leccia takes out a paper and pen and begins to draw.) Here is the sea, here is the shore, and this borderline is constantly moving, and it is completely white. I like the colour white. For me, it is the same as creativity, like a white cloth or a sheet of white paper. At the same time, the sea is never the same, it changes from day to day. That is why it takes a long time to comprehend the significance of the sea, and for me it is also a question of Zen philosophy, of being right in front of. Right now, I am in front of you. But, in order to be able to understand you, and you me, we need these waves. *Sea* is a work about contact, communication.

Roos The problem *Sea* faces me with has to do with my viewpoint – since I do not see it as a symbolic work (that is one of its most distinctive qualities). I wonder how I am going to talk and write about it. Or is that entire ambition in itself an impossibility, something that can already be intimated from the abstract image the work invokes, despite the expressive waves, a still centre of a circle. Minimal, exact, absolutely in the right place, i.e. perhaps my linguistic problem is a consequence of the fact that you have specifically succeeded in bringing your mode of artistic expression to this simple, unerasable point?

Leccia If I continue with my demonstration, perhaps you will get a hint. Here is the shore, here is the sea, and I am standing up on the top of the mountain. Suddenly I realised that I wanted to take a picture with my camera rotated to an unnatural angle. Why, I do not know. I have spent twenty years on this beach in Corsica, where I have my house.

Roos Interesting, since when we look at the work we do not think at all about how it has been made, technically. But there is, then, a slight abnormal twist, an angling that make the normal scene a little out of line, just small enough so that we barely see it as a deviation.

Leccia For me, it is a demonstration of the way a usual situation becomes unusual with another meaning.

Roos Is this a special insight that has to do with Zen, this slight twist that makes the everyday noticeable, clearly apparent?

Leccia My works are about starting off from very normal circumstances, and via small changes getting them into focus, making them clearer. Displacing things a bit so that something will stand out more clearly. For me, Zen is not about mysticism, but mostly about a slight twist, turning the camera. I know a mathematics researcher, who told me that in new mathematics people are investigating turbulence. When he saw my work he specifically saw a parallel with new mathematics. And, here, we can draw a parallel with our own life. In principle, we have millions of possibilities. Sitting on chairs here in this café is one of the most everyday things we can do without reflecting on it. For me, just such a situation can be very stimulating to work with artistically. It takes so little for a new meaning to take over. I work rapidly, and I only discover the meanings afterwards.

Roos I wonder why the visuality present, for example, in *Sea* is so inspiring. Is it because in 1995 our hyped visuality really welcomes something that is capable of relieving the mind of the excess of visual images that are there? A purification?

Leccia It is certainly quite correct to call *Sea* a kind of cleansing device. It situates itself before philosophy, before reasoning. It is primary, simple and pure. And that is why it is probably also possible to see a mass of meanings in it.

Roos Even if it fulfils those criteria, it is usual for a work simply to make you as the viewer bored; nothing happens. With *Sea*, the opposite happens, without our having to make an effort to mobilise any form of interest.

Leccia (Laughs) That is the magic of art.

I was still interested in the work I mentioned at the beginning of this piece, the second before the kiss, and I asked Leccia the simple question: The kiss work? Leccia took out his pen again.

Leccia I'll explain. There are two spotlights shining on each other, one to one. No light escapes, it does not light up something as is usually the case, but here light meets light, and for me that constellation is Zen.

Now I understood that this explanation applied to another work that was actually called *The Kiss*, and that the second before the kiss is another work. My slip of the tongue had, in fact, been correct. To return to my introductory remark about the centre point and the circle, I think that it is specifically this that is the distinctive quality of Leccia's practice. The work attains the same abstract level, the centre point, even if the mode of visual presentation can vary in the most surprising ways.

Siksi 1/1995. Translated by Mike Garner

Anne Katrine Dolven
Nordic Arts Centre, Helsinki

From Surface to Space

When Anne Katrine Dolven last exhibited in Helsinki, three years ago, she participated in a group exhibition organised by the Nordic Art Centre, *The Dark Green*, with young Norwegian painters. *The Dark Green* underlined the tendency that marked Nordic 80s painting, a re-invigoration of the Romantic tradition in landscape painting. Dolven's works at the time had colours associated with nature and the shapes evoked archaic symbols.

In the three years since then, Dolven's painting has changed in an interesting way. Gone are elements that could be understood as representations and thereby connected to meanings. The colour has also changed. In her paintings Dolven tries out shades of white, which have been achieved through the technique of working the paint. In this way colour is submitted to a transformation and becomes an aspect of the painting's material extension. Sometimes the surface has a structure reminiscent of a thin layer of plaster, sometimes the surface looks like white, hard stone carved with surgical precision. Slight tinges of yellow enter into the picture at those very locations where the possibilities for variation of the white have been exhausted. The paintings are dominated by horizontal and vertical fields, expressed in the same austere and laconic way as the colours.

In this sense Dolven's painting is close to Modernist art's claim of purity, i.e. an art limited solely to what it may express in itself. By analogy to this, representation and other significant signs are renounced. But this renunciation need not be clear cut, it can also mean that art moves closer towards absolutely secret language, that art refers to what we can think and imagine but not show. Dolven has created a structure that expressly functions through this kind of paradoxical negation. The structure refers to something we can imagine but does not show it. We encounter the external side of something, and through recognition of the external the idea of the internal is implied.

Although Dolven's painting is free of articulated references and in that sense pure we still encounter a fiction, which is not literary but rather spatial by nature. It is this connection to spatiality that leads Dolven's paint-

144

ing into exciting areas. The paintings oscillate between their surface and objects outside them and so are part of the same room where the spectator is located or, to put it the other way round, the spectator becomes part of the painting's space. What happens in the intersection between the spectator's space and the fictitious spatiality that the paintings bring out?

Placeless places, closed forbidden rooms, corridors that lead to more corridors; a long, narrow room like a tunnel, in which nearness and distance are drawn to each other and split up in an endless movement. Spaces where speech and event remain outside what is being said and what is happening. The wasteland of the real as the uncharted zones of the internal.

Hufvudstadsbladet 7 June 1991

Anders Tomren
Galerie Artek, Helsinki

Positive in White

Anders Tomren's exhibition is a nice surprise on the sculpture front. His works have found their integrity and from that they work their way towards a place and a mental state where something significant happens: in relation to the notion of sculpture as a medium and art historical category, and in relation to the viewer and her references in relation to the juncture of concrete and imagined reality.

The effect of Tomren's sculptures is extremely multi-dimensional, it feels as if the sculptures had invisible engines, producing effects that expose the viewer to a cross-current. Immediately as we enter the gallery something happens. The otherwise sleek gallery looks almost shabby when we compare it to Tomren's clinically white objects of melamine and other industrial materials. The surface is clean, hard and brutal with no trace of craftsmanship, no presence of the hand or references to the organically physical.

If we think of the objects in relation to their category, sculpture, we can draw some quick conclusions that prove how difficult Tomren's works are to place within the familiar classification systems for sculpture. Sculpture, which historically was considered one of the major visual arts, attained its position through its capacity for representation, according to which its æsthetic value was measured. Marcel Duchamp negated this at the beginning of the 20th century. The urinal he exhibited as a work of art was a readymade object without conscious æsthetic value, a use-object. Tomren's works referring to furniture at first challenge our dependency on language-based interpretation. One work looks like a mirrored cupboard, another one like a shelf, but they signal something more, which makes it possible to claim that the works are not furniture, and not readymades either, since they are unique productions crafted by the artist. Nor do the objects belong with those minimalist sculptures that aimed at interacting directly with the viewer in a kind of spatial drama, through the omission of the distancing plinth.

Minimalist sculpture functioned directly in space, but Tomren's works all have a base. The three sacks on the floor sit on a circular platform, whereas the 'mirrored cupboard' of the work *Nude* has a rectangular base and *Real II*, for instance, rests on a solid plinth. On the other hand we can't claim that Tomren is a clear-cut conceptualist, since in conceptual art the meaning and intention of the work replaced the process of creating real objects in space. On the contrary, the uniqueness of Tomren's sculpture springs from the fact that the works are very palpable, real objects in space, even if language cannot single out a conceptual notion to describe them. They do not picture objects from the real world, but in a way produce a realism of their own that lives in a unique order. As an instrument, we could use Jean-François Lyotard's analysis of the orders of the figure. Lyotard's analysis produces three orders, of which the first two are anchored in Modernism. The first is the optical, what we empirically say that we see, the object bound by its contours. The second order was what Modernism strove for: to find the formal conditions for exposing 'pure' form, to find an invisible structure that highlighted pure form.

Lyotard calls the third order that of the matrix. This is what interests me in Tomren's work, since the sculptures take us further to something unknown that surpasses their existence as concrete objects in space. The work *I, I, I* in particular hints at this. Three sacks in clinical white, each on its own low platform on the floor and with a legend referring to an understanding of the self. The order of the matrix, according to Lyotard, operates underground. It is invisible, but conveys impulses to the surface level that disturb the claims made by what is concrete and visible. Tomren's surface is systematic and pulled together by accurate forms, which underpins what the matrix achieves, a kind of constancy of the mental flow. The activity of the matrix is about constancy of the mental flow. The activity of the matrix is 'hitting' us, and it is this consistent pulse that we find in Tomren's work. To quote Lyotard, the imagination may be in constant motion, its conceptions and content may be marked by instability, but beneath this is a form, a rhythm, a pulse. This rare version of the notion of form is what Tomren is working with, the visible form of the sculptures reveal the order of the matrix whereby form delves into conceptions and re-emerges as rhythm, as pulse.

Hufvudstadsbladet November 1995

Marja Kanervo
Kunsthalle Helsinki

Modulations in Space

Marja Kanervo (born 1958) made her debut in 1981 and since then she has been working tirelessly with solo and group exhibitions, among these her participation at the São Paulo Biennial in 1989.

The Kunsthalle, planned by Hilding Ekelund in the 1920s, is with regard to the interior a place with a conspicuous touch of solemnity. In particular the many stairs leading up to the exhibition space itself awaken the feeling that we are about to step inside a kind of temple for the arts. For an artist working with installation it is expressly the space with all its qualities that becomes the starting point. The task Kanervo had to resolve was, then, not an easy one – finding a combination that brings together the venerable Kunsthalle and installation art of the 1990s, especially since the latter is based on concepts like time and space.

The condition for an installation to function is that the viewer becomes present, that she is seized in such a way that she physically establishes a relation to space. Something must happen by way of spatiality so that the viewer becomes involved and reacts with sharpened sensitivity to detail, contour, structure and nuance. The experience can be related to the instinctive, sudden feeling through which we sense the presence of another person on the physical level before it can be confirmed by the eye. There is no doubt that Kanervo supremely dominates this sphere. We react immediately to her solution for the staircase, where she has covered the walls with wax panels, each bearing the imprint of her own back. The monumental entrance is transformed at once into contours of something human enticing us with its being turned-away. What is fragmentary and shattered captures our attention more effectively than an unambiguous whole. If we look back at Kanervo's production we notice that she has often used this very trait, the repetition of units that sometimes form a series.

On my way up the Kunsthalle's stairs I reflect on Ekelund's commendable spatial plan, which makes the visitor unconsciously turn left, to the room with the beautiful tall and narrow window stretching from floor to ceiling. Kanervo's installation also follows Ekelund's routes, for in this first room there is a decisive thematic take on spatiality with the consequence that Kanervo manages to rid the Kunsthalle of its quality as a kunsthalle (institution). Before, we always knew where the boundaries of this room were, but now they are unclear. Where does the room begin? Where does it end? The room has been transformed into a realm of transparency and reflection. The architectural whole is dissolved. Kanervo has reproduced the room's windows along with details we usually do not notice and then she has placed the photographs under plexiglass of different hues. For instance on the floor right under the tall and narrow window we find its structure repeated in dark violet and black. As we look down we see the real window being reflected in the photograph.

A form of transgression has occurred. The suppressed structure in the first room rubs off on our experience of the other rooms. We are prepared to orient ourselves in a spatiality that functions according to the conditions created by Kanervo; the Kunsthalle itself becomes overshadowed. In the following room there is darkness and light contrasting with one another. On almost the whole floor burning candles have been placed, reflected in glass surfaces placed between them. On the walls there are pictures of bricks that are probably taken from the inner walls.

In front of Kanervo's earlier candle installations I have felt a little vague, ambivalent. It is beautiful of course, but does it come too close to being pathetic? But here at the Kunsthalle my attitude is somewhat changed, since the exhibition's scope exposes a significant feature of Kanervo's strategy. This is particularly palpable in those works where the material is, for instance, oil or birds' feathers soaked in the same devastating fluid. It is as if the outer world were entering into the works through the material, like the oil that reminds us of ecological disaster. From this point of view it is not so far-fetched to understand the candles as memorial images for collective traumas.

The rear room as well is occupied by a concept that has seized it completely. One of the walls is covered in silk tissue smeared with cooking oil, which has transformed the tissue into a transparent film. Some of the oil has spilled onto the floor, which is also dressed with the same kind of paper. The transparent stains on the floor lay bare neat rows of numbers that denote various measurements for the building at hand. The elements of live process that often appear in Kanervo's installations here take on a threatening expression. As time passes the room is changed by the black oil slowly dripping from two tubs. When the exhibition period is over the whole white floor will most probably be ruined.

The epilogue is to be found in the smaller rooms – an epilogue just as dense as the rest of the exhibition. The back imprints in the staircase are given an equivalent that transcends the private, and the circle is completed. On the wall there is a rug woven from birds' feathers impregnated with oil. The oil tub nearby has an impenetrable black surface. It is not difficult to imagine which real-life drama this could be about.

Hufvudstadsbladet 28 August 1992

Eva Löfdahl
Chemical Research Laboratory, Stockholm University

Abstraction and Space but Also, and Also

Whenever we have to use words as tools for expressing something about Eva Löfdahl's work we should acknowledge our handicap as soon as possible. There will be stammering and a farewell to eloquence (or at least to our dependence on it).

I would use the expression 'cutting the words', as if I were cutting paper dolls and hoping that the outlines would be precise enough to let us sense a skeleton behind the flat pieces, giving them some volume. I decided to try and achieve this with the smallest possible verbal apparatus. Only the bare necessities.

The brief I have been given is to talk about the notion of space in relation to Eva Löfdahl's work. It is important to say 'notion' here, because I soon realised that what we usually mean by the pictorial space of a work and its relation to real space does not at all exist in Eva Löfdahl's work or is not relevant to it. This means that she does not work with pictorial space in the art historical sense; the notion of space has some other significance in relation to her practice. Something else. What?

For the longest time I have been looking at Jacques Lacan's diagrams, his graphic display of thoughts. Particularly when the text turned into question marks it was a release to study the diagrams. I often asked myself why the diagram says something else than the text pages. Understanding the same thing in different ways, with different and limited means. Above all, the diagrams began to influence my interpretation of Lacan's theory, they began to say something more about it – about the Law, about Structure – well, you know the vocabulary. These concepts for the given, for conditions and for fundament suddenly open up in different directions. The abstraction entered a space and became three-dimensional, visual.

With fresh experience of the significance of the Modernist grid, I am not referring to the kind of system that was in fact delineating, excluding, autonomous, aimed at creating an essence in me, when I speak of figure and diagram and order. Instead I intend to use these notions as a means of conveying that abstraction might presuppose a room for existence, i.e. that it might have to be made three-dimensional. When for instance Eva Löfdahl's work is mentioned, there is often talk of absurd sculpture. Absurd means counter-rational. This her sculptures are definitely not, although they might easily be presented as such if we only considered how they look and then compared them with other things in reality.

References. Lyotard has discussed orders. The first two we know. The first is what we empirically see, the object as it is seen, the object bound by its contours. The second order is to do with formal possibilities that condition visuality as such and how it may be presented; the level where pure 'form' operates as a principle of coordination, unity, structure – *visual but unseen*. This is what Modernism wanted to rule over.

But the third order makes me think of abstraction in space, and also of what is induced and created because of it. It makes me think of Eva Löfdahl's work. The third order is what Lyotard calls the matrix. With that he means an order whose operations are removed from the visible, altogether *underground, out of sight* and, it should be added in reference to Löfdahl's work, *in space*, i.e. in relation to its spatial, three-dimensional environs. How can phenomenological and psychoanalytical spatiality be united?

Play with words. *Spatium* means 'space in between', *spatiosus* means 'with large in-between spaces', *spatulum* means 'a small spade-like implement' (for making in-between-spaces). And what about the teaspoon? What does it do? It also reaches into what is inside to make space, not just a space in between.

The underworld. And up. And down. Eva Löfdahl's work balances between spatialities. Bits of forms may take shape and become clearly recognisable, and space of the third order appears as space for the unconscious. This space is 'unrepresentable', but it is represented in Löfdahl's work: a block of contradictions. In reality it exists as projections of various 'figures' that emerge out of the 'depth' of its 'space': slip of the tongue, daydream, fantasy etc.

In Eva Löfdahl's work these figures are not projections; they are realised as the third order. In principle this order works underground, but when abstraction is realised as three-dimensionality it may gain visibility, concrete presence.

Lecture 1 November 1995

Rita Roos kritik

Rita Roos (1956–1996) i Helsingfors, juli 1996

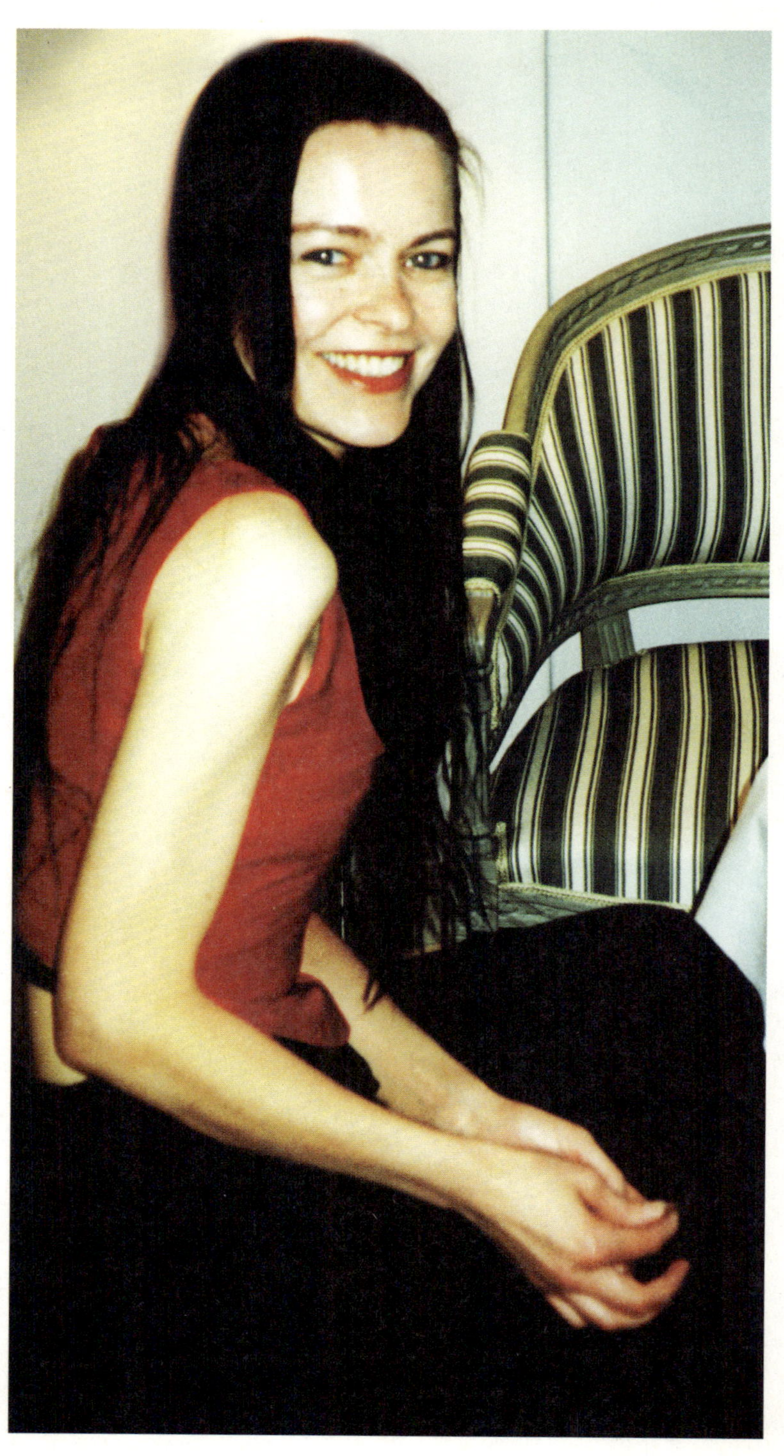

För tio år sedan rycktes Rita Roos bort, hastigt och oväntat, mitt i en period av intensiv aktivitet. Hon var konstkritiker i Hufvudstadsbladet i Helsingfors, finländsk redaktör för den nordiska konsttidskriften Siksi, föreläsare i konstteori vid Konstakademin i Trondheim i Norge. Hon var en passionerat uppmärksam iakttagare, läsare och samtalspartner.

Denna bok utges till minne av en älskad syster, nära vän och uppskattad kollega. Men den är inte avsedd enbart för dem som hade förmånen att känna Rita Roos och följa hennes gärning i dagspressen, konsttidskrifter, utställningskataloger och monografier.

Rita Roos' texter kännetecknas precis som hon själv av inlevelse och nyfikenhet, men också av kritisk distans, lyssnande och förmågan att verkligen se. Hon hade den ovanliga begåvningen att intensivt bemöta det hon skrev om. Med skarpsynt intellekt och intelligent öga närmade hon sig konstverket och konstnärskapet. När man läser Rita Roos' texter får man vara med henne och se och uppleva och tänka. Hennes språk är ett redskap som hon använder för att skriva sig in i konsten, skriva med konsten snarare än om den.

Detta är en bok om konstkritik, men den berättar också om ett skrivande som var ett ständigt fortlöpande tänkande. I texterna prövar och undersöker Rita Roos de tankar och idéer som hon var upptagen av och utvecklar dem i mötet med konstverket. Vi får möta något så ovanligt som en nära dialog mellan skribenten och konsten, mellan det iakttagna och dess expansion i tanken. Resultatet är inträngande och förbehållslösa texter som med precision lyckas synliggöra och förmedla verkets meningsskapande plan.

Detta urval av Rita Roos' texter presenteras både på svenska och i engelsk översättning. Vi hoppas att boken skall läsas också av dem som inte tidigare känt till en av Nordens främsta konstskribenter, och att hennes texter skall uppskattas både för vad de säger om konsten och för vad de säger om Rita Roos själv.

Vi har ordnat ett urval av Rita Roos' publicerade texter i ett ganska öppet tematiskt kretslopp med avdelningsrubriker som citerar brottstycken ur texterna. Boken fokuserar på områden som upptog henne, och som kanske kunde formuleras så här: "gränsen", "rösten", "bilden", "metoden", "överskridandet", "världen", "vertikaliteten".

Lund i september 2006

Anders Kreuger och Nina Roos

kolofon

Rita Roos. Kritik

Text: Rita Roos
Redigering: Anders Kreuger, Nina Roos
Fotografi: Marianna Uutinen
Design: Daiva Kišūnaitė
Tryck: Logotipas, Vilnius 2006

Förläggare:

Veenman Publishers/Gijs Stork
Sevillaweg 140
NL-3047 AL Rotterdam, Nederländerna
Tel. +31 10 2453333, fax. +31 10 2453344, info@veenmanpublishers.com

ISBN: 9086900399
EAN: 9789086900398
© Nina Roos

Tack till: Kristin Bergaust, Yane Calovski, Anne-Karin Furunes,
Maaretta Jaukkuri, Iréne Kreuger, Pyry Nykyri, Ann-Mari Roos,
Gertrud Sandqvist, Mikko Zenger

Denna bok utges med stöd från Suomen Kulttuurirahasto,
Svenska kulturfonden och Kunstakademiet i Trondheim, NTNU

Distribution:

D.A.P.
155 Sixth Avenue, 2nd floor
New York, NY 10013, USA, dap@dapinc.com

Idea Books
Nieuwe Herengracht 11
1011 RK Amsterdam-NL, Nederländerna, idea@ideabooks.nl

Art Data
12 Bell Industrial Estate
50 Cunnington Street
W4 5HB London, England, info@artdata.co.uk

innehållsförteckning

Identitet – jaget
Museet för nutidskonst, Helsingfors

En anvisad identitet

Efter 80-talets livliga hårklyveri kring begrepp som identitet, jaget och subjektet tenderar det man i dag försöker sammanfatta exempelvis om identiteten att framstå som en aning enfaldigt vilket blir särskilt påtagligt då man betänker att begreppet bygger på mångfaldighet.

Nåväl, utställningen i Museet för nutidskonst med ryska och finländska konstnärer har "identitet – jaget" som tema, vilket än en gång, liksom många av 80-talets tematiskt uppbyggda utställningar, aktualiserar förhållandet mellan konst och teori. Teori är inte konst och konst är inte teori. Det här låter som en självklarhet men det är just den poäng som en del av 80-talets utställningar missade i den mån konstverket hanterades som ett renodlat objekt för kunskap uteslutande de kvaliteter som föll utanför den anvisade tolkningsramen.

Det kvistiga beträffande den aktuella utställningen ansluter sig till frågan, på vilken nivå opererar identitets- och jagbegreppet? På sätt och vis är svaret enkelt, ja nästan för enkelt. För det första arbetar ifrågavarande konstnärer konceptuellt med tonvikt på det uttänkta och vissa av verken tycks vara gjorda utgående från utställningens tema. Delvis som en följd av det här kommer verken att belysa ämnet på ett sätt som fungerar som en bekräftelse på den lacanska uppfattningen om jaget och i detta avseende blir infallsvinkeln förutsebar; verken når precis så långt Lacan menar att vi kan nå i vårt sökande efter kunskap om vårt jag. Enligt Lacan kan det vi vet om jaget knappast ens kallas för kunskap, snarare konstruktioner kring något som visar sig genom sina förklädnader, som ett symptom som ständigt undflyr vår självkännedom. Det *Identitet*-utställningen utökar är följaktligen förrådet av konstruktioner, det som faller utanför ramen är den kvalitet ett konstverk har potentiell möjlighet att förverkliga; att förekomma, föregå given kunskap, att få konstruktionerna att krackelera.

Att en konstnärlig undersökning kan åstadkomma en blottande sprickbildning är i och för sig inget nytt. Man behöver bara referera till Marcel Duchamps glasarbeten som med tanke på jagbegreppet är särdeles intressanta, för Duchamps metod kan förstås som en extrem tillämpning av

konstruktionens princip, men på så sätt att resultatet inte handlar om en logisk struktur utan motsatsen, en avgrund bortom vårt strukturerande medvetande som förklädnaderna suveränt och samtidigt skenbart lyckas dölja. En konstnärlig undersökning på denna nivå är alltså möjlig utan att mångfalden utesluts. Därför är det heller ingen tillfällighet att Duchamps glasarbeten skulle kunna analyseras utgående från de senaste årtiondenas vokabulär kring jaget och identiteten: kvinnligt, manligt, begär, brist, jagets förhållande till konventionen m.m.

Det som gör *Identitet* till en bra utställning är i första hand den exakthet och träffsäkerhet som finns i de enskilda verken. Eija-Liisa Ahtila är den av konstnärerna som lyckas skapa ett slags avbrott eller diskontinuitet i förhållande till en normaliserad vardagsuppfattning, förutsatt att hennes tre stycken tre minuter långa filmer *Okay, We* och *Gray* visas i sitt avsedda sammanhang, insprängda mitt i programutbudet på en kommersiell TV-kanal. Ahtilas androgyna kvinna som vankar omkring i en lägenhet, talande både med mans- och kvinnoröst, kunde väl lämpa sig som inslag i reklampausen för *The Bold and the Beautiful*, och hennes tre kvinnor i en hiss, upptagna av en kärnkatastrof vore lämpliga att visas efter tvättmedelsreklamen där kvinnorna nästan besatt analyserar smutsfläckens mysterium.

Om identiteten uppfattas som en kulturellt och samhälleligt styrd konstruktion, då kan man säga att Juri Leidermans spelbord är dess levande metafor. Varje dag under utställningens lopp byter diverse föremål plats på ett numrerat och inrutat spelfält. Ifall två av föremålen råkar få samma nummerplacering frisläpps en mus som är gömd under bordet.

Upptrappning och nedtrappning av en anvisad identitet – Pekka Niskanens rekonstruktion av mediafenomenet Stefan Lindfors med hjälp av en fiktiv intervju och en samling av Lindfors' designmöbler blir den punkt där identitetens förankring i en verklig människa suddas ut och jaget rör sig på en yta från vilken alla de egenskaper som är nödvändiga för en medialansering fritt kan plockas. Och nedtrappningen då? I Juha-Pekka Hotinens *Andra hands man* är det en lindrig defekt i konstnärens ena arm som är svaret på frågan, vad är det för fel med mig? Via diagnostisering av skadan och analys av symptomen avslutas ämnet med terapeutisk manikyrsession i den professionella manikyrstol som är ställd mitt i rummet.

I rummet bredvid den lindforska exhibitionismen fokuserar Gia Rigvavas videoinstallation på levande ögon. Effekten av ögonen som rör

sig på videoskärmarna är på något sätt förbryllande. Även om materialet är icke manipulerat kommer jag inte att tänka på de här ögonen som själens speglar utan de verkar mer kliniska som levande organ.

Då det mesta har sagts och ältats angående identitet och jaget utan att man känner sig ett dyft klokare är det dags att ta en titt på Pentti Koskinens melonhuvud, d.v.s. hälften av ett melonhuvud är fäst vid väggen i det bakersta rummet ledsagat av ett fotografi där Koskinens huvud har förvandlats till melonens andra hälft.

Hufvudstadsbladet 16 december 1993

Nationalgalleriet Zacheta, Warszawa

Hvar är din broder, Abel?

Zacheta, museet för samtida konst i Warszawa, är inrymt i en av de få byggnader som blev besparad förintelse under kampen om Warszawa. Tyskarna som höll staden ockuperad 1939–44 hade i byggnaden sitt nöjeshus, ett kasino.

Det judiska ghettot återhämtade sig aldrig. Anda Rottenberg, chef för Zacheta och kurator för utställningen *Hvar är din broder, Abel?* för mig omkring i Warszawa med bil. Stadsplanen är som en öppen bok för metodisk grymhet; endast några byggnader i ghettot överlevde våldet, här och där finns det oförklarligt tomma områden, skarvar och återuppbyggnadsprojekt som är ställda sida vid sida liksom främlingar.

Då sade Herren till Kain: ”Hvar är din broder, Abel?” Han svarade: ”Jag vet icke; skall jag taga vara på min broder?” Då sade han: ”Hvad har du gjort? Hör, din broders blod ropar till mig från jorden.”

Hurudan är en utställning som i dag heter *Hvar är din broder, Abel?* 90-talets konst som översvämmats med bekännelser: jag är homosexuell, jag har aids, jag är svart, jag är ”white trash” och sedan en teoretisk diskurs som kretsat kring jag-tecknets bräckliga grundvalar och frågat: Vem är det som talar? Utställningen i Zacheta är varken lätt att beskriva eller förklara.

17

Den är en av de utställningar som lyckats, som har den kvalitet att den förutsätter att du stiger in, går genom salarna, bland verken. När man märker att det är Abel, den dräpte brodern, som är den mest närvarande av de två, då vet man att temat fungerar, att utställningen har förmågan att föra apparaten av symboler och metaforer tillbaka till jorden, till ett tillstånd som har sin mentala konkretion i de utställda verken. För att därefter åter igen kastas ut i den tillspetsade kontext den bibliska frågan framtvingar. Miroslaws Balkas korridor med svagt gula, tvåldoftande väggar är mer än sitt yttre. De markerar platsen för en rit, antingen skrämmande eller vällustig. Skalan rör sig mellan extrema poler, att tvätta sig för att bli människovärdig eller att tvätta sig för att bli värdig döden. I Christian Boltanskis installation *Neighbours* läser en röst upp anonyma namn ur en telefonkatalog samtidigt som man ser sitt eget ansikte reflekteras i blanksvarta ytor. Namnlistor. Lista på pristagare, utvalda, dödsdömda, vinnare, förlorare. Ett namn som kunde vara vem som helst. Lawrence Weiners text på en av väggarna är en efterlängtad prolog för lagtavlorna (min föreställning ser dem alltid som stenblock): *Wet sand and small stones placed in the sun to dry (All mixed together).*

Skriften i Bibeln är renodlad så till vida att den skrivandes problem, att oupphörligt befinna sig på avdrift från den meningens närvaro han sökte, är eliminerat. Gränser är satta för skriftens mångfald genom att Bibeln omfattar en enhet där kontexten fungerar som dogm, en dogm som omfattar t.o.m. Skriftens egen historia. Och det avgörande som gör Bibeln till Bibel är detta att bortom tecknena skapas en närvaro av något som står utanför differensernas spel, Gud. Ett samtal med Herren sker därför alltid med Herrens diskurs. Utställningen i Zacheta är tillämpning av en annan möjlighet. Den fråga Herren ställer till Kain klipps ur Skriften och prövas i ett visuellt språk som däremot inte kräver, inte straffar, d.v.s. är utan etiska imperativ. Verken i Zacheta, i närvaro av den bibliska frågan, tillämpar ett slags "neutralitetens etik", ifall Barthes ursäktar ett fritt lån av sitt uttryck. Barthes talar om Skriften som norm, Texten som ett fält för förförelse för att sedan i slutet av sjuttiotalet tillföra uttrycket det neutralas etik med vilket han avser ett språk som inte begär utan älskar; något ickeaggressivt, något ickegenitalt, att vilja leva utan att bemäktiga sig. Verken i Zacheta kräver ingenting men väcker mycket.

Vem är min broder? Tänk att för omväxlings skull kunna ställa en fråga som inte handlar om identitet utan om gemenskap och frändskap. Vi

har och har haft system som operar enligt solidaritets- och enhets-principen, men ofta med konsekvensen att den andres broder förintats eller nedtystats. Tomasz Kiznys verk *The Verdict* består av två sekvenser av svartvita fotografier: fotografier av dödsdömda från KGB:s centralarkiv och samtida fotografier från Moskvas tunnelbana med slumrande, efter-middagströtta människor. Porträtten av de dödsdömda förseddes vid arkiveringen med exakta uppgifter. Personens namn, yrke, datum för exekutionen och dess orsak: dödad 1938 på grund av oönskad politisk verksamhet. Vad mer finns det att tillägga då även frågorna fått tystna?

Siksi 3/1995

Muu-galleriet, Helsingfors

Jouni Kujansuu

I fönstret till Muu-galleriet exponerade Jouni Kujansuu ett svartvitt natu-ralistiskt fotografi av en man i jeans med armarna i en lovande "begär-gest", den som används när T-skjortan dras upp för att blotta torson. Gesten i fotografiet hade i det här fallet en annorlunda funktion – kroppens mellanparti var inpackat i degmassa som mannen som ett lager plastiskt fett försökte töja ut och dra upp mot sina axlar. Vid samma tidpunkt lanse-rades Calvin Kleins nya reklamaffischer på stan, en skock tomt stirrande ungdomar (Kate Moss & Company) med anorektiskt tunna armar och ben. Samma gest, mannen som begärligt drar upp sin T-skjorta, syntes även i Kleins reklam.

Vem är han, denne man som exponerar sig som ett begärligt åtråvärt objekt? Somliga föds till män andra till kvinnor, javisst det vet vi. Men vad jag är, och vad det vill säga för mig att vara man eller kvinna, det är en fråga som det oaktat oupphörligen ställs och som inte kan besvaras av en eller annan naturlig, definitiv konklusion. Och detta är givet i kulturen (eller i det omedvetna) där det finns en ofullföljd skrift som ställer frågor om vår mentala könsidentitet. Och vad vi gör, var och en på sitt sätt, är att om och om igen försöka "skriva in" oss i denna för att där finna vår

särskilda plats.

Att hitta igenom djungeln av osäkra självdefinitioner, att leva med dem, är något annat än det som självbekännelsekonsten manifesterar. Mätt på jagexcessens estetik som gör påståenden av områden som egentligen visar sig i skuggan av sina symtom, skeptisk gentemot tendensen som för fram ett multinationellt-massmedialt visuellt språk som skall uttrycka jaget, finner jag angelägna "antipoänger" i Kujansuus utställning som mer handlar om att relatera till ett svart, sjukt område än om påståendet att jaget vet.

Förutom det tidigare omtalade fotografiet finns det ett annat med liknande naturalism. En ung man riktar heroiskt och samtidigt aningslöst blicken uppåt med degmassa som pinsam peruk (tänker på brittiskt rättsväsende där lagen utövas av aktörer i peruk). Fotot är inte enbart pinsamt utan det personifierar skammen, att tro att allt är väl och inte själv märka att något är på tok (trots att alla redan skrattar). Skammen över att stigmat syns; det förbjudna, bortdrivna, äckliga, smutsiga. Antingen som hos anorektiker som försöker hålla sin kropp ren genom kontroll över den oral-anala passagen. Eller som hetsätaren som stundom spränger kroppens gränser för att försvinna i tomhet, bli ingenting, ett slutet tillstånd.

Det som Kujansuu gjort i sina övriga fotografier är att lyfta fram degmassan som det snedvridna, förbjudna tröst- och hetsobjektet. Att vårda och ta hand om det mest hatade och avskydda har här förts till en punkt som får degmassan att ingå i en ritual som förädlar det abjektala. Degen är bl.a. flätad i ett mönster som associerar till köksrutigt, färgen som sköljt över är svagt grön, reminiscens av trygghet. En annan klump är syntetiskt grön, en tredje varmbrun. Tillståndet är regressionens med en symptomskapande överhet, här representerad av estetiken – i verkligheten av fadern som skall klippa av banden till det mjölk- och degdoftande köket, modern, det symbiotiska. Fotografierna har en inneboende farlighet genom att deras estetik motverkar det brutala avklippandet, snittet mellan realt och symboliskt. De kvarhåller de två instanser som borde ersätta varandra, återkallar dem båda samtidigt.

Siksi 4/1995

Hans Hamid Rasmussen
Nordiskt konstcentrum, Helsingfors

Fremmed

Kallsvett och vämjelse i tidig morgonnatt. Hans Hamid Rasmussens broderi av deformerade foster på ljus linnelärft är i drömmen utklippta och omvandlade till förtorkade klumpar i klinisk sjukhusmiljö. De slängs bort under tystnad fylld av stumt obehag, någon måste ju ta i klumparna för att få bort dem.

Hans Hamid Rasmussens historia är långt från kliniskt sjukhus. Född i Algeriet 1963, norsk mor, arabisk far; föräldrarnas politiska engagemang tvang familjen fly via Ungern till Norge. Då var Rasmussen sex år. Hittar i mitt uppslagsverk en bild från Algeriet. En man står på en platå framför staden El Hamel som ligger nere i en dalgång. Min fokusering gäller mannen, inlindad i vitt tyg från huvud till fötter, endast den mörka ansikts-tavlan är synlig.

Rasmussens utställning Fremmed i Galleri Augusta visar tre områden: broderi på vit linnelärft, teckningar, samt en installation i två delar – en "honungsvägg" och ett stycke text skriven på väggen. Vid första bekant-skap verkar områdena visa en "normal" välgjord helhet. Efterbilderna däremot pekar mot annat håll. Texten på väggen om honung, barn, gråt, varm mjölk är en tröstevisa som skulle behöva en person, en röst för att inte orden skall stå där som enbart attraktiv konstruktion, ursprungna ur ett kulturbundet utsägande. Och vidare, Rasmussens teckningar är prov på den begåvade handens förmåga att besvärja föreställningarna.

Broderierna med vanskapta fosterliknande varelser befinner sig "i skillnad" till det övriga, de är en del av utställningen som i samklang med sin teknik, att sy in, knyter ihop något – en främling?

Främlingen sägs (enligt Kristeva) skydda sitt omedvetna på andra sidan gränsen. Här avser Kristeva det nya språk främlingen lärt sig och som är fördömt att fungera utanför det omedvetna. Då jag ser Hans Hamid Rasmussens broderi blir jag förvissad om att dess konstnärliga kvalitet precis har att göra med det att Rasmussen i sitt broderande lyckas bryta in i det som finns på den andra sidan, det fungerar som en navelsträng transponerande livsupprätthållande substans. Sålunda finns inte utställ-

ningens egentliga "främlingsskap" i broderierna utan i teckningarna och installationen där uttrycket befinner sig på igenkännbar uttrycksnivå.

Mardrömmen om förtorkat foster, bilden av den draperade herden ovanför El Hamel, osynliga arabiska kvinnor, sönderslitna kroppar och mycket därtill finns i den ostrukturerade massa som Rasmussens broderi absorberat upp. Hans Hamid Rasmussens foster är fullständigt ogripbara och träffar som en vass nål betraktarens egen molande kuslighet.

Siksi 3/1995

Jan Kaila
Målarförbundets galleri, Helsingfors

Porkalablå parentes

Varför favoriserade ryssarna på Porkala en speciell blå färg? Denna något tunga blå nyans brukades både inomhus och utomhus under Porkalas röda parentes 1944–56 då Finlands sydspets förvandlats till rysk militärbas. Befolkningen var evakuerad och tio gånger fler ryssar hade möblerat om udden enligt principerna för ett militärt provisorium. Kanske den blå färgen hade blivit överflödig i en nation som signalerade rött. En annan egenhet, ryssarna (av vilka många var unga män i värnplikt) tyckte om att tapetsera. I gamla Porkalahus hittar man fortfarande lager på lager av vanligtvis blommiga tapeter. Kanske ett till – när det kom ett nytt befäl till territoriet markerade han sig genom ett nytt val av väggblommor.

Jan Kaila gör i sin utställning om Porkala-parentesen det långsökta närsökt. Sedan 1990 har Kaila rört sig i sin hemtrakt kring Kyrkslätt och samlat material om det ryska Porkala och om ryssen som för finländaren är bärare av dubbelt stigma: främling, fiende. 150 ryska föremål, två filmer som ryssarna glömt kvar på Porkala, Komsomol-aktivistens anteckningar från 1951 och fotografier ur Bertil Sjöholms album 1956 utgör utställningen. Kaila har alltså inte själv fotograferat utan valt fram ett material som han visar med justeringar jämförbara med finmekanikens dunlätta åtgärder.

Tanken bakom urvalet och bildernas format är konsekvent. Sättet på vilket Kaila visar det dokumentära materialet styrs av en värdefull insikt om fotografiet och dess användningsmöjlighet i fallet Porkala. Urvalet Kaila gjort förenas av en enkel faktor, för bilderna handlar uttryckligen om fotograferandet som ritual. Denna faktor har Kaila finkänsligt format till ett instrument som förmår avlägsna det tabulagda och parentetiska lager för lager. Ett skikt handlar om den formella "diskreta" diskurs som förts i ämnet (som politiskt kapitel har Porkala skötts oroande smärtfritt). Ett annat lager är den täta djungel av finländarens komplexa sociala fantasier om "ryssen" och gränszonen, som kring Porkala tillförde ytterligare en gräns innanför gränsen. När finländarna återvände 1956 försökte de göra sig av med främlingen just på ett sätt som går igen i Kailas utställning. De som återvände rev bort lager efter lager av ryssarnas blommiga tapeter.

Fotograferandet blir en ritual när det sker med anledning av något, det som formar uddarna i livet: de första stegen, förändringarna, flytta in, flytta bort, gifta sig, fira födelsedag. Även den äldsta ser ofta glad ut på ett foto. Så som Kaila noterat under sin rundvandring i Porkalatrakten. Då finländarna skulle flytta bort från udden tog de fram kameran vilket resulterade i muntra flyttningsbilder med släkt och vänner. Tragiken i uppbrottet blev på fotot det motsatta genom att den fotografiska akten mer kom att handla om fotografens och objektens ömsesidiga relation.

> Endast så: genom inbillningskraften satt i nollpunktens ställe är vi i stånd att se ett ansikte. (Walter Benjamin)

Genom att Kaila undvikit att förse utställningen med annat än renodlat rituellt material förs inget utomstående samtal i fotografierna. Istället upprättas en kontakt mellan bilderna och betraktaren vilken får dennes historiskt och politiskt betingade nätverk av föreställningar om Porkala-parentesen att tillintetgöras. Effekten uppstår genom ett slags kontrastverkan, främlingen, fienden ser fullständigt normal ut. Inget stigma syns.

Det fotografi som förföljer en genom utställningen, där de flesta bilderna uttrycker kamratskap männen emellan, är fotot av en kvinna med två barn i famnen. Det speciella är inte det att hon troligen är hustru till en Komsomol-aktivist utan att hon är en kvinna som vet att hon är älskad. Detta syns på samma sätt som den fotografiska aktens ögonblickliga moment syns. Ett av barnen riktar sin blick bort från kameran mot något som sker vid sidan om fotografen.

Parentetiskt liv: kamratskap, kärlek, tuggummiseg vardag. Ett stycke ur Komsomol-aktivistens anteckningar:

Får inte på något sätt skrivet brev till Zorin.

1. Måste skriva brev till Remirjasovs kolchos.

2. Måste byta böckerna *Hur stålet härdades*, *Livsklipp*, *Av allt hjärta*, *Gyllene stjärnans riddare*, *Levande vatten*.

3. Måste organisera agitationsarbetet. Måste tala med folk – dit han reser.

När Bertil Sjöholm återvände den femte februari, dagen efter att de civila tilläts besöka Porkala, fotograferade han snöklädda hus denna kalla februaridag. Husen ser ut som om de alltid sett likadana ut.

Siksi 3/1994

Regeländring: ramar, redskap, roller
Litauisk samtidskonst i Södertälje, Norrtälje och Västerås, 1996

Regeländring – ett konkret brott mot den korrekta distansen

En regeländring väntar att nå fram likt en transitpassagerare som tappat bort sitt identitetsbevis och därmed också sitt ansikte. Hindren handlar dock inte om eventuella problem vid säkerhets- och passkontroll utan om att landa på territorier, mentala och sociala, som ännu inte är ockuperade av en färdigskriven, legitimerande diskurs. När det som kännetecknar stabila tillstånd, att kritiska ögonblick egentligen är skenbarheter, de äventyrar ingenting, hotar ingen för de är produkter av ett system som redan förutsatt dem – när detta inte finns, var är vi då?

Inte i Västerås i SAS-hotellets skybar som är motsatsen, en idealisk plats för att beskriva ett annat tecken för stabilitet, den korrekta distansen. Uppifrån ser staden ut som den helhet den är avsedd att vara. Inga bitar eller läsbarheter är synliga, också rörelsen där nere tycks korrekt följa ett givet mönster, allt från röken i industripiporna till hemsamariterna som förverkligar åldringsvård, och vårdarna som utför lokalvård.

Regler plus råd, rön och hjälp finns till handa för varje nivå, för allt och alla.

Korrekt distans som attityd. Tänker på kungahusets Ken och Barbie på besök i ett av de baltiska länderna. Scenariot var perfekt, folkmassorna viftade med vimplar framför näsan på de välklädda kungligheterna och Sverige blev det samma som i barndomens fantasier: sockerkaka, polkagris, lakritsbåt… Skärande bristningar, tomrum mellan erfarenhet och erfarenhet.

I centrum av Vilnius finns en populär bar, NATO-baren, planerad och inredd av arkitekt Valdas Ozarinskas. Dörren till platsen ser ut som vilken som helst ytterdörr i Vilnius. Men, där inne. Musiken är aggressiv, hårt påskruvad, inredningen är militantisk och brutal, gevär, metall, mörker och rök. När man sitter i en av de låga fåtöljerna känns det som att vara i en officersklubb där drinken ger tillfällig avkoppling från förödelseplanering. Har ingen liknande upplevelse av rollbyte i social miljö att referera till. Kan inte avgöra vad som är ironi, vad som är allvar, var gränsen går mellan iscensättning och realitet. Insåg senare att jag letade efter fel sak eller annorlunda uttryckt, att avsaknaden av det jag letade efter just var symptomatiskt för situationen i Vilnius. För närvarande finns där inget system som skulle kunna fungera enligt "korrekta" regler, utan man lever i ett tillstånd av förändring, mitt i det, avsaknaden av ett ovanför. Även en besökare tappar bort sina distanserade verktyg. Aggressiv musik förföljer en till toaletten, ett elegant kabinett i metall, där man skräms av sin egen spegelbild.

Det som i den Lacanska psykoanalysen går under benämningen Herrens diskurs är frånvarande, d.v.s. den diskurs som upprätthåller illusionen att världen är hel och harmonisk samt garanterar stabilitet. Således utesluter den hot om förändring och människan kan leva vidare i sin förutfattade mening om sig själv. Denna diskurs rymmer i själva verket inte något hat, eftersom ingen människa i själva verket egentligen identifierar sig med Herren eller Mästaren. Han bara finns där, och människan underordnar sig honom som något självklart. I NATO-baren finns ingen självklarhet, bara mutationer av frigjord energi.

Filosofen Sven-Olof Wallenstein gör i sin essä *Det utvidgade fältet – från högmodernism till konceptualism* ett intressant antagande, att det moderna konstbegreppet är på väg att genomgå en fundamental mutation. Men i så fall i riktning mot vad? frågar sig Wallenstein. "En generaliserad medvetande-, design-, media- och kommunikationsteori, informationsteknologi, en de sociala processernas estetik."

De elva konstnärerna från Vilnius som deltar i utställningen *Regel-*

ändring (i Norrtälje, Södertälje och Västerås) formar en triangel av orden: ramar, redskap, roller. I det här fallet behöver man inte tvivla på orden. I Litauen finns ingen som helst anledning att följa den korrekta distansens restriktioner, överlevnaden kommer först.

Konsumtionens högsäte i Södertälje, köpcentret, har fått en utvidgning. Platsen för konst och kultur, Konsthallen är transformerad till en kufisk affär vars estetik och funktion är en avvikelse från de övriga butikernas. En tröja har virkats av människohår (Eglė Rakauskaitės verk), vem vill köpa? En fotbollsmönstrad jacka i utsökt silke (Sandra Straukaitės) är på catwalk. Gintaras Makarevičius står naken med ett gevär av trä större än mannen själv. Med vem krigar han? Är det erfarenhet av kaos och desillusion som gör de litauiska konstnärerna så suveräna visavi förmågan att bära med sig, i sitt verk, dess kontext? Som om det vore i direkt kontakt med kontexten, som om de visste att betydelsen skapas ur sammanhanget, och att sammanhanget är gränslöst ifall det inte preciseras.

S & P Stanikas' installationer reser sig med en sällan skådad förmåga ur ruinerna av ett kollapsat psyke. Ofta störande, ofullständigt och brutalt, på gränsen till fulhet. Att förändra är att förlora kontroll över gammalt material; brott som begåtts, desillusioner som fått dig att drunkna, ord som kastats ut i vanmakt och hysteri. Som en verklighetens Fågel Fenix putsar Stanikas askan från vindarna, klär upp sig och sätter på en ny skiva. En ny dag kan börja, banaliteterna kommer även denna gång att uthärdas.

få konstruktionerna att krackelera

Francesca Woodman
Finlands fotografiska museum, Helsingfors

Kameran som själsfrände

De uppgifter jag har om Francesca Woodmans personhistoria är knapphändiga. Woodman föddes 1958 i Denver av föräldrar med italienskt påbrå. Sin uppväxt tillbringade hon både i USA och Italien. Hon började fotografera vid 14 års ålder och år 1975 inledde hon sina studier vid Rhode Island School of Design. Tre år senare flyttade hon till New York. I januari 1981 publicerade hon serien *Some Disordered Interior Geometries*, några veckor senare begick hon självmord. De aktuella fotografierna är alltså gjorda av en ung kvinna i åldern av 15 till 22 år.

Även om Woodmans fotografier undersöker kvinnan och kvinnligheten är det missledande att betrakta henne som en förelöpare till 80-talets iscensatta konceptuella fotografiska praktik som riktar en medveten kritik mot det andra könets position i vår kultur. Woodman manipulerar inte med det fotografiska medlets inneboende konventioner – hon befattar sig inte med det fixerade seendets tekniker, hon använder inte kameran för att synliggöra distansen mellan subjekt och objekt. Hennes relation till kameran är en annan, den är en själsfrände, ett fogligt redskap med nästan magiska egenskaper som tillåter henne att fånga sådant som inte är omedelbart tillgängligt för ögat. Fotograferandet blir en handling med ständig psykologisk relevans.

Önskar man placera Woodmans bilder i ett fotografiskt sammanhang finner man anspelningar på viktorianska fotografer som Clementina Hawarden och Julia Margaret Cameron beträffande det inslag av drömsk och romantisk teatralitet som finns i fotografierna. Men likheten till den här traditionen är skenbar, den erbjuder endast ett visuellt ramverk för bildernas kritiska moment i vilket kvinnokroppen framträder som betydelsebärare. I det här sammanhanget har kvinnokroppen mycket litet att göra med traditionell fotografisk skönhet, sambandet kan närmast beskrivas som ett brott mot det skönas retorik. Däremot är det möjligt att se en påverkan från symbolismen och surrealismen där det omedvetna utgör föremålet för den konstnärliga undersökningen.

Då jag studerar Francesca Woodmans fotografier är det framför allt en

fråga som sysselsätter mig: Vad är det hon försökte se eller uppenbara genom de här avbildningarna av sig själv? Det är som om utgångspunkten ofta skulle vara ett tillstånd där människan inte längre kan sägas ha en kropp – som om en kritisk gräns suddats ut och kamerans uppgift är att visa bilderna av en kropp som rör sig på gränserna mellan olika tillstånd.

I fotografierna finns en inneboende ambivalens. Dels finns det en strävan att oförmedlat nå det råa och obearbetade, det som placerar sig före symboliseringen, dels är Woodman i sin praktik uttryckligen beroende av bilden som förmedlande länk och därför kommer också många av hennes fotografier att präglas av ett mångbottnat bildbegrepp. Exempelvis i serien *Self-Deceit* (Självbedrägeri) ser vi hur den nakna kvinnan leker ett slags katt-och-råttalek med en spegel i ett övrigt tomt rum. Hon försöker på olika sätt, förgäves, komma undan spegeln eller snarare spegelbilden. Då Woodman i sina fotografier ofta hanterar speglar och glasskivor är det svårt att låta bli att associera till spegelstadiets drama i vilket barnet genom spegelbilden uppfattar sig som en hel gestalt. Genom att barnet inte omfattar sig självt utan bilden av sig blir gestalten liksom alla bilder illusorisk. *Self-Deceit* ter sig som ett misskännande riktat mot det egna jaget. "Bilden är i mitt öga. Men jag är inte i bilden", för att citera Lacan. I många av fotografierna upphävs avbildningen av kroppen, kroppen ser ut att försvinna och ersätts av ett tecken eller ett spår. Det kan vara frågan om ett bränt avtryck av en kropp eller en skugglik gestalt.

Flera av de utställda fotografierna går en annan väg, problematiken förs upp till symbolens plan. Kroppen omges av tyger, växter, pälsbitar, pärlor. I de här bilderna upprättar Woodman en personlig symbolisk ordning, ett uttryck för den omedvetna fantasin. Symbolernas förmåga att förtäta och förskjuta betydelsen underbyggs av Woodmans träffsäkra fokusering. Det är som om hon lämnat en del av miljön orörd. Platsen utgörs ofta av ett stökigt eller övergivet rum. Där någonstans framträder kristallklart uttänkt och genomförd en scen med en stark symbolisk laddning.

Hufvudstadsbladet 2 april 1993

Gerhard Richter
Moderna Museet, Stockholm

Skamlös frihet

Vid öppningen 1958 visade Moderna Museet Picassos omdiskuterade verk *Guernica.* Cirkeln sluts, Gerhard Richters retropektiva utställning, omfattande ett hundratal verk, blir museets sista i den gamla byggnaden. Efter att ha sett utställningen är jag redo att kalla denne man, utbildad i klassisk målarkonst, en av samtidens mest betydelsefulla målare, vilket förstås väcker många frågor. Vilka är kriterierna för ett dylikt omdöme, vad motiverar benämningen visavi Richter?

Inledningsvis kan jag inte låta bli att tala om upplevelsen, att vandra omkring bland Richters verk ger en sällsynt delikat sådan. Därtill är utställningen utsökt hängd som ett resultat av kurator Kasper Königs och Richters samarbete. För det andra, att analytiskt påvisa Richters betydelse är ett mångbottnat företag och dömt att misslyckas ifall det inte förankras i Richters måleriska egenart. Flera av de instrument som brukas i analys av samtidskonsten blir plötsligt inför Richtens produktion förvridna och obrukbara. Redan ett uttryck som "tidsenligt måleri", eller vår vana att lineärt hantera "måleriets utveckling" med rubriker som sekelskiftesmåleri, det moderna genombrottet, den postmoderna upplösningen, blir hotade. Detta är en bland många av Richters förtjänster. Den inblick som utställningen ger i måleriet är oförutsebar och den bärs utan tvivel upp av konstnärens passionerade relation till sitt medium.

Det är omöjligt att påvisa Richters betydelse genom att hänvisa till ett av verken som den måleriska undersökningens höjdpunkt. Bakom den här omständigheten döljer sig Richters egenart, sättet på vilket han hanterar sitt medium implicerar ett intressant drag av skamlöshet; Richter målar i olika stilar, han växlar mellan dem och använder dem parallellt. Fotorealism, landskapsmåleri, abstrakt expressionism, porträtt av människor och "porträtt" av färger förekommer. Det kontroversiella draget är följaktligen inte synligt i uttrycket, i själva verket, utan det manifesteras genom den skamlösa frihet Richter anammat i förhållande till måleriets värdeladdade hierarkier. Han rör sig transversalt och därför behövs det ett hundratal verk för att man skall upptäcka den richterska destinationen: hur hans

djupt rotade misstro mot estetiska utopier omvandlas till ett betydelsefullt pussel med flera parallella lösningar.

Enligt min tolkning utgör Richters användning av stilar inte ett självändamål. Inte heller skriver jag under den uppfattning som en del skribenter för fram då de talar om en indifferens som typisk för Richters förhållningssätt, d.v.s. att han genom stilvariationer tömmer måleriet på betydelser och sålunda utarmar sitt medium. Jag tror det motsatta, att de olika stilarna för Richter tjänar som nödvändiga passager för att komma det han letar efter på spåren, att hans måleri egentligen handlar om excesser kring begäret efter begäret; det som blir kvar efter insikten att begärets objekt är omöjligt att måla.

Stilen ger ett slags nödvändig materialisering som kompenserar det tomrum det frånvarande objektet kvarlämnat. Av denna anledning håller jag inte med dem som kallar Richters attityd distanserad. Det som är närvarande i målningarna förlänas närvaro just på grund av det att hela företaget upprättats av en specifik människa i en specifik situation. Den skönhet man ser i Richters verk anger ingen slutpunkt, den liksom drivs vidare och får liv av ett slags inbyggt sår eller ickeöverensstämmelse. Insikten om att det finns ett richterskt moment i målningarna, lika starkt som osynligt, är dock oerhört svår att analytiskt bekräfta. "Att måla är ren idioti men ändå så meningsfullt", säger han själv.

När Richter målar använder han ofta ett fotografi som förlaga. Enligt ett uttalande målar han inte av fotografiet utan han vill måla det. Är det fråga om att återupprätta ett minne av något förgånget som utan hjälp av målandet vore förlorat? Exempelvis hans landskapsmålningar har föregåtts av tusentals fotografier, sist och slutligen är det endast ett fåtal av dem som berör det han letar efter, det han inte visste han sökte.

Sviten *18 October 1977* som handlar om RAF-medlemmarnas sista levnadstid, målade han först 1988 efter att i åratal samlat på dokumentärt material. De gråsvarta fotorealistiska målningarna med en speciell suddig effekt som gör bilden otydlig har i Moderna Museet fått ett eget rum där de avgränsat hänger. Det är döden man ser. Richter beskriver ett tragiskt kapitel av tysk samtidshistoria uteslutande utgående från några människors levnadsöden.

Att Richter är mästare i att finna den rätta nivån för sin känslighet blir tydligt då man studerar målningen *Betty*, ett porträtt i färg han målade av sin unga dotter medan han höll på med *18 October 1977*. Betty visar inte sitt

ansikte, hon sitter med huvudet halvt bortvänt. Finns det någon annan möjlighet än att låta betraktaren endast i föreställningen se den unga kvinnans aningslösa ansiktsdrag – efter att man sett målningen *Död* där en av RAF-kvinnorna ligger med bruten nacke. När Richter var färdig med sviten målade han ett antal abstrakta verk i rött.

Skönhet som bär på sin skada, samstämmighet över disharmoniska element, skapar kärnan i Richters talangfullhet och just denna karaktäristik bekräftas genom upphängningen i museets sal ett plan upp. Den här lilla utställningen i utställningen fungerar som en bild som leder rätt in i den richterska passagen. Nere vid trappan två verk, en stor målning av en naken kvinna som går nerför en trappa, intill denna en liten "traditionell" vy från Venedig med en pojke som sitter vid en kanal och tittar ner i vattnet. Då man går uppför trappan rör man sig mot en utsökt avbild av blommor. Inne i rummet konfronteras man direkt med det plan som Richters användning av givna strukturer (repertoaren av stilar) möjligen är avsedd att leda fram till – en lockelse att se, leta, lyssna, möta väcks till liv.

Här uppe försonas en väl vald samling av icke-samstämmiga uttryck som finner en punkt där ett meningsbärande sammanhang kan vidkännas. En kort beskrivning: Porträttet av Betty i närhet till "porträtt" av färger, liksom tagna ur en färgkarta, färgerna överförs och transformeras därefter i ett litet abstrakt, expressionistiskt verk. Mitt emot Betty står en ställning som bär upp fyra glasskivor som kan vändas i vardera riktningen. Richters nyaste verk *Bach*-serien bildar en annan av utställningens fullträffar. Väldiga dukar med färg så tunt påstruken att man nästan ser igenom färghinnan. Ett analytiskt sinne glömmer bort sig, totalt absorberat av seendet.

Hufvudstadsbladet 16 april 1994

Intervju med psykoanalytikern Iréne Matthis

Bekanta sig med gamla, livlösa ord på nytt. Ord vars betydelseinnehåll stått stilla och så småningom tystnat. När Iréne Matthis inledde sin föreläsning *Strangebody* i Malmö öppnade hon med en gång en bortglömd dörr.

Vad hon sade var att tro inverkar på kroppen, att vad vi fantiserar och föreställer oss genljuder även på det kroppsliga planet. Hon refererade bl.a. till Claude Lévi-Strauss som i sina studier av myter noterade ordets läkande kraft genom dess förmåga att benämna det tidigare opåverkbara.

Detta skedde i maj, när jag i september åkte till Stockholm för att samtala med Iréne Matthis hade jag nyss sett Catherine Bigelows film *Strange Days* som åtminstone för mig gav föraning om den "medvetanderevolution" cyberspace-teknologin kunde medföra icke minst visavi förhållandet mellan verbalt språk och visualitet. Filmens huvudperson producerar och säljer cyberspace-band, d.v.s. han erbjuder sina kunder upplevelser som finns på cyberband och överförs till mottagaren via en hjälmliknande apparat. Ordet upplevelse är här egentligen fullständigt otillräckligt för att beskriva det som överförs till mottagaren: han är den persons verklighet som haft andningsapparaten på sitt huvud (skyddad av peruk). Såsom en av kunderna i filmen säger efter sin resa i cyberspace: han var en 18-årig flicka i duschen, han såg vad hon såg, kände vad hon kände, han var lika med hennes kropp under duschsekvensen. Konsekvensen blir ju då att "upplevelser" kan konsumeras när som helst, var som helst, och det som konsumeras kan vara allt från mord till kärlek – och därmed förlorar det filosofiska spörsmålet om jag kan känna vad du känner sin grund.

Med kristallklar skärpa analyserade Matthis mina frågor om vad virtualverkligheten kunde betyda från en psykoanalytisk synvinkel sett.

Matthis Principen att materialet är lagrat är den samma för hjärnans del, det vi upplevt i våra liv är "lagrat" i vår hjärna. Den avgörande skillnaden mellan det du berättade om cyberspace-mekaniken och hjärnan är att när människan minns finns det en rörelse i återberättandet; minnet varierar beroende på tidpunkt, livssituation och plats m.m. Det vi minns kan vi emellertid förhålla oss till på olika sätt, förenklat uttryckt: som tecken eller som symbol. Tecknet fungerar på samma sätt som cyberspace-bandet, där relationen mellan tecknet och det tecknet refererar till är direkt. Man kan säga att tecknet liksom klibbar vid situationen. Symbolen å andra sidan har tagit ett steg vidare, till en abstraherad nivå, den uppväcker inte situationen som sådan utan konceptet. Symbolen väcker således till liv minnet av situationen vilket betyder att vi kan leka med den, den klibbar inte längre fast vid oss, den ger oss distans. Tecknet sitter ovillkorligen fast liksom huden medan symbolen är som en klänning vi kan välja att ta av och på.

Roos Det du säger om skillnaden mellan tecken och symbol får mig att tänka på den tendens som just nu är synlig i konsten, unga konstnärer är upptagna av "det verkliga tinget", försöker etablera ett direkt förhållningssätt till verkligheten exempelvis såsom i det man kallar trash- och slackerart. Problemet enligt mig är att projektet ofta misslyckas, verket är stumt, utestänger dialog. Kunde det här just bero på att verket fungerar på tecknets nivå, det klibbar fast vid något som inte öppnar sig för kommunikation?

Matthis Ja, det är svårt att kommunicera med tecknet. Jag tänker på konceptkonstnärens pragmatiska prövning i rummet där han försöker finna ut varför det just skall vara på ett sätt och inte på ett annat, d.v.s. det gäller för honom att finna exakthet för hur verket skall fungera i rummet för tecknet går direkt in i kroppen, det talar direkt till oss utan att vi behöver förstå konstverket som sådant.

Roos Då kunde man alltså säga att det jag nämnde som misslyckad funktion hos trash- och slackerart beror på det att konstnären inte fått tecknet att tala utanför sin egen kropp, det når inte fram till betraktaren.

Cyberspace, hur tror du att det kommer att förändra vårt sätt att se och tänka? Hörde nyss tiden i virtuell verklighet omtalas som "dream time".

Matthis Att det kommer att göra det är klart. Går man in i virtuella rum som om det vore fråga om verklig tid måste det ju, när man går ut ur dem, färga sättet för hur den verkliga världen uppfattas emedan det vi upplevt finns kvar i vår hjärna. Fastän det är förstås svårt att föreställa sig hur detta kommer att vara – på samma sätt som vi har svårt att föreställa oss verkligheten i kulturer som enbart är muntliga. Walter J. Ong redogör i sin bok *Muntlig och skriftlig kultur* för hur dylika kulturer fungerat. Bl.a. minneskonstnärer i Afrika arbetade genom att stryka ut och förändra berättelsen, den var aldrig den samma berättad en andra gång. Även sättet för hur en historisk händelse beskrevs såg annorlunda ut än i vår kultur. Exempelvis beskrevs händelserna som förlopp enligt flodens mönster. Tiden uppfattades således i rumsliga termer, för rummet kände de till även om de inte fick grepp om själva tiden. "Den nya virtuella verkligheten" ger oss kanske ett nytt sätt att se och tänka, för tiden blir igen rumslig. Vi hamnar i ett slags visuellt förkroppsligande av minnet och tiden.

Roos Vad håller du för tillfället på med i din teoretiska verksamhet?

Matthis I korthet kunde det beskrivas som förhållandet mellan kropp och språk; språnget eller klyftan mellan kropp och "mind" (jag använder hellre engelskans *mind* än det svenska ordet själ). Hos patienten är det psykosomatiska symptomet ett slags tecken som klibbar vid kroppen och styr de mentala processerna. Om man lyckas göra tecknet till en symbol kan förändring inträda, för symbolen har många värden. Tolkningen är således ett abstraherande av teckenfunktionen till en symbolnivå som är möjlig att förändra. Det är det här språnget, från kropp till språk, som jag försöker kartlägga. Språnget manifesteras på många plan, exempelvis i relationen mellan patient och läkare, mannen och den hysteriska kvinnan. Ett hysteriskt symptom avslöjar klyftan mellan kropp och själ, i hysterin ser lidandets form en negation, ett tecken för ett förnekande som kroppen utsätts för. Att få tag i detta och börja symbolisera det är bara möjligt i relation till andra, till någon utanför att rikta sig mot.

Paletten 2–3/1996

Ars 95, Museet för nutidskonst, Helsingfors
Intervju med Anish Kapoor

Att förlänga ögonblicket av tilltro

Anish Kapoor, född 1954 i Bombay, är son till en indier och hans mamma är judisk irakier. Efter sin konstnärliga utbildning i London på 70-talet har Kapoor varit verksam i Storbritannien och flitigt uppträtt i internationella sammanhang. Kapoor har tillfört skulpturen "något": samtidigt enkelt och totalt suggestivt. Speciellt under de senaste åren är det ett djupblått, mörkt, gränslöst hål man mött i hans verk. På *Ars 95* har man nu tillfälle att se hans verk *My body your body* (1993).

Roos Jag har ett enkelt exempel beträffande det sätt på vilket dina verk frammanar de fundamentala verben – att se, att titta på, att förnimma. Ofta kan man undra över vad betraktaren egentligen ser och hur han ser, men inför dina verk får man en känsla att det är möjligt att dela någonting; vad

jag ser sammanfaller med vad du ser.

Kapoor En stor del av mina arbeten under de senaste sju åren har handlat om hinnan – ytan av ett objekt – kontaktpunkten mellan föremålet och världen. Den förvirring som existerar visavi förhållandet mellan kropp och öga, hand och öga kopplar jag till just ytan som skinn, hud, hölje – något som ser mycket verkligt ut men dock är mycket enkelt. Frågetecknet finns alltid där: var finns början, var finns slutet? Och man stöter på lingvistiska problem; man kan inte beskriva med ord för här ingår en rent abstrakt dimension, illusorisk och flyktig, som lever i fantasin. Vad som intresserar mig är att abstraktion på den här nivån blir oren, blir vulgär när kroppen kommer in i bilden. Och det är då när kroppen inträder som det verkligen blir intressant. Förstår du vad jag menar?

Roos Jag minns en tanke jag fick när jag läste en text om dina arbeten – det är ju framför allt tomrummet (hålet) som diskussionerna handlat om. I en intervju sade du att det är betraktaren som har det avgörande valet på sin lott, att stiga ner eller inte i det lockande, sugande djupet. Men man stiger inte ner för var man hamnar är ju okänt, att stiga ner i hålet förutsätter en föreställning om vad som följer därpå, fantasier om ett post-tillstånd. Dina arbeten med ett mörkt, oändligt hål beskriver det här utan ord. Någonstans har du sagt att du vill berätta en "annan" historia, ett berättande utan en narrativ följd; på sätt och vis kan man säga att föreställningarna kring att stiga ner i hålet just handlar om ett annat slag av berättande.

Kapoor Det talas mycket nuförtiden om tomrummet, som om hela mytologin kring nedfärden nyupptäckts – den platonska föreställningen om människan i grottan, Kristi färd till limbus, eller Edvard Munchs resa till branten av vansinne. Dessa är, på sätt och vis, alla bilder av vad vi ser som den negativa sidan av psyket. Jag tror det finns en annan form av detta, som är lika gåtfull, men inte negativ. Kunde faktiskt vara frågan om ett positivt försvinnande, att färdas nedåt i positiv bemärkelse. Men problemet är att då man talar så här kommer man alltför nära ett slags religiöst språk.

Roos En positiv variant av att stiga ner i det okända? Jag kan inte tro att någon skulle kunna tänka sig den möjligheten utan att relatera rörelsen till en plats, därför att det som är inbyggt i psyket från allra första början är insikten om att du har varit beroende av någon annan människa. Ser man så här på saken, kunde man säga att rädslan gäller en möjlig förlust av ens

bakgrund som på något underligt sätt "håller oss fyllda", ger oss ett koncept för utsträckning och varande i tiden.

Kapoor Jag träffade en gång en person i Grekland vars far var en psykoanalytiker som använde LSD för att föra människor tillbaka till deras upplevelser före födseln, och sonen hade alltså också varit där. Jag försökte tala med honom om hur det var.

Åtminstone är det en perfekt idé om återkomst eller nedfärd. Till slut kunde han endast konstatera att han faktiskt var oförmögen att ge upplevelsen verkliga ord även om han visste hur det kändes. Och jag förstod inte mer än tidigare – således vad vi förmår är att endast tala metaforiskt om ämnet.

Roos Ja, religionen gör det, och i olika kulturer har man olika ritualer som tar hand om detta tysta område. Men å andra sidan, det här är inte ditt problem för ditt område är det visuella. Du kan exempelvis visualisera det slag av upplevelse din grekiska vän var oförmögen att beskriva i ord.

Kapoor För det första saknar vi ett verbalt språk för det här, för det andra har vi inte heller något visuellt språk att ta till. Det bästa vi har är ett slags mellanliggande, otydligt rum. Vad jag försöker föreslå är att det finns någonting mer exakt än otydlighet, och jag tror... När man tänker på alla de här historierna av Dante, alla historier om mörk nedstigning; de blir uppenbara i det ögonblick man fysiskt börjar hantera ämnet. Som bildkonstnär behöver man faktiskt inte bära med dig det mytologiska bagaget, det infinner sig. Jag tror att i och med att jag blivit mer säker på vad jag försöker göra behöver jag allt mindre använda det mytologiska för det är där ändå.

Roos Men, refererande till dina verk, är det tänkbart att du trots allt arbetar med vissa gränser kring abstraktioner. Den visuella processen är inte totalt öppen, även om abstraktionen får löpa enormt fritt på ett plan förutsätter visualiseringen mycket exakta gränser.

Kapoor Det intressanta med skulptur är att då den befinner sig i rummet blir den teatral. Den blir av nödvändighet berättande för du har det här och det där ögonblicket och då du går omkring i rummet uppstår olika sekvenser och moment. Vad jag försöker göra är att avgränsa den här aspekten så mycket som möjligt. Så nästan alla arbeten jag gjort är frontala, du står rakt framför dem och där är det, verket. Vad jag avser är att reducera det narrativa momentet till ett enda perspektiv, till ett minimum.

Anledningen är mycket enkel. Då man gör en begränsning och använder endast en riktning inträder tidsaspekten. Tiden blir inte symmetrisk utan den tillhör en sinnesstämning. Denna sinnesstämning i sin tur är förankrad i ett moment av närvaro, det är frågan om det mycket, mycket närvarande ögonblicket. Det sublima är nu, som Baudrillard förklarade på 60-talet.

Roos Kanske den primära basen för frontaliteten är kopplad till den psykiska utvecklingen, till ansikte-mot-ansikte-kontakten, eller mer exakt till speglingen?

Kapoor En relation där vi är ansikte mot ansikte, inte framför eller bakom är ett receptivt tillstånd, och detta är viktigt för mina verk. Det sublima är här, just nu och sålunda blir färden neråt mot något annat förkroppsligad, den existerar endast i relationen och genom relationen. Då kan man säga att det sublima inte existerar i det abstrakta utan endast i ett bestämt ögonblick, för en bestämd tid.

Roos En kort sammanfattning av ditt verk, *My body our body* (1993) här i Helsingfors – som betraktare undrar man: hur långt in vågar jag gå?

Kapoor Min intention är att tänja ut precis det där ögonblicket, för efter en stund kommer vi på hur djupet tekniskt sett fungerar, vi gör det till någonting vi kan förstå. Jag är oerhört intresserad av att försöka förlänga ögonblicket av tilltro till vad man ser, hur långt kan det bli? Ett ögonblick av tro – man tror på vad man ser och glömmer att förstå. Det är ungefär som att få syn på ett utsökt ansikte hos ett litet barn. Du är helt slagen av förundran, vilket ting! Sedan, naturligtvis ser man på det som vilket som helst barn och ögonblicket är förbi.

Roos En sista fråga, jag är nyfiken på hur det var att vara sjutton år och komma till London efter att ha vuxit upp i Bombay?

Kapoor Egentligen var jag nitton, för jag tillbringade två år i Israel. Rätt så svårt. Jag vet inte varför men det var rätt så desorienterande. Allt kändes förvånansvärt bekant och otroligt främmande, förvirrande. Jag hade vuxit upp i en kontext där den enda möjligheten, ifall man ville bli konstnär, skulle ha varit att följa någonslags västerländsk avantgarde-modell, men i termer av mina egna erfarenheter var det ingen idé med detta. Det kändes som ett utanför. Det var först efter att jag kommit på ett sätt att handskas

med innebörden i att vara indier som jag kunde finna ett språk som hade
någon mening för mig och mina erfarenheter. Nu befinner jag mig i en
position där frågan om att vara indier eller inte inte är avgörande, den är
totalt irrelevant för vad jag sysslar med för mitt språk här har sin egen bas.

Roos Du hade alltså ingen modell för hur bete sig som konstnär, ingen tradition att falla tillbaka på, då du kom till London?

Kapoor Det är riktigt, det fanns helt enkelt inte någon modell att ta till.
Visserligen fanns det konstnärer som On Kawara, men On Kawara arbetade i avantgarde-traditionen. Där fanns Nam June Paik som då hade gjort
några filmer men fortfarande i ovannämnda tradition. Och sedan Naguchi
som tog några steg utåt, men fortfarande mycket försiktiga. Men tidpunkten var den rätta för en öppning som kom att gälla hela den kulturella
ramen. Det hermetiska synsättet på kultur upplöstes, och detta hände
överallt, samtidigt, inom musik, teater, visuell konst.

Siksi 1/1995

Lone Høyer Hansen
Nordiskt konstcentrum, Helsingfors

Mot den oartikulerade formen

När man synar Lone Høyer Hansens verk i Strandkasernen är föränderlighet den dominanta egenskapen. Verken ser olika ut, de förefaller inte
utgå från ett homogent visuellt uttryck. Om man vill leta efter en utgångspunkt för Høyer Hansens skulpturala undersökning finns den således på
ett annat plan än det formellt visuella, något som för övrigt genomgående
kännetecknar ung dansk skulptur.

Under vandringen bland Høyer Hansens skulpturer återkommer
ständigt samma fråga: finns det en plausibel utgångspunkt som skulle
kunna sammanfatta det heterogena utan att tvinga in det i analys som
reducerar dess komplexitet, för det är samtidigt svårt att utesluta det faktum att Høyer Hansens undersökning av skulpturen följer vissa spår, som

om den letade efter någonting, möjligen uttryckbart som ett slags gestaltning eller konkretion av tingens icke-logiska tillstånd.

I en färsk intervju säger Høyer Hansen att hon började studera vid Konstakademin i Köpenhamn (1980–85) för att Willy Ørskov där undervisade i skulptur. Hon hade läst hans bok *Reading Objects* och gillade den, dels för att Ørskov gav skulpturen ett språk och dels för att hans utgångspunkt alltid fanns i den verkliga världen. Tolkar man begreppet det verkliga helt ordagrant skulle det närmast gälla det som är synligt i Høyer Hanses 80-talsarbeten, exempelvis i *Pascal* eller *Still-Life* där byggstenarna utgörs av vardagliga föremål. Men i förhållande till hennes skulpturala undersökning som sådan har det verkliga en relevans som går utöver de igenkännbara objekten. Skulpturerna befattar sig inte med metafysiska spekulationer om kroppar och former utan de kan genomgående relateras till den verkliga världen genom att Høyer Hansen lyckas parallellställa skulpturens existens med verklighetens.

Helheten består av kroppar och tomrum, emedan förnimmelsen i sig hävdar att kroppar existerar, och förnimmelsen är den bas utgående från vilken vi drar slutsatser då vi resonerar om det okända, för att citera ett avsnitt ur epikureisk filosofi där det verkligas komplexitet sammanfattas på ett mycket odramatiserat sätt. I Høyer Hansens arbeten blir skulpturen en kropp jämställd med vår egen kropp i rummet, men med den skillnaden att skulpturen dessutom förkroppsligar det okända, tingens icke-logiska tillstånd genom att få detta att framstå som en realitet bland andra.

Förverkligandet, förkroppsligandet av ett immateriellt tillstånd i Høyer Hansens senaste arbeten löper hand i hand med det hur artikuleringen av formen utvecklats. I 80-talsverken med de vardagliga föremålen kunde artikuleringen kallas för ett slags fördubbling, en upprepning av ett bekant föremål placeras i ett sammanhang som förskjuter innebörden i en bestämd riktning. Jämför man detta med språket skulle det vara frågan om att underordna sig det symboliska (i lacansk bemärkelse). Efter att Høyer Hansen uteslutit de vardagliga objekten går utvecklingen mot en oartikulerad form, en form som inte entydigt underordnar sig det symboliska, som inte betecknar sig själv genom att förtydliga sig utan i stället representerar ett okluvet tillstånd där subjektet inte är givet utan det alstras.

Verket *Dårporträtt* (1990) består av en gruppering av utdragna former som vi gestaltar som antydningar av långa, böjda nackar med huvuden vars ansikten ständigt förblir bortvända. De osynliga ansiktenas frusna

mimik är liksom förskjuten till förhållandet mellan figurernas nacke och huvud. Trots skulpturens envetna närvaro och konkretion i rummet utesluts inte förnimmelsen att Dårporträtten likaväl kunde sägas handla om reminiscensen av en ögonblicklig, förbiilande otäck känsla av att ha tappat bort sig, oförmögen att finna de förlösande orden.

Puntello-verken (1993) är tvådelade, den ena delen består av regelbundna järnlådor med blänkande yta, den andra av mjukt formade bronsklumpar som balanserar intill, bredvid eller på järnlådan genom en kontaktpunkt som får det hela att se orimligt bräckligt ut. Den här bräckligheten, känslan av att bronsklumpen vid minsta skakning kommer att rubbas är fröet till den sammandrabbning mellan den stabila "minimalistiska" formen och den oartikulerade störningen. Den minimalistiska kroppen råkar ut för något som är starkare än det objektiva, rationella och mätbara, liksom ett begärande subjekt placerats in för att dra intresset mot de möjligheter ett tillblivande alstrar.

Hufvudstadsbladet 16 oktober 1993

Jussi Niva och Nina Roos
Sara Hildéns konstmuseum, Tammerfors, 1994

Delad glädje är dubbel glädje

Dela rum

Även om rumslighet varit ett nyckelord i analys av Jussi Nivas och Nina Roos' arbeten tänker jag nu skjuta ordet åt sidan. Det är fortsättningen som intresserar mig, vad som kommer att hända då deras verk delar rum i Sara Hildéns konstmuseum.

När Jussi Niva och Nina Roos träffas för att planera utställningen har jag en färdig fråga i bakfickan: vilken är anledningen till att ni ställer ut tillsammans? Snart glömde jag dock att fråga, upptagen som jag var med att lyssna, inte så mycket på innehållet i vad de två sade utan det sätt de kommunicerade på. Medlet var egentligen inte språket utan deras arbeten

och jag befann mig utanför. Jag märkte att verken i takt med tiden hade fått olika benämningar och smeknamn som för mig var obekanta. Närmast påminde situationen om en sådan där ett invant par umgås kring en gemensam angelägenhet som inbegriper ett självklart plan av delad insikt. Nästa gång vi sågs ställde jag min fråga. Paus. Plus ett lakoniskt svar av Niva.

Jussi Niva Därför att vi velat se våra arbeten tillsammans. Det finns ett behov hos Nina och mig att se de egna verken i umgänge med verk som liksom från början och parallellt levt med ens eget arbetande. Och en tillfredsställelse som möjligen väntar betraktaren sedan när utställningen är färdig och arbetena får klara sig själva och leva på varandras villkor. Nina är faktiskt den enda konstnär vars arbeten väckt en omedelbar lust att låta dem kommunicera med mina egna. Vi ville från början utesluta koncept, rubrik, tema, namn, kurator. Sedan två år tillbaka har vi på olika sätt sysslat med den här utställningen. Som jag tidigare sade, det finns ett ömsesidigt behov och en lust att låta verken umgås med varandra.

Rita Roos Så man får vänta och se vad som kommer att ske. Genom att ni båda i ert konstnärskap aktualiserar rumslighet föreställer jag mig ett slags fruktbart korsdrag i det verkliga rummet vilket driver upp glidningen mellan verklighetens fysiska dimensioner och föreställningens oändliga potential till transformationer.

Barndomen

Rita Roos Berätta en minnesvärd episod från barndomen?

Jussi Niva Jag minns när jag fick upp ögonen för Ninas arbeten. Hon gick då det sista året på Konstakademin och arbetade med en stark grön färg. Alltid då jag tittade in pekade hon på olika moment i målningarna och undrade svagt hoppfullt, börjar inte det här se "fel" ut? Är det inte "på snedden"? Kort därefter lämnade hon duken, hittade zinkplåten och fick fatt på "felaktigheten".

Nina Roos Din beskrivning handlar väl om min ansats att försöka finna en egen "brottsplats", d.v.s. en plats för mitt måleri från vilken jag dels kunde bryta med det jag uppfattade som ett hinder, måleriet med stort m och dels kunde påbörja en undersökning på egna villkor. För övrigt Jussi, dina barndomsarbeten förknippar jag med målningarna med organiska motiv. Det var väl blommor?

Jussi Niva Jag tröttnade rätt så snart på de organiska snäck- och svamp-formerna. Bakgrunden, det sekundära, fascinerade mig plötsligt och jag renodlade den som separat visuellt objekt. Konsekvensen blev den att mål-ningarna i form av ett slags väggpanel ingrep på ett fysiskt sätt i det verk-liga rummet.

Den enögde

Rita Roos Nu vill jag höra historien om hur du missade kaffekoppen.

Jussi Niva Under resan fick jag en svår ögoninfektion och behandlingen gjorde att mitt högra öga var ett dygn helt övertäckt. Jag fick reda mig med fel öga, på så sätt fel som då en högerhänt måste skriva med vänster hand. Med ens begrep jag mig inte på den välbekanta och trygga tredimensio-naliteten. Med ett öga gick det inte att gestalta närliggande avstånd. Jag var i färd med att gripa tag i föremål innan jag ens vidrört dem, i trappor-na steg jag ut i det tomma och snubblade även på plan mark. Situationen var som tvådimensionella fragment varav man försöker bygga en rumslig verklighet. På samma sätt som antingen höger- eller vänsterhäntheten bestämmer logiken för hur handen fungerar, gestaltar antingen-eller-synen i första hand tredimensionalitet.

Rita Roos På tal om detta, jag undrar om *I Spy with My Eyes*-serien är ett slags guidad tur i perceptionens mysterier? Du specialtillverkade monokroma målningar för autentiska lägenheter och därefter fotograferade du scenen.

Jussi Niva Jag fotograferade *I Spy*-arbetena med panoramakamera. Dess bild motsvarar läget hos en betraktare i rörelse där bilden skapas likaväl av redan passerade, nyss sedda Saker som av sådana som finns framför en. Bilden är snarare en pensling av det sedda som koordinerar avstånd och förhållanden mellan storlekar i stället för att bygga detaljer. Ett enögt nor-malobjektiv förstärker fokuseringen, då igen ett panorerat vardagsrum kan betraktas som en bild i sig själv. Den motsvarar på ett naturligt sätt si-tuationen att vara i rummet. Du vet exempelvis hur du skall röra dig där. De målningar jag gjort intar i vart och ett rum sin egen plats. De är egentli-gen den enögdes hjälpmedel för att gestalta avstånd genom att mäta eller täcka över, försöket att förändra läget.

Ögat och Marianne-karamellen

Rita Roos I Jussi Nivas arbeten finns en förmedlare, redskapsbegreppet är artikulerat. Visualiteten hanteras pragmatiskt trots att det inte finns anledning att använda ordet om resultatet, de faktiska verken. I vilket fall som helst, när Niva arbetar behöver han inte praktikens krumsprång, processen ter sig relativt rationell och tydlig. I det här avseendet är ni varandras raka motsatser?

Nina Roos Det är svårt att göra jämförelser och analysera skillnad men olikhet finns. Jag kan försöka förklara den genom ett "symptom" jag funderat över. Jag har inte körkort och kommer heller inte att skaffa mig ett sådant. Anledningen är på samma gång mycket enkel och komplex. När du kör bil är du tvungen att reagera på omvärlden motoriskt genom att avläsa den genom en viss uppsättning koder, signalfärger, trafikmärken, rörelsemönster. Det är för mig helt enkelt omöjligt (och högst antagligen livsfarligt) att inordna mig i den här typen av visuell styrning. Mitt måleri är motsatsen, att om och om igen orientera mig i en rumslighet där det inte finns någon given plats från vilken jag själv eller det som finns utanför kan zoomas in. Visualitet, det som kommer in genom ögat, kan jag inte separera eller avskärma från annat slag av sinnlighet. Därför är måleriet mitt medel, redan färgen innehåller en outtömlig potential, och sedan att använda den och samtidigt utesluta och frångå det som är visuellt igenkännbart. Exempelvis häromdagen när jag målade och var upptagen av ett rött streck på vit färg kände jag en verklig smak av Marianne-karamell i min mun.

Rita Roos Det låter som om du rörde dig i betydelsens gränssituationer. Vanligen anger man då två typer av fall, antingen ett tillstånd där betydelsen ännu inte är, eller ett annat där den inte längre kan uttryckas. Jag undrar om det i ditt måleri kunde vara frågan om en tredje variant, möjliggjord just genom att din praktik inte är verbal utan måleriets. Alltså, det som intresserar mig är att även om man som betraktare inför ditt måleri kan erfara ett "betydelsens gränstillstånd" är det samtidigt möjligt att etablera kommunikation med verket, man lämnas inte utanför. Min tanke är att det inte är frågan om ett tillstånd före tecknet eller efter tecknets upplösning utan ett tredje alternativ, en parallellkommunikation vid sidan om det som sker på det symboliska planet. En kommunikation där symbolerna ersatts med fästepunkter i måleriets specifika materialitet.

45

Nina Roos Ljudar rimligt, med förbehållet att du inte tänker referera till Julia Kristevas tankar om skapandets förhållande till moderskroppen eller snarare förlusten av den. Trots att det inte är min uppgift att tolka mina målningar gör den terminologin mig en aning skeptisk?

Rita Roos På vilket sätt skeptisk?

Nina Roos Helt enkelt därför att ett ord som exempelvis moderskropp är alldeles för visuellt och konkret (även om det ju också är en abstraktion) när saken handlar om måleriet. Då sitter man igen genom språket fast i representationernas nätverk, ett plan jag försöker frångå, d.v.s. måleriets bilder. Bakvänt på något sätt.

Rita Roos Allvarligt talat; vad jag här tänker på relaterar sig till begreppet förfrämligande. Då vår kunskap om världen enligt lacansk terminologi är grundlagd på den imaginära identifikationen (via speglingen) hamnar vi i ett tillstånd av förfrämligande. Vårt jag har egentligen sin bas i ett något som finns utanför oss själva. Vad jag vill påstå är att dina målningar frångår förfrämligandet, vi kan liksom assimileras i dem, gå in i dem via sinnena. De fungerar som fästepunkter för ett slags överraskande assimilation fullständigt oberoende av den symboliska framställningens lagar. Den rumsliga desorientering du jobbar med relaterar jag till en avsaknad av just den gräns som separerar, och samtidigt skapar jaget och därigenom också den Andre, den plats det talas från. Målningarna realiserar en sinnlig utopi, förnimmelsen av att kunna röra och orientera sig obehindrat genom att utanförskapet saknas. Ett förverkligande som enligt logikens principer är en omöjlighet.

Nina Roos Jag förstår. Men det motsäger inte det att jag är upptagen av tydligheten. Inte som förenkling utan som en sekundsnabb realisering av ett moment där en fysiskt kännbar tydlighet, målad, transponeras likt en nervimpuls till något annat. För mig är detta verklig realism.

Smalt och brett. Tjockt och tunt

Skillnaden som förutsättning för kommunikation att både se en sak och en annan fastän de varken är lika eller olika varandra. Jussi Niva mäter och beräknar storlekar, avstånd och proportioner. I Glo-galleriet år 1990 ställde han fram sina mätinstrument och betraktaren kunde ta ett direkt steg in i åtgärdernas dynamik. Också Nivas seende i färg följer gränser som nog-

grant testats. Som om vi genom färgläggningen av snölandskapen i *Snow-Clad* eller genom regnbågen i *Borrowed Landscape* fick delaktighet i en extrem visualitet. Ögat är här nog för upplevelsen av fysisk närvaro.

I den japanska kulturen uttrycks förhållandet till det främmande med ord som tjockt och tunt. Behändiga ord att använda i en kultur där relationen till främlingen hanteras genom en form av sammansmältning istället för gränsdragning. När något utifrånkommande blir för mycket, för tjockt gör japanen det tunnare, han skär bort och skapar en ny form.

När jag i samband med Nina Roos' måleri tänker på ordet materialitet associerar jag det precis till detta enkla, att färgen genom att växla mellan tjockt och tunt ständigt ger målningen fästepunkter. I Roos' sätt att arbeta med färg och akrylglas finns en inbyggd garanti för att gränsernas försvinnande inte blir detsamma som ett möte med tomrummet. Så länge vi förnimmer, förnimmer tjockt och tunt är vi fysiskt närvarande.

Konstnären och arbetsmetoden

Eva Löfdahls konstnärliga verksamhet har varit en av de riktgivande krafterna i den svenska 80-talskonsten. En intellektuell hållning, kopplingar mellan det litterära och det visuella, en fokusering på vissa strategiska termer (t.ex. "glappet", det "vanliga", "mellanrum" och "mellanområden") utgör drag som utmärkte det svenska 80-talet. Grupperingar som Wallda och ibid har redan nu fått en legendarisk klang. Wallda-konstnärerna bestående av Max Book, Eva Löfdahl och Stig Sjölund hade i början av 80-talet en gemensam ateljé i Årsta där de bl.a. framförde en rad kabaréföreställningar. Löfdahl var också en av deltagarna i utställningen *ibid. II* i Münchenbryggeriet i Stockholm.

Det är omöjligt att göra en kortfattad presentation av Löfdahls konstnärskap då det kännetecknas av överraskningar, tvära kast och ombytlighet vad utförandet och det yttre beträffar. Tekniken och medlen växlar, Löfdahl har arbetat med måleri, objekt, skulptur m.m. Men då man följer upp hennes produktion genom åren synliggörs dock en helhet eller ett sammanhängande område någonstans "bakom" eller "under" det yttre. Då jag träffade Eva Löfdahl för ett samtal var det framför allt de här nivåerna jag var nyfiken på. Hurudan är hennes konstnärliga process och metod? Hur ser intentionen ut i förhållande till resultatet? Ja, enligt vilka banor löper tankarna?

Roos Det finns ett intressant och exceptionellt drag som genomgående utmärker dina arbeten, de så att säga "fastnar" direkt. Ingenting blir oklart i relationen mellan det man ser och det man memorerar. Kan du kommentera det här?

Löfdahl Det är otroligt viktigt för mig att det är så tydligt, att komplikationen inte ligger där. För om det finns en komplikation i själva seendet, i perceptionsprocessen tror man ju ofta att man nått målet när man till slut upptäcker det oklara. Om verket är såpass enkelt att man omedelbart kan se det och dessutom minnas minnesbilden kan man bearbeta det i efterhand på ett helt annat sätt. Och komplext uppbyggt, både formellt och icke-formellt, språkligt och icke-språkligt – med många nivåer blandade,

skulle alltsammans försvinna om det inte fanns den här tydligheten att nagla fast vid. Det jag gör skulle försvinna i världen, överhuvudtaget inte fästa någonstans.

Roos Hur blir då någonting till? Hur ser den processen ut?

Löfdahl Det är frågan om ett dubbelriktat skeende. Många gånger har jag en aning och en struktur eller, ja, struktur är kanske det bästa ordet fastän det är väldigt vagt. En sådan struktur kan på samma sätt som poesins vara sammansatt av olika komponenter. Där kan ingå ett betydelseplan, ett formellt plan, ett rytmiskt plan, ett dynamiskt plan. Och när jag anar vad jag är intresserad av letar jag efter det. Jag kan också analysera baklänges om jag blir väldigt fascinerad av något. Den och den saken berörde mig, vad beror det på? Vad finns det för kvaliteter som gjorde att jag intresserade mig för just detta?

Roos Det är alltså i ett tidigt skede du medvetet börjar göra val och en analys av dem?

Löfdahl Processen pågår på något sätt hela tiden. Det är svårt att avgränsa starten på en specifik sak. På ett sätt är det så enkelt som – vad är jag intresserad av? Märkvärdigare än så är det inte. Ta nu t.ex. ordet genomsläpplighet. Det finns någonting i genomsläppligheten som intresserar mig. En annan kvalitet jag sysselsatt mig med är accelerering, eller snarare det ögonblick som uppstår då ett flygplan upphör att accelerera och i stället planar ut litet grann. Men det är väl först genom utförandet som det jag säger blir begripligt. Kastar jag ur mig ord som genomsläpplighet, flygplan, accelerering, kärl utan botten, tofsmössor saknas sammanhanget.

Roos Genomgående tycks din konstnärliga praktik röra sig på ett plan som träffar kritiska moment. Du fångar något som inte konstruerar sig logiskt men som ändå visuellt sett fungerar som en logisk konstruktion. Du gör föremål man uppfattar som upp- och nervända fastän de i faktiskt avseende inte är upp och ner, eller du framkallar en spegelvändhet som inte bygger på ett logiskt riktigt förhållande. Då konstruktionen är komplicerad – hur långt kan du styra avsikten i förhållande till resultatet?

Löfdahl Jag tycker nog att jag kan komma fram till ett beslut, avgöra om det är rätt eller inte, utan att jag helt har dragit upp problematiken till ett verbalt plan. Det här är en del av den dubbelsidighet vi talade om i början.

Jag är ute efter något men inte förrän jag gör en självanalys av responsen på olika saker blir jag riktigt klar över vad det första var. Tidigare har jag gått mer metodiskt tillväga då jag tog en massa foton. Först i efterhand då jag tittade på filmerna märkte jag att jag tagit samma bild t.ex. åtta gånger. Då blir det uppenbart att jag är ute efter någon specifik egenskap som finns där, varför upprepar jag annars?

Roos Det här vi talat om, kan man kalla det för ett slags metod som du utvecklat för ditt konstnärliga arbete?

Löfdahl Ja, det är väl just det jag beskrivit. Därtill samlar jag på mig en del föremål och konstellationer som jag vet att är bra på något sätt och som jag senare kan få användning för.

Hufvudstadsbladet 5 november 1992

Sounds in White Rabbit Fur. A Theory of the Visuality of Sound

Siksi 4/1996 (se den engelska översättningen sid. 51)

Ernst Mether-Borgström
Monografi, Otava, Helsingfors 1996

Lyssna en andra gång, noggrant

Fyra år sedan skrev jag för första gången om Ernst Mether-Borgströms verk. Jag erinrar mig ivern inför insikten som verken öppnade. Ibland är klarhet ett blixtsnabbt skeende. Mether-Borgströms gouacher övertygade mig om att den tolkande instansen missar skarven, de moment i en målning, i ett konstnärskap som inte ryms inom den aktuella kategorins (-ismens) ramar. Att läsa om Mether-Borgströms konst inom modellen för "den nya bilden", d.v.s. modernismens genombrott, är en annan sak än att

följa den visuella tråd Mether-Borgström arbetat med, ja, allt sedan han i slutet av 1930-talet inledde sin konstnärliga utbildning.

Även den här gränsdragningen är en konstruktion. Vem kan egentligen analysera fram hur ett konstnärskap får sin början och av vilken anledning? För att inte tala om omöjligheten att bestämma en konstnärs specifika visuella tänkande. Nästan ironiskt gentemot vedertagen definition av konkret konst – en konst som är totalt frigjord från direkt intryck och återgivning av naturen – framstår det lakoniska yttrande Mether-Borgström gjorde under ett samtal denna vår: "Sedan liten pojke har jag varit intresserad av biologi och av att vistas i naturen."

En bit till faller på sin plats. Jag kommer att erinra mig de skisser jag sett där Mether-Borgström tecknat totempålar med ett symbolspråk som visar livet som en organisk strukturerad form, och teckningarna med cirkusmotiv där rytmen och rörelserna följer den cirkelformade scenens form. Om en konstnär är intresserad av organiserade former såsom strukturerna i naturen kan man även förstå att denne är intresserad av att arbeta med olika grader och nivåer av formernas visualisering. Eller annorlunda uttryckt, att förhållandet mellan föreställande och nonfigurativ konst är en utmaning; två poler på samma skala och inte en väsensskild motsättning. Tittar man på ett stycke natur i mikroskop ser man inte längre måleriska färger utan välordnade system av celler. Skillnaden gäller sättet på vilket man ser och hur man väljer att återge detta.

Angående Mether-Borgströms intresse för naturen ville jag veta litet mera, är det något speciellt som lockar? Igen fick jag ett klart svar: dofterna. Doft, form, rörelse och färg. "Färgerna använder jag som verktyg för att få dem att leva mot varandra och matcha så att de bildar kraftfält som påverkar tittaren."

Vi som skriver har mycket att lära oss. Att våga lämna tryggheten i att applicera en färdig modell på ett konstnärskap och istället vända på tolkningens problematik med frågan, vilken slags modell för tänkandet, livet, verkligheten, måleriet kan ett specifikt konstnärskap ge oss?

Mether-Borgströms arbeten väcker behovet att nyansera den favoritterm som brukats i samband med konkret konst, formen. Ett nyanserat förslag, adekvat för Mether-Borgströms praktik, skulle möjligen kunna handla om ett formbegrepp som inte går att reduceras till geometriska konturer utan är istället förknippat med en komplex sammanfogning av de visuella elementen på så sätt att det riktar sig till alla våra sinnen sam-

tidigt. Tänker man så här kommer man litet närmare en beskrivning av det konstnärliga register Mether-Borgström rör sig med. Bland konstnärens skulpturer finns en grupp han kallar "semafor-mobiler". Semafor-mobilen är motordriven och går ett varv runt på en minut. Under denna minut genomgår den fyra olika skeden där "färg- och formbrickorna" intar fyra olika konstellationer. Man kunde alltså säga att en semafor-mobil producerar fyra dynamisk växelverkan. Mether-Borgström, intresserad av att utforska det nya, och ständigt beredd att lämna det invanda, lyckas med sin intention. Det är som om hans verk, vart och ett, är permanenta strukturer för perception och framförallt av vårt sätt att uppfatta förhållandet mellan figur och bakgrund. När Mether-Borgström i målningarna av stort format, som i exempelvis *Sirius*, fyllt dukens yta har vi ett slags unikt kosmos att förnimma; lagarna det lyder under är okända och samtidigt ytterst väl-lustiga för våra sinnen att utforska.

För sin utställning på Galerie Artek 1977 publicerade Mether-Borgström *7 teser*. Där kan man läsa bl.a. följande:

Man väntar sig fel saker av konsten, man har kommit in genom fel dörr. Konsten arbetar indirekt, den påverkar källan. Vi får lov att börja om från början. Bildkonsten bör för det första vara medveten om sina gränser och sin uppgift, skydda sin identitet. Den har sin egen "nisch" att leva av i den intellektuella ekologin.

Vi bör känna vår begränsning, inte låta oss integreras av element som är främmande för vår specifika sektor. Vårt medium är färgen och formen och vad vi med deras tillhjälp kan uttrycka, icke ordet, icke teknologin, icke sensationsmakeri eller show, icke ytlig dekoration, för att ta några exempel ur den rika flora av missbegrepp, som konsten gjort sig skyldig till.

År 1995 tål dessa att läsas på nytt. Tankeställare. Framförallt den dolda förvissning som framkommer ur textfragmenten, att bildkonsten handlar om något specifikt, väsensskilt från övriga uttryck. Icke ordet – Mether-Borgström har rätt. Bildens förhållande till ordet har under de senaste åren varit den fråga som uppmärksammats inom den teoretiska diskursen. Skillnaden dem emellan är viktig. Ordet och isynnerhet den teoretiska diskursen riktar sig direkt till en samtalspartner, till en annan person, medan bildkonsten agerar på ett annat sätt. Den har sin avstamp i en handling, den handling genom vilken konstnären skapat sin bild. Därigenom

blir det konstnärliga mediet samtidigt den aktiverande passage som öppnar kommunikation med betraktaren. Det specifika i ett verk handlar således inte enbart om generella omständigheter för dess medium utan i högsta grad om hur konstnären i minsta detalj tillämpar de redskap han valt. Med detta avser jag exempelvis det hur Mether-Borgströms målningar förmår kvarhålla närvaron av handlingen att måla. Spåret kan vara ett litet glapp mellan två färgfält, ett punctum i form av en överraskande, sned linje eller ett oväntat, "mether-borgströmskt" färgval.

Mether-Borgströms produktion bildar en klassiker med det främsta förtecknet att verken enbart liknar sig själva – resultatet av att konstnären sökt lösa de utmaningar han fascinerat gett sig i kast med. Fortfarande är Mether-Borgström upptagen av att komma vidare – sysselsätter sig med tanken att försöka lösa problemen med alla prima-måleri på stor duk.

Den fråga jag själv sysselsätter mig med och lämnar öppen handlar om hur man genom orden skall förmå uttrycka det specifikt "mether-borgströmska". Det att varje verk hålls i liv; när man börjar betrakta det förlorar man sig i Mether-Borgströms kosmos. Kommer att tänka på den verkliga innebörden i ordet klassiker, att vara oberoende av tiden, stundens här-och-nu och överleva realtidens begränsningar. Mether-Borgströms verk lämnar dörren öppen för betraktaren, även för den framtida.

Marko Vuokola och Pasi Karjula

Det gyllene konceptet i funktion

Marko Vuokola och Pasi Karjula är två finländska bildkonstnärer som nu och då dyker upp som ett arbetspar vid sidan av sin enskilda praktik. Praktik är det tacksammaste ordet för att karaktärisera deras konstnärliga värld: den visuella produkten, konceptuellt renodlad och förtätad, bär inom sig sin förutsättning, en konkret undersökande arbetsprocess genom vilken visualitetens fascinations- och fixeringspunkter silas och separeras till minsta fungerande entitet.

Samla och hålla på plats

Våren 1994 sammanfattar Marko Vuokola sitt huvudbry med planeringen av ett nytt arbete på följande vis. Jag behöver guld, närmare bestämt guldtråd, hur skall jag få sådan? Strax efter midsommaren åker Vuokola och Karjula till Lappland med den envisa föresatsen att vaska fram behövlig mängd guld. Den planerade två veckors vistelsen växer till fem. Guldfebern angriper de två. Att resa till Lappland i detta syfte visar sig bli fruktbart i en överraskande, komplex bemärkelse. En guldgrävare förverkligar sin legend, den spinner ett nätverk av tyst samförstånd guldgrävarna emellan. Varje vår när isen tinat inleds säsongen. Guldgrävarna anländer, reser sin temporära boplats och sätter igång. Hårt arbete, att gräva, att bygga rännor i vilka vattnet silar jorden, att leva mer eller mindre i periferin till den fasta bebyggelsen och nära sig med förhoppningen att just denna sommar gör jag fyndet, hittar den guldklimp som väntar på att bli funnen. "Maahinen" har förstås också ett finger med i spelet, det gäller att blidka henne, härskarinnan över de lapska guldmarkerna. Karjula och Vuokola var måna om att hålla "Maahinen" på gott humör, hon var ju egentligen hela projektets förutsättning och därmed förlänade de henne en egen kultplats med därtill hörande skulptur i trä.

Visa, berätta och relatera

Guldgrävarens arbetsplats är avslöjande. Den ser ut som sin skapare, präglad av dennes egenheter. De tekniska rännkonstruktionerna där jorden silas är skräddarsydda för respektive guldgrävare, d.v.s. deras funktion styrs av drömmen om guldet. En är besatt av tanken på att fånga en så stor guldklimp att den även fångas upp av legenden, en annan är besatt av de tunnaste guldkorn, en tredje av samlandet i sig, och de tekniska patentlösningarna ser ut därefter.

Arbeta och hålla fast vid

Legenden berättar följande. En man frågar guldgrävaren, varför all denna möda, är det verkligen värt besväret att för några futtiga gram minutiöst granska stenbit efter stenbit. Guldgrävaren svarar inte, han svarar genom att placera i tvivlarens hand en liten bit guld. Guld glimmar, guld är både lätt och tungt och dessutom segt. Ett gram guld kan genom modern teknologi förvandlas till två och en halv kilometer guldtråd.

Guld gömmer en kod, oantastbar för diverse dechiffreringsförsök och just därför är ämnet absolut, perfekt. Alkemin har genom tiderna kännetecknats av spekulativ naturvetenskap och humaniora i nära förening, både metallurgiska experiment och filosofi om livets uppkomst och beskaffenhet. Det här hade Karjula och Vuokola inte erfarenhet av, de hade inte känt den viktlösa tyngden av ett guldkorn i sin hand. När detta var gjort fick mysteriet tag i dem. Guld är ett märkligt ämne, som blir ännu märkligare i föreställningarna efter fem veckors hårt arbete vid Palsinoja i Lappland. Sålunda, att gräva guld är lika mycket fantasins som kroppens arbete. Gunnar Ekelöf skriver om alkemisten:

> Jag söker ett värdelöst guld
> ett guld som gör värdelöst
> guldet, allt guld!
> Med brända händer håller jag degeln i handen.
>
> Jord, vatten, luft, eld!
>
> Det är först när de döda och levande möts
> som Det Stora Felet skall uppenbaras –

Form Function 4/1994

Claude Rutault
Museet för nutidskonst, Helsingfors

Definition/metod nr 175 (1989–1990), utdrag

Konstvännens möte med nutidskonsten utfaller inte alltid väl. I värsta fall uteblir mötet. Ett talande exempel är Claude Rutaults installation i Studio N. En icke uppmärksam besökare löper risk att passera utställningen utan att ens upptäcka att det finns en installation i ifrågavarande utrymme.

Det paradoxala är att Rutault i sitt begreppsliga system uttryckligen vänder sig till konstvännen/-samlaren. Sedan 1973 har Rutault skrivit det han benämner definition/metoder, anvisningar för hur ett arbete skall

förverkligas. Många faktorer lämnas öppna och det återstår för konstvännen/-samlaren att ta ställning till exempelvis färg, storlek, placering, material, mängden av element. I sin intention är konstnären klart uttalad. Han är intresserad av målningen med betoningen på att måla och att låta bli att måla. Den bild Rutault eftersträvar är frigjord från splittrande faktorer som "skönhet", "representation", "känsloinnehåll" m.m.

Rutaults konceptuella projekt placerar konstvärldens uppsättning av relationer (konstnär, konstverk, konstvän/-samlare/betraktare, utställningsinstitution) i ett noggrant uttänkt system. Konstnären delegerar ett medverkande som på sätt och vis kan presenteras som en skräddarsydd, konstsociologisk modell. Att förverkliga anvisningarna i definition/metoderna kan innebära t.ex. en process som fortsätter med jämna intervaller och upphör först i samband med antingen samlarens eller konstnärens död.

I *Definition/metod 69* (1978) står bl.a. följande: "Varje år målas en ny tavla i samma färg som bakgrundsväggen. Samlaren väljer varje år den duk som skall målas. Sålunda har samlaren det andra året två kilramsdukar med samma färg som bakgrundsväggen, det tredje året tre... För arbetet uppbärs årsavgift. Arbetet får sin slutgiltiga form, då den ena parten – konstnären eller samlaren – dör."

Systemet förutsätter av betraktaren en problematiserande attityd, raka motsatsen till den som präglas av det "kantska spöket". I Kants tradition var estetikens enda upphöjda mål att tillfredsställa smaken, och sålunda uteslöts alla andra aspekter. Enligt smakens protokoll betyder bedömning av ett konstverk detsamma som en oreflekterande, naturlig reaktion; bedömningen befattar sig inte med betydelsen eller innehållet hos det man ser. Som en konsekvens av det här förnekas i synnerhet hänvisande kopplingar mellan verket och teoretiska frågor. I ett ytterlighetsfall såsom Rutaults konceptuella installation kan en dylik attityd betyda det absurda att konstverket blir osynligt för betraktaren.

Rutaults arbete i Studio N går under beteckningen utdrag (fra. *extraits*). Enligt anvisningarna skall ett utdrag bestå av minst sex delarbeten som plockats från tidigare definition/metoder, vilka dessutom har förverkligats åtminstone en gång. Förverkligandet av utdragen lämnar ännu större rörelserum än definition/metoderna. Processen är hejdad i ett så pass tidigt skede att betraktarens ansvar för den slutliga målningen blivit större; konstnärens betoning ligger vid den omålade målningen.

Endast en bakgrundsvägg är målad i en röd nyans med tillhörande tavla i samma färg. På golvet finns en hög med färgade pappersark, ur en monter kan man välja det önskade materialet. De vita väggarna har varit föremål för konstnärens format- och formprövningar i blyerts.

Elementens kontinuitet, sekvenser för verkets förverkligande, den försvinnande målningen är namn för utdragen vilka hänvisar på tänkbara problem som betraktaren/skaparen av den egentliga målningen har att ta ställning till. T.ex. elementens kontinuitet är ett arbete som består av en serie kvadrater i ökande storlek. Den sista kvadraten har endast ett hörn utmärkt – hur långt skall serien få fortsätta eller skall den sista, ofärdiga kvadraten suddas ut? Det finns nästan en oändlig mängd variationsmöjligheter som underlag för betraktaren då denne ger sig i kast med måleriet.

Ur kritikerns synvinkel finns det en fascinerande poäng med Rutaults installation. Det slutgiltiga resultatet, den målning betraktaren härleder ur utdragen, är oåtkomlig för varje kritiskt öga.

Hufvudstadsbladet 28 februari 1992

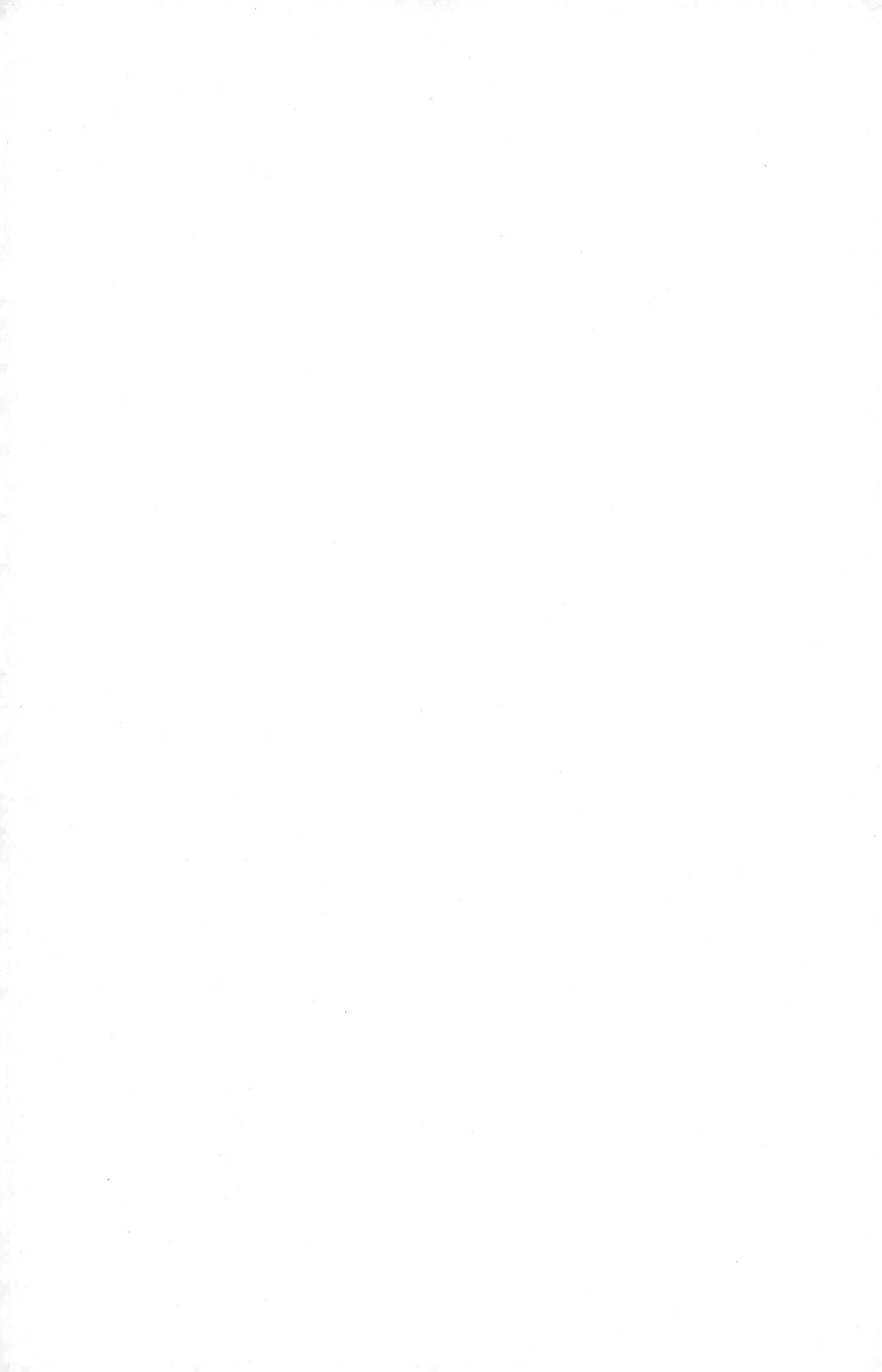

Silja Rantanen
Helsingfors konsthall

Måleriets sanning och målarens kontrakt

När en målning är bra är den överlägsen ordet och separerad från ordet, den är både utan ett namn och mer än ett namn. Tolkningen, namngivandet, är således från början dömd till en mer eller mindre misslyckad position i förhållande till verket. Risken för reduktion finns brännande nära; verket offras, blir ett föremål för teorin som börjar förutbestämma sitt objekt i stället för motsatsen.

Att just Silja Rantanens målningar från tioårsperioden 1983–93 ger upphov till den här reflexionen har en enkel anledning. Utställningen ger möjlighet att se och förstå samband som uttryckligen föds ur måleriet, i förhållandet mellan 80- och 90-talets produktion. Målningar med namn som *Kupolens snitt och segment* (1983), *Deposizione* (1982, 1983) och *Popflätning* (1993) binds nu här samman av sin inbördes och i varandra gripande komplexitet. Och det finns ett inslag av något jag önskar kalla för hundraprocentigt vilket är exakt den typ av kvalitet som kommer i kläm i diskrepansen mellan det som är gjort, målningen, och namngivandet, texten.

Mitt vanskliga företag att använda ett ord som hundraprocentig blir ännu mer vanskligt då jag ämnar koppla det till sanningsbegreppet i alldeles speciell bemärkelse. Men först, tillbaka till startpunkten. I sitt arbete går Rantanen tillväga som en arkitekt vars primära förutsättning är att känna till grunden. I det här fallet är basen måleriets konventioner, d.v.s. de överenskommelser som styrt och styr bilduppfattningen – medeltidens, förrenässansens, den japanska konstens. Studiet av en förrenässansmålning blir för Rantanen utgångspunkten för ett subjektivt kontrakt mellan konstnären och målningen: rummet i bilden, rummet i rummet där målningen befinner sig och sedan rumsligheten förvandlad till några enkla former och lysande färg som i målningen *Padua*. Möjligheterna är således många i Rantanens studium av kulturen och resultatet får betydelser vi inte kan förutse. Mönster, scheman, modeller, förebilder omsätts till en slutpunkt med en väsentlig egenskap, den överträffar motivet och intentionen. En sanning är upprättad och dess värde kan inte anges utgående från likhet med motivet (det igenkännbart avbildade) utan den är enbart

lik sig själv.

Då man talar om sanning i måleriet hamnar man alltså inför en intressant omständighet; en sanning kan igenkännas utan att dock likna något annat, tidigare givet. Dess enda förutsättning är egentligen det som ingår i kontraktet mellan konstnären och måleriet vilket i bästa fall ansluter sig till ett slags moraliskt tänkande. Rantanens målningar *Den goda viljan* (1993) och *Ett gott samvete* (1992) relaterar till detta, båda arbetena är måleriets målningar kommenterande moral och förpliktelser. I mitten ser vi ett gult fält omringat av tunna "ramar" av färg, de oskrivna lagarna. För att inte tala om löftet i de två verken *Come più belli li sapranno fare* (underförstått, att måla så vackert jag förmår).

Det som är sanning i bildkonsten skiljer sig från andra konstområdens sanningar, den upprättas med andra medel. Även om detta låter som en självklarhet är det just i detta avseende en bra målare är oförutsebar. I Rantanens senaste *Deposizione*-verk (Nedtagningen från korset) ser vi två stegar ställda mot var sin korsarm, frontalt avbildande. Studerar man de två stegarna upptäcker man sitt eget ögas benägenhet till normaliserande osanning – man vill se dem som rakt stående objekt och man försöker se dem som sådana. Det är ögat som skapar den här illusionen, det är svårt att direkt godta sanningen att de två stegarna faktiskt rör sig i mycket långsam takt mot varandra, allt närmare korsets mitt. Via minimala avståndsskillnader underbyggda av objektens färgkonturer nås sålunda verkets sanna eller egentliga innebörd.

Utställningens nyaste arbeten är schematiska framställningar av hur en vetelängd flätas, d.v.s. det här är det man vill tro att man ser. Men målningarna går utanför avbildningen, representationen är enbart ett medel för att nå fram till den nivå där den egentliga innebörden uppdagas. I diptyken *Popflätning* vänds avbildningen av hur en vetelängd flätas till en fråga om måleriets komplexitet via ett avgörande moment. En sekvens av den gulorange degen fortsätter över målningens andra halva där bakgrunden är lilafärgad och just därför är vetelängdens ändor målade på ett annat sätt, andra penseldrag, en annan färgnyans i jämförelse med den del av längden som befinner sig mot den ljusa bakgrunden. Målningen lyder under måleriets villkor och blir plötsligt transparent i den bemärkelse att själva avbildningen antar en sekundär plats i förhållande till det ting måleriet framställer.

Hufvudstadsbladet 1 september 1993

Jussi Niva
Galerie Artek, Helsingfors

Mitt öga spejar och spanar

Jussi Nivas utställning i Galerie Artek väcker uppriktig nyfikenhet. Minns ett ögonblick av reflektion under Venedigbiennalen sommaren 1993 framför Nivas installation *Borrowed Landscape* (Lånat landskap). Vad jag spekulerade över var rimligheten i försöket att räkna ut hur Nivas arbeten kommer att utvecklas efter detta för jämför man exempelvis *Lånat landskap* med installationen på Documentautställningen i Kassel året innan hittar man ett konsekvent "Jussi Niva-förhållningssätt" till måleriet. Jag envisas att tala om måleriet även om fotografi ingår i Nivas installationer av den enkla anledning att hans tänkande komponeras av måleriets primära byggstenar: färg, form, yta, rum, verklighet och illusion.

Den visuella tydligheten som karaktäriserar verken utsäger att Niva är måleriets pragmatiker *par excellence*. Det är via ett välriktat utförande som de intressanta vinklingarna artikuleras och får fysisk prägel vilket räddar installationerna från renodlad konceptualism. Redan i ett tidigt skede förekom ordet mekanik i verkens titlar vilket ju syftar på funktion och rörelse. År 1990 skrev Niva, som en kommentar till sin utställning på Glogalleriet, en dialog mellan en lantmätare och en byggare där de två diskuterade olika sätt att förhålla sig till en specifik plats med anledning av det gemensamma uppdraget att bygga. På samma sätt som de båda diskuterade platsens egenskaper i syfte att skapa ett konkret och synligt resultat analyserar Niva rumsligheten – hans konstnärliga handlande vittnar om medveten kontroll och manipulering av redskapen.

En kort resumé som vägledning för den aktuella utställningen Galerie Artek. Documenta-arbetet bestod av två delar: en panelmålning som följde väggens yta och linjer samt ett fotografi som autentiskt avbildade den nyss nämnda målningen i rummet, dock i förminskad skala. Istället för att fungera som en målning kändes färgfältspanelen närmast som ett påtagligt fysiskt objekt som occuperat ett hörn av rummet. Först via fotografiets distanserande effekt framstod målningen som en målning. Däremot, stående framför panelen hamnade betraktaren i ett nätverk av relationer genom att färgfälten öppnade nya rum i rummet.

Nivas installation i Venedig får en så här i efterhand att leta efter en översättningsmotsvarighet till engelskans "viewing situation", ett uttryck som understryker att situationen är avsedd att upplevas via synen, seendet.

Nivas installationer är egentligen lika med den helshetssituation som utgår från betraktaren i den stund denne står i samma rum som verken och låter sitt öga pendla mellan olika perceptionsmässiga alternativ. Som en osynlig regissör kontrollerar Niva det visuella händelseförloppet.

I Venedig-paviljongen kunde betraktaren plötsligt relatera sin närvaro till tre olika landskap: det verkliga landskapet utanför, den "kuliss" Niva ställt i rummet med ett målat atmosfäriskt landskap och slutligen fotografierna på väggen av ett snöklätt finländskt skogslandskap.

Vad som hände sedan var att man som betraktare hamnade mitt i ett landskap där nivåerna mellan illusion och verklighet försköts i olika riktningar.

Härmed har texten nått fram till realtiden, d.v.s. till Nivas utställning i Galerie Artek. Dryftandet av ett landskap har bytts ut mot en granskning av interiörer, vilket samtidigt betyder ett steg mot ett mer privat och intimt område. För sina nya verk har Niva valt ut en grupp av hem, verkliga hem, och låtit dessa bli substansen för hela utställningen. Varje arbete består av två delar, ett fotografi av ett rum och en hög av målade dukar ställda mot väggen nedanför. "Formeln" för installationerna är mycket tydlig och klar och därför vill man som skribent undvika att läsa in komplikationer på plan där konstnären genom sin klartänkthet och sitt pragmatiska grepp lyckats undvika dem.

Däremot aktualiseras en fruktbar komplikation som berör måleriets och rumslighetens grundfrågor i det ögonblick betraktarens perception börjar uppfatta den i verken inbyggda mekaniken. Det visar sig att de monokromt målade dukarna på marken inte alls fungerar som redskap för Nivas operationer i interiörerna. Den staplade högen av dukar är liksom lyft ur fotografierna som i sin tur inte alls handlar om ett stilrent studium av hem och inredning. Tvärtom har Niva "stigmatiserat" interiörerna med hjälp av målningarna vars format och färger är skräddarsydda för respektive lägenhet. Målningarna skär igenom rummet, bildar ett snitt som ingriper i rummets givna linjer, färger och former. De märker ut, täcker över, avgränsar, grupperar, sammanfattar olika aspekter av rummet och dess inredning.

Denna mekanik kunde likväl vara en beskrivning av hur ett abstrakt

tänkande fungerar, men det intressanta är att Niva framställer denna operation genom enbart visuella medel.

Här har vi kärnan i Nivas konstnärliga praktik – ett erkännande av ögat och dess perception som meningsskapande instans. Och resultatet bekräftar verklighetens oförsonlighet med sitt öde, att vara något annat än den ser ut att vara.

Titeln för varje verk börjar med orden *I Spy with My Eyes Something Being...* och sedan följer exempelvis tillägget *Earth-Coloured*, vilket syftar på den färg Niva valt ut som representerande interiörens nyckelfärg.

Denna lek, att speja och spana och låta ögat följa färgsättningen, är egentligen hämtad ur en färgläggningsbok avsedd för ett barn. Enkelt.

Lika enkelt är det att avgöra ifall Niva lyckats som visuell regissör. Detta går att bevisa genom den omsvängning vår tolkning genomgår; vi tolkar inte lägenheterna voyeuristiskt, som tecken för privata hem, utan som en skådeplats för visuella händelser.

Hufvudstadsbladet 26 augusti 1994

Håkan Rehnberg
Galerie Artek, Helsingfors

Drömmens syster

Fem stycken av Håkan Rehnbergs i övrigt namnlösa målningar i Galerie Artek har fått en hänvisning. Inom parentes står ordet Hérodiade skrivet vilket syftar på ett av Mallarmés lyriska huvudverk *Scènes d'Hérodiade* (1871) – den dikt om Salome och Johannes döparen där Hérodiade förkroppsligar drömmen om renhet.

Det är alltså Hérodiade som träder fram för Håkan Rehnberg i ett skede då han uttrycker ett allt mer renodlat intresse för det måleriska.

Under 80-talet rörde sig Rehnbergs praktik i fältet mellan måleri och skulptur.

Sviten *Moira* från år 1988 blev en vändpunkt. Dess gula och grå nyanser är pålagda med kniv, ibland mycket pastost och det skulpturala är

endast en reminiscens.

Den vertikala och horisontala delning av färgytorna som ännu var synlig i *Moira* har Rehnberg nu övergett. Markeringen av en gräns har fått ge vika för något som i stället blivit ett tillstånd där handlingen att måla är aktualiserad.

Vi ser hur färgen expanderar över ytan, fyller den och samtidigt upprätthåller en form av transparens. På de ställen där underlaget akrylglaset är synligt är det som om rörelsen gått den motsatta vägen, färgen har vikit undan i syfte att blottlägga.

Rörelsen är dubbel, den stryker över ytan och går igenom den.

I ett samtal refererade Håkan Rehnberg till en rimfrostig fönsteryta då han ville beteckna det tillstånd av blottlagd existens som finns bakom ridån av vetandet och tänkandet. Suddar vi ut rimfrosten försvinner det osynliga som tecknas fram.

Ifall ytan varit helt täckt av det vita skulle vi haft blott en ridå till.

Den hårfina balanseringen mellan ett täckande och ett blottläggande framträder i en sekvens bestående av tre målningar.

I den första målningen breder den opala gula färgen ut sig från ytans mitt, i den tredje är kontrollen och den lugna behärskade rörelsen totalt bruten.

Rehnbergs måleri närmar sig allt mer ett område som blir problematiskt i förhållande till språket för det handlar uttryckligen om det som faller utanför tematisering och reduktion till begrepp.

Däremot gäller Rehnbergs undersökning måleriets specifika möjlighet att framföra något som enbart kan ta form genom och i handlingen att måla.

Måleriet blir markören av en plats där ett framträdande äger rum – uttrycket får en struktur utan att det uttryckta formuleras eller ges ett innehåll.

I den här meningen kan man säga att Rehnberg har förverkligat drömmen om renhet. Det finns en plats för tomheten som dock inte handlar om bristen utan om något som är öppet för något annat.

Det vi konfronteras med är således handlingen att måla och dess rytm som hoplänkar momenten.

Att leta efter former är lönlöst emedan det för Rehnbergs del är frågan om ett måleri som börjar vid den punkt där formen blivit oformlighet, i dess syfte att fungera som rimfrosten på fönsterrutan.

Beträffande Mallarmé sägs det att hans konstnärliga produktion vilade

på den frustrerande insikten att vi lever i en värld där handlingen ej är drömmens syster.

Rehnbergs särpräglade måleri kunde vara en av dess systrar. I en orangeröd målning tränger färgens rörelse in från alla håll för att i mitten ebba ut i ett lugnare område, inte orörligt utan snarare möter vi ett stilla fallande.

Hufvudstadsbladet 23 oktober 1992

Carolus Enckell
Galerie Artek, Helsingfors

Målningen som genomlyst medvetande

Carolus Enckells måleri vilar på och är beroende av sitt medium, ljuset och färgen, in i det yttersta. Det abstrakta hos Carolus Enckell hör inte hemma bland formella konstruktioner eller bland idé- eller känslomässiga uttryck. Det har funnit sin egen väg i korspunkten mellan det allmänna och det specifika.

I konsthallen där Carolus Enckell för två år sedan ställde ut i egenskap av Årets konstnär var tillfället utmärkt för ett studium av t.ex. måleriets nyanser, att ställa färg vid färg för att se skillnaden dem emellan, för att få syn på nyansen som fanns där, mellan, osynlig. Ett studium som till sitt väsen närmade sig övningar i andlighet, sträckande sig bortom bilden som materialiserad verklighet.

I Galerie Artek uppmärksammar man ett måleri som bär drag av förtätning och frigjordhet – en kombination som i sig verkar omöjlig. Lika omöjligt som det låter då man talar om målningen som förmedlare mellan den inre och yttre verkligheten. Men måleri är något annat än filosofi, det kan ha egenskaper som bara delvis kan omfattas av tanken.

Vid ingången till galleriet finns ett mycket litet arbete i olja på zink som fängslar blicken, *Fra Angelico-rött*. Det vitala röda är ställt bredvid den vita färgen. Penseldragen är sinnligt påtagliga vittnesbärare för handlingen att måla – spår av ett förflutet nu som förenar målningen med det levande nuet.

Carolus Enckells målningar är ett med måleriets möjlighet att vara en förmedlande yta mellan den inre och den yttre verkligheten där ytan omvandlats till relationer av färg och ljus. Ju mer jag fördjupar mig i målningarna desto mer benägen blir jag att vända en aning på förhållandet mellan bilden och det inre och yttre. Bilden som förmedlande yta anger i Carolus Enckells fall inte en gränsplats utan motsatsen, det gränslösa vars metafor skulle kunna vara ett medvetande som är fullständigt genomskinligt. Målningens inre öppnar sig mot det yttre och tvärtom vilket betyder att positionerna aldrig blir absoluta. Porten och fönstret som ofta förekommer som element i Carolus Enckells målningar karaktäriseras just av denna dubbla optik, blicken som både ser in och ut. Därför är det svårt att veta om det är jag, betraktaren som tar emot eller ger innebörd.

Verken *Morandis fönster* och *Vitt rum* är på sätt och vis förbundna vid varandra – fönstret som utgångspunkt, det vita rummet som den efterlängtade platsen. Morandi, en säregen konstnär som livet igenom målade utsikten från sitt fönster, sökte kanske på det sättet nå bortom det synliga. Det är en tilltalande tanke att föreställa sig att Morandi fördjupade sig i ett och samma landskap tills det närvarande blev så välbekant att han därigenom förmådde se det frånvarande.

Förtätning infinner sig i galleriets centrala rum. Två stora målningar (diptyk och triptyk) är ställda mitt emot varandra. Verket *Caput mortuum* har fått sitt namn av den speciella röda färg som i motsats till Fra Angelico-rött är det levrade blodets färg.

> Frågan, frågan, – i blodet är den, där ej ser ditt öga, i det skuldlöst
> stilla som en mänska bär
> (Gunnar Björling, *Vilande dag*)

Målningen lever i kraft av färgerna och hur dessa strukits på duken. Processen kunde vara livsförloppets, och tystnaden efteråt. En tät caput mortuum-röd yta är ställd ovanför en ogenomtränglig mörkblå. Ungefär i mitten av målningen finner vi det förlösande momentet, en ljus, himmelsblå färg är försiktigt påstruken så att det mellan penseldragen blir rum för luft och ljus. En ständig upprepning finns i form av det gula, gula intervaller som skapar förtröstansfull kontinuitet.

Hufvudstadsbladet 18 september 1992

Henry Wuorila-Stenberg
Galerie Artek, Helsingfors

Hur det är

Henry Wuorila-Stenbergs nya målningar artikulerar ett område som både
är intressant och "svårt". Det svåra gäller inte måleriet i sig eller upplevelsen av det utan följande steg, att föra fram upplevelsen till ett medvetet
plan. Namnet på en av de utställda målningarna, *Det finns ingen säkerhet*,
säger precis det som man inför sina ansatser till tolkning får lov att
acceptera.

Ännu för fyra år sedan var det möjligt att tala om Henry Wuorila-
Stenbergs arbeten utgående från begrepp som det rena måleriet, vilket ju
anspelar på ett vedertaget modernistiskt förhållningssätt med bl.a.
föreställningen om en inre upplevelse som kan finna sitt uttryck i det rena
måleriet. Då man vandrar bland Wuorila-Stenbergs målningar i Galerie
Artek blir man övertygad om att något avgörande skett, en förändring
som inte låter sig infångas av en tolkning präglad av kritisk distans och
formell analys som huvudsakligt verktyg. Målningarna har helt enkelt
inget "utseende" som kunde tjäna som underlag för en formell analys. Att
kalla dessa arbeten för antingen abstrakta eller figurativa, eller att leta efter
symboler och metaforer leder ingen vart. Målningarna viker undan denna
typ av formell karaktärisering. I stället får man lov att ställa frågan annorlunda, ja, att ta ställning till det enskilda verket och undersöka det i termer
av närhet, relation eller sammanhang.

Målningarna i galleriets stora rum är riktgivande för det processartade
tillstånd som Wuorila-Stenberg framkallat. Anledningen till att just de här
arbetena fungerar som det kritiska momentet i helheten blir uppenbar då
man stiger in i salen – perceptionen prövas i en dubbelbottnad process. På
avstånd träffas ögat av visionära glimtar som stiger ut ur målningarnas
avgränsade yta. I verket *Till det försvunna* är det ett vitt flöde som utvidgar
sig, motsvarande den gränslöshet vi exempelvis förknippar med himlen. I
verket *På golvet* är det starkt gula, böljande linjer som bryter ut ur den
mörka massan. Målningen *Dit varifrån det kommer* är liksom påfågelns
skrud översköljd med ett teckenregn. Gula cirkelformade linjer med en
inre kärna av blått och svart kretsar både lugnt och oroligt kring duken. En

relation till tiden upprättas, det gäller sekunden, perceptionens ögonblick gör anspråk på förståelse.

När ögonblicket viker undan, när man förflyttar sig närmare målningarna förändras deras relation till tiden. Ögonblickets punktuella tid ersätts av den utsträckta i och med att en annan dimension av målningen blir synlig. Nu blir de visionära glimtarna sekundära i förhållande till den täta massa av färg som ger ytan dess struktur. Färgen är pålagd i tjocka lager som genomgått omsorgsfull bearbetning. Ytan skapar det nätverk genom vilket allt annat i målningen blir till; den ger målningen en plats, en historia och ett djup. De två formerna för tid förutsätter varandra. De temporära momenten ger liv åt den mörka massa som annars vore tom som ytan på en skorpa. Och ögonblicken skulle inte framträda utan förankring i en bakgrund, en plats.

Genom sin förankring i tiden och platsen handlar de här målningarna i sista hand om ett bland många möjliga uttryck för jaget. Ingenting är dock självklart, ingenting är säkert. Den jag-uttryckande tendensen avvisas i en del av målningarna genom att den strukturerade ytan är en annan funktion, att med vitt täcka in och följa störande element som ställvis lyckas skymta fram som tunna hinnor av färg. Den här längtan efter ljus och därmed också en längtan efter en viss form av estetik har dock sitt pris. Det som faller utanför blir oönskat, måste förnekas och målas över.

Henry Wuorila-Stenberg gör det inte lätt för sig. Utställningen innehåller ännu en tredje sammanhängande grupp av arbeten som uttryckligen handlar om måleriet genom att målningarna utgår från ett motiv, horisontlinjen som blivit nästan en estetisk konvention. Betraktaren kan inte undgå alla de associationer som är förknippade med motivet. Det som de övriga målningarna uttryckt, utan retorik och citat, väger allt tyngre i närheten av dessa expressivt "vackra" bilder.

Hufvudstadsbladet 11 december 1992

En mera föreställande konst
Amos Andersons konstmuseum, Helsingfors

Infratunna skillnader

Marcel Duchamp använder ordet infratunn när han dryftar frågan om vad ett estetiskt omdöme egentligen är. Enligt Duchamp är ett estetiskt omdöme en talakt som spänner sig exempelvis mellan två påståenden som det här är en målning/det här är inte en målning.

Mellan de två påståendena finns en infratunn passage och en obestämd skillnad, någonting som inte har ett namn och allra minst ett begrepp emedan ett estetiskt omdöme är ett experiment som flyr den begreppsliga fattningsförmågan. När sedan Duchamp fick ingående frågor om hur han definierar det infratunna svarade han lakoniskt att man endast kan ge exempel på det, inte förklaring.

Den observanta läsaren undrar antagligen i det här skedet vad Duchamp och hans utsagor har att göra i en recension av en utställning med rubriken *En mera föreställande konst* där tre unga konstnärer från Sverige, som håller på att avsluta sina studier vid Kungliga konsthögskolan, ställer ut tillsammans med målaren Hannele Kumpulainen från Finland. Svaret då?

Utställningen som ingår i Helsingfors festspels program och är sammanställd av konstnär Silja Rantanen, är en renodlad förevisning av ett synsätt på det problematiska bildbegreppet där härvan av frågor är oändlig. Vad är en bild? Hurudant är avbildningens förhållande till det den avbildar? Vad skiljer ett bruksföremål från ett readymade-konstverk?

Såsom känt är motsatsen mellan föreställande och ickeföreställande konst en konstruktion. Istället gäller det en glidning mellan olika aspekter: det som bilden visar på, som den fångar in och håller fram för våra iakttagelser och det som gör infångandet eller avbildandet möjligt, d.v.s. bilden som medium. Betraktaren kommer sedan med det avgörande tillägget, vad han föreställer sig framför bilden, vad han uppfattar att han ser. Precis här, i skärningspunkten mellan de olika aspekterna upprättar utställningen *En mera föreställande konst* en infratunn passage så att uttrycken mera föreställande konst/mindre föreställande konst vardera biter sig själva och dessutom varandra i svansen.

För att återknyta till inledningen, till Duchamps begrepp om det infratunna, önskar jag tillämpa hans metod att ge exempel, inte förklaring. Som kuriositet kan nämnas några av Duchamps exempel på vad det infratunna är. Värmen hos en sittplats (som någon just har lämnat) är infratunn. När tobaksröken även doftar av den mun som inhalerat den ingår de två odörerna ett infratunt förbund.

I Amos Andersons konstmuseum har vi en prydlig utställning, förbryllande lätt att titta på och förbryllande rik i de föreställningar den sätter i gång. Carl Nyström håller på med att teckna fram sin ateljé med ett annat medium än teckningens, installationens. I museet finns ramverket av ett rum som motsvarar konturerna av den autentiska ateljén. Under utställningens lopp, på morgonen innan museet öppnar, möblerar Nyström om i rummet, flyttar på saker och ting och finslipar detaljerna i inredningen. För att rummet är så minutiöst autentiskt förhåller man sig till det med respektfylld distans. Man håller sig utanför, som om rummet existerade i form av en teckning. Också Karin Ohlins svarta, omsorgsfullt lackerade träpiano äger den autentiska infratunna beviskraft som får det stumma pianot att ingå i en föreställning som Ohlin de facto inte avbildar men skapar. Pianot väcker en brutal impuls att öppna locket och höra ljud, pröva hur det låter, att bryta upp den förstärkta stumheten.

Nina von Schmalensee utövar total kontroll i sitt måleri, även över verkligheten eller annorlunda uttryckt över måleriets förhållande till förebilden. Hon väljer ett motiv, gör en konkret modell av det, alltså ett objekt som hon sedan målat av. Den verklighetstrogna modellen är en stum kopia av någonting i förhållande till det vad den blir då hon målat den. Hon målar inte av den utan målar den till någonting som är mer än verkligheten. Hur hon använder sitt medium, måleriet, sker på hennes egna villkor och hon får en verklighet vars motiv stämmer överens med modellens men är annorlunda, hör till en annan "värld av väsen".

Finländskan Hannele Kumpulainens måleri bär upp en föreställning om ett slags målerisk tradition. När man tittar på hennes målningar i Amos Andersons konstmuseum får man känslan av att befinna sig i ett historiskt museum där variationerna i stil och uttryck följer vedertagna konsthistoriska indelningar. Denna anakronism, känslan av förskjutna tidsperspektiv beror delvis på att Kumpulainen använt sig av kompositioner som är lånade från italienskt renässansmåleri, men frånsett det här finns det även ett annat drag i hennes måleri som får det att verka "klas-

siskt". Tyngdpunkten, och själva innehållet i måleriet, är nära kopplat till det sätt på vilket målningen är målad. Varje målning är ett slags nomadisk karaktär i ett landskap som upprättas inom dukens gränser.

Hufvudstadsbladet 24 september 1995

Gloria Patri – patologi utan namngivare

Av föreläsarna på symposiet i Malmö var Mary Kelly den enda som arbetar med konstnärlig praktik. Jag samtalade med Kelly under öppningen av Gloria Patri på Malmö konstmuseum, dagen innan hade hon föreläst med rubriken *Miming the Master – Boy-Things, Bad Girls and Femmes Vitales*. Fortfarande starkt påverkad av Kellys teoretiska grepp, att läsa Lacan och Freud utgående från insikten att dessa analytiker blivit mästare på/genom att observera kvinnlig psykopatologi, riktade jag Kelly en fråga om förhållandet mellan hennes olika former av verksamhet.

Kelly När jag talar är skillnaden grundläggande beträffande det om jag presenterar ett teoretiskt resonemang som under föreläsningen eller om jag talar om mina konstnärliga verk. Verket är alltid en visualisering som fungerar i kraft av seendet, och denna process hjälper mig att tänka. Hur jag strukturerar verket visuellt handlar om exakthet, nedskärning av möjligheter. Objekten i installationen måste vara på sin rätta plats för att seendet skall fungera, för att det teoretiskt-abstrakta plan jag eftersträvar skall nås.

Roos Du har tidigare sagt att du har svårt att skilja mellan text och bild, dina installationer *Post Partum*, *Interim* och nu *Gloria Patri* består alla av objekt och text, den är rösten från en människa. I *Interims* corpus-del gällde rösterna kvinnans begär efter njutning, och verket upplevt från en kvinnlig position betydde lycksaligt igenkännande. Samtidigt problematiserades motpolens, den manliga positionens oförmåga att höra kvinnlig röst ifall den inte hänger med som ett attribut till hennes fysiska, verkliga kropp, d.v.s. den yta på vilken det manliga psyket kan inskriva sin egen röst, sitt begär.

Kelly Hur mina verk har utvecklats handlar också om hur feminismen har förgrenat sig under de senaste tjugo åren, från *Post Partums* tillblivelse (det verk där Mary Kelly dokumenterat i enlighet med lacanskt tänkande sin sons första sju år, d.v.s. till den tidpunkt då han inträdde i den symboliska ordningen) fram till dagens värld med en vardag fylld av incidenter som påvisar hur kvinnan behärskar ett slags imitation av mästaren, d.v.s. infogar sig i den manliga diskursen. Tänk bara på händelser som Gulfkriget

med kvinnan som deltagare i armén. Berättelserna i *Gloria Patri* påminner om dem i "Pecunia" (delen "pengar" i *Interim*), de är fyllda av objekt från vardagslivet, liksom förankrade i realvärlden.

I det föregående verket *Interim* befattade sig delarna "Pecunia", "Historia" ouch "Potestas" med diskurser för herraväldet, imiterande röster tillhörande dem som härskat med makt och pengar. *Gloria Patri* är annorlunda, dess psykologiska tillstånd är skrämmande i sin kombination av extrema poler av maskulinitetens psykopatologi; både den offentliga varianten, kriget, och det privata moment där det förbjudna hackar hål i den psykologiska ordning som det symboliska givit sig ut för att garantera. Kelly har nu skiftat metod, sina observationer om det maskulina artikulerar hon inte längre med en distans som skulle skydda det kvinnligas integritet, istället korrelerar hennes metod med ämnets patologi.

Tunn, hård, blänkande aluminium. Högst upp plattor med förskjutna symboler för insignier hämtade från amerikansk militär. Nästa serie, sex troféer med textsnuttar som Kelly plockat från nyhetsprogram där amerikanska soldater i Gulfkriget gör kommentarer: "Kick ass", "...Busting our butts to get it right", "... Letting loose and hitting 'em with all we got". Varje trofé kröns av en tredimensionell mansfigur som håller upp var sin bokstav av ordet GLORIA. Längst ner den tredje serien, sex sköldar med inskriven texthistoria.

När blicken vandrar längs med de blänkande objekten, när den avläser krigets heroism, och när den slutligen fattar vad historien handlar om, då önskar den sluta sig inför den psykologiska visualiseringen. Min tanke relaterar till två ord Kelly använde i sin föreläsning, "display" och "camouflage". Översatt betyder display att visa upp, spela ut, och camouflage är enligt ordlistan det samma som vilseledande maskering eller (skydds)förklädnad. Det som Kelly gör i sin installation är att hon visar att det som den maskulina patologin ytterst, i sista instans kamouflerar är kamouflaget, d.v.s. att verkligheten i den manliga diskursen är ett instrument för jagets självbekräftande funktioner. På så sätt kommer patologin att maskera sig som normal vardag och verklighet. Uppvisningen är lömsk, den igenkänns inte som ett fenomen skapat för scenen, det som spelas ut finns redan inskrivet i ontologins definition för varandet. Och sålunda kommer det som i den manliga diskursen har status av att vara naturligt och normalt att vara något som likväl följer patologins krav.

Julia Kristeva ställer i sin artikel *The True-Real* en intressant fråga. Hur

är det möjligt att "the true-real", d.v.s. det som är det *reella* i lacansk bety-delse, trots alla mekanismer som upprättats för att hålla det undan läcker igenom, att dess förekomst är en ständigt hotande rimlighet? Att den enor-ma skräcken för denna främmande, oönskade sanning inte utesluter dess förekomst i det sociala kontraktet. Precis den här typen av läckage är det vad Kelly använt sin röst till i berättelserna i *Glora Patri*. Rösten när nivån av ejakuleringens negation, istället för att bekräfta basen för den falliska symbolen, fråntas den.

Det sista vi samtalade om gällde möjligheten att ett manligt psyke är oförmöget att identifiera sig med rösten, den är för real, för förbjuden och därmed utesluten. Men som suverän mästare i kamouflage kommer Kelly med sitt sista drag. Berättelserna avslutas med den som handlar om hur Mary Lou imiterar mannens röst i gymet: "… Fit in. Weigh in at the right weight and defeat her rivals. She breathed out heavily. Hard-hearted? Not at all, she told herself: It was a hard life. What she had was hard-earned and if anyone objected, well, that was, she spat on the floor, hard luck."

Paletten 2–3/1996

Rosemarie Trockel
Museet för nutidskonst, Helsingfors

Yllet, spegeln och spisen

Rosemarie Trockels utställning i "skulptursalen" i Ateneum är ett fint exempel på hur en till formatet liten presentation också kan fungera som en representativ introduktion till ett konstnärskap vars främsta känne-tecken är mångtydighet.

Då Trockel under åren 1974–78 studerade måleri vid konst- och konst-industriskolan (*Werkkunstschule*) i Köln dominerades den tyska konstvärl-den framför allt av Joseph Beuys och de neoexpressionistiska målarna såsom Georg Baselitz och Anselm Kiefer. Det var också vid den här tid-punkten som ovannämnda målare trädde in på den amerikanska konstsce-nen vars marknad följaktligen kom att domineras av män vars arbeten gick

upp i skyhöga priser. I kontrast till detta kunde en annan tendens skönjas, företrädd av kvinnliga konstnärer som Sherrie Levine, Cindy Sherman, Barbara Kruger och Jenny Holzer. Typiskt för dessa amerikanskors strategi var konfiskering av bilder och texter från massmedierna, med hjälp av vilka de ifrågasatte avbildningarnas förmåga att referera till verkligheten. Bilder om kvinnan behöver nödvändigtvis inte sammanfalla med bilder av verkliga kvinnor.

Vad det konstnärliga uttrycket gäller har Trockel gått en annan väg än sina amerikanska kolleger också om de formats av en gemensam tidsanda och medvetenhet. Beträffande Trockel kan vissa influenser spåras till Joseph Beuys och den europeiska surrealismen. Arvet från Beuys förmedlar ett synsätt där konstens beroende av sociala strukturer uppmärksammas genom en praktik som kunde kallas för multikonstnärlig. En av Trockels metoder, att ställa fram objekt i vitriner, påminner t.ex. om etnografins och antropologins sätt att strukturera information. De objekt Trockel ställer fram varierar beträffande tillverkningssättet, det kan vara frågan om allt från ready-made till egenhändigt konstruerade föremål vars karaktär växlar mellan konceptuell stramhet och expressivitet.

Att tolka Trockels konst är en paradoxal aktivitet genom att man då försöker fixera en betydelse till någonting som medvetet är konstruerat med förtecken som "motsätter sig förklaring". Det problematiska och utmanande med Trockels verk tror jag att beror på det att när Trockel behandlar det kvinnliga finns det alltid närvarande en underliggande nivå som står för glappen. I dessa glapp tecknas det kvinnliga fram som en mental konstruktion, osynlig, undanglidande, skriven mellan raderna. Bilden för den här skulle kunna vara ellipsen, den oavslutade kroklinjen. "Att vara kvinna är att vara någonting som inte kan avgränsas i en sluten av lagen bestämd skrift. Kvinnan med stort K existerar därför inte som universell bestämmelse", för att citera Jacques Lacan. Symptomatiskt nog så kombinerar Trockel ofta sina objekt med satser vars betydelser vanligen blir förvridna – dessutom är alltsammans kryddat med en förträfflig humor. Trockel förhåller sig alltså till sitt ämne indirekt genom förmedling av två olika register: den mentala bildens och språkets. Den rätlinjiga förståelsen är ersatt av kroklinjens krumelurer. Dolda möjligheter i form av föreställningar och fantasier manas fram.

För sina syften använder sig Trockel av surrealismens teknik, att blanda samman det bekanta med det främmande. Hennes verk kan läsas som

en rebus, en bildgåta där delarna inte nödvändigtvis hör ihop. I synnerhet gäller detta objekten i vitrinerna. Det enda sättet att förstå en rebus är att betrakta delarna en efter en. Man kan inte följa argumentationen men om man är villig att koncentrera sig på ett fragment i taget kan mycket förstås. Möjligen är det vår vana vid diskursiv läsning som stör oss inför mötet med Trockels arbeten, men liksom i drömmen kan en tydning vara värdefull även om vissa delar förblir dunkla.

I de två vitrinerna i "skulptursalen" finner man en oanad rikedom på fyndigheter ifall man ger sig i kast med rebusen. Arbetet *Profumo* är en enkel liten spegel i silver. Då man tittar in i den ser man inte sin egen spegelbild utan en livboj i rött och vitt vars förlaga i ylle hänger ovanför rummets dörr. En mängd associationer infinner sig: allt från Narkissos som förälskade sig i sin egen spegelbild till Lacans teori om Den Andre i spegeln. Är livbojen utkastad för Narkissos eller för någonting annat? Ja, det finns ännu en historia som anknyter till namnet Profumo. Nyckelfiguren i "Profumoskandalen", Christine Keeler, var den kvinna som samtidigt hade en affär med den brittiske försvarsministern Profumo och den ryske marinattachén Ivanov. Det torde vara självklart hur den affären slutade. Profumo sjönk oavsett livbojen som lömskt nog var tillverkad av ylle.

Munplastiken (*Mundplastik*) består av ett litet tuggat tuggummi som doppats i silver. Att tala är silver, att tiga är guld, enligt ordspråket. I det här fallet blir det omsvängt, den som tuggar talar knappast även om tuggandet kan uppfattas som ljudlöst pratande, aktiviteten kan vara lika febril. Tystheten når sin höjdpunkt i verket Jag skulle alltid vilja vara någonting speciellt. De grandiosa visionerna har fått ett platt fall. Vi ser ett långsmalt objekt inlindat med vitt bandage. Den ena ändan liknar huvudet av en hund med en mun som likaså är ordentligt inpaketerad. Bandet som är knutet kring hundens nacke väntar redan på sin husse.

Trockels stora stickade arbeten associerar till traditionellt, kvinnligt handarbete. Men det som tidigare gått under benämningen hantverk har Trockel upphöjt till "högkonst", till samma nivå som gällde för de manliga 80-talsmålarna. Att koppla samman det stickade med hantverk är bedrägligt i Trockels fall då arbetena de facto är maskintillverkade och dessutom dataprogrammerade beträffande sitt mönster. En yllestickning, som dock inte finns med på den här utställningen, kunde vara en prolog för de aktuella verken. Prologen är försedd med Descartes' grundtes (stickad

i ylle) *cogito ergo sum* (jag tänker, alltså existerar jag). Tesen har på senare tid aktualiserats av Lacan som menar att satsen i stället borde lyda: "Jag är inte, där som jag är min tankes leksak. Jag tänker på det jag är, där som jag inte tänker att jag tänker." Med andra ord i det omedvetna, där också Trockels yllestickningar med sina mönster som liknar Rorschach-testet befinner sig – mönstren har samma blå färg som de kända bläckplumparna.

I ett angränsande utrymme som i vanliga fall tjänstgör som städskrubb har Trockel installerat en köksvrå. Kökets attribut spisen och diskhon finns på sina sedvanliga platser och dessutom på väggen, för där har Trockel placerat ett konstverk som består av vit metall och två spisplattor, ett fulllödigt verk i minimalismens anda. På diskbänken finns en tom tallrik som dock har den löftesrika inskriptionen *Wurst und Fleisch*.

Hufvudstadsbladet 4 september 1992

Marianna Uutinen
Galerie Anhava, Helsingfors

Ja och nej i bubbelplast

Marianna Uutinens målningar i Galerie Anhava är den här gången enkla att beskriva.

Akrylfärg har strukits på bubbelplast resulterande i helt monokroma arbeten. Sin tidigare teknik att spritsa ut färgen över duken har Uutinen nu övergett. Däremot fortsätter hon att undersöka och blottlägga den villkorlighet den konstnärliga utsagan vilar på, och hon lyckas få grunden att svikta.

Uutinens nya arbeten kunde kallas för målningar om bubbelplast, d.v.s. både material, utseende och innehåll sammanfaller. Alltsammans handlar om plast.

De färger Uutinen valt är precis sådana som man finner i plastleksaker, plastämbar, badrumsinredning m.m. Nyanserna är insmickrande och sötaktiga. Uutinens långt drivna anpassning till materialets villkor överensstämmer med modernismens centrala tes – det är medlet som är

avgörande för det konstnärliga uttryckets utseende.

Måleriets problem blir det artegna mediets problem, formen beror av det specifika materialet och vice versa. Alltså Uutinens förhållande till plasten uppvisar samma logik som modernismens förhållande till duken.

Det är bara det att konsekvensen av Uutinens tillvägagångssätt blir "felaktig". Genom målningarnas associationer till plast, framför allt till billiga plastföremål, för hon in en verklighet som ligger utanför den rena konstens intresse.

Taktiken är dubbel, den opererar med hjälp av två begrepp som ständigt motverkar varandra, anpassning och destruering.

Denna dubbla taktik kunde jämföras med ett språk där varje ord har två betydelser som pekar åt olika håll. Inför ett sådant språk blir vi osäkra på talarens intention: är den ena betydelsen egentligen ett kamouflage för den andra eller tvärtom.

Uutinen lyckas på ett suveränt sätt säga både ja och nej. Hennes målningar uppfyller beträffande format och färg måtten för det vi betecknar som vedertaget måleri samtidigt som de är utmärkta representanter för den "låga" smaken och estetiken.

Hufvudstadsbladet 17 mars 1993

Peter Bonde, Claus Carstensen, Erik A. Frandsen
Nordiskt Konstcentrum, Helsingfors

Tre danskar

På inbjudningskortet för utställningen i Strandkasernen finns tre foton av tre skrynkliga spädbarn, Frandsen, Carstensen och Bonde. På kortets andra sida står det präntat "måleri". Man får sig en tankeställare, vänder på kortet och absorberas ånyo av de tre nyfödda. Med ett frågetecken i bagaget beger man sig således ut till ön – senare fattar man att det här var det första skedet i killarnas direkt cyniska strategi, så väl uttänkt och genomförd att den är svår att avfärda.

I det första rummet slänger Bonde, Carstensen och Frandsen skräp i

ansiktet på betraktaren. Deras gemensamma verk *67 timmar samarbete* utbreder sig över golvet, d.v.s. arbetet är lika med allt det avfall som kan tänkas ha uppstått under 67 timmar av arbete: odiskade tallrikar och glas, fyllda askkoppar, tomma ölburkar och inte att förglömma "bananflugorna" som envist kretsar över fruktsalen. Den uppretade betraktaren står där mitt bland avfallet utan att finna verktyg för någon slags motattack, vilket jag misstänker är precis den effekt konstnärerna velat uppnå. Genom att de upprättat ett tätt möbiusband mellan konsten och livet blir konsekvensen den att det ena fungerar legitimerande för det andra och vice versa. Frågar man sig om detta kan kallas för konst hamnar man inför det faktum att själva konstbegreppet i grunden är en konstruktion eller en överenskommelse och därför kastar verket 67 timmar samarbete bollen till institutionen – i avseende på dess konstutnämnande och konstlegitimerande funktion. Avfallet i Strandkasernen får stå kvar som konst, annars hade städerskan sopat undan det.

Efter samarbetsprojektet artikulerar sig de tre konstnärerna på en annan nivå. Hur långsökt det än låter så är det trots allt spädbarnsfotona och skräpet som ger nyckeln till den underliggande attityden. Fotografiets tre nyfödda är fortfarande ett med modern, inneslutna i symbiosens fullständiga trygghet. Tilliten är ännu inte hotad. Men senare, när barnet upptäcker att det finns skillnader – mellan det självt och andra, och framför allt mellan det självt och modern sker mötet med den andre i hat och bortstötning. Som en röd tråd i danskarnas praktik formar sig kretsgången mellan dessa två grundkänslor, tillit och trygghet kontra hat och bortstötning. Att ställa ut skräp blir den inledande, absoluta manifestationen av önskan att driva bort, stöta ifrån sig.

I Claus Carstensens verk får bortstötandet relevans på ett samhälleligt plan som opposition mot tvång och gränser. För det här syftet använder sig Carstensen av samhällets symboliserande mekanismer. Sjutton stycken gröna flagglika dukar som hänger i rad från taket upprepar ett emblem, cirkeln och stjärnan. Avslöjaren av den konstnärliga strategin blir bokstäverna och texten som finns inskrivna i emblemet. Förkortningen F.A.I.A.T. kunde betyda (ifall man utgår från utställningens katalog) familjer mot hot och terror. Samtidigt varnar texten för något naket ont som hotar. Det intressanta är att språket skapar ett främlingskap. Vem är det som talar, vem hotar vem? Sålunda avslöjas också språket som representant för det symboliska vilket ju är den ordning subjektet å ena sidan

invigs i och måste underordna sig i och med att det börjar tala under loppet av det andra levnadsåret. I Carstensens verk ligger betoningen vid underordnandet; reaktioner mot tvånget att underordna sig en social, språklig värld av lagmässighet och reglering.

Peter Bonde går till attack mot måleriet, samtidigt skamlöst och humoristiskt. Mest skamlös är han mot sig själv genom att attacken uttryckligen riktar sig mot de målningar han skapat. Bondes olika varianter av abstrakt måleri har råkat ut för infantil vandalisering. Liksom i Carstensens fall är taktiken dubbel – han både utnyttjar och förlöjligar den ordning språket representerar. En brun monokrom målning har en etikett med texten "Brown Flowers", ett annat arbete har texten "Bror Lort". Mitt bland målningarna hänger två plastkassar med all världens skräp.

Ett ihållande lallande hörs från det bakersta rummet där Erik A. Frandsen, som för övrigt var en av de fyra nordiska Documenta-konstnärerna, har installerat sig. Det entoniga gnolandet kommer från en video med ett rött öga i närbild. Då man förenar ljudet och ögats rörelser etableras en rytm, nästan som ögat stod för andningen. En kontrast till det här utgör de färglösa kolteckningarna på väggen som upprepar bilden av en androgyn kvinna, möjligen i förpuberteten. Cirkeln sluter sig. Den råa taktiken avslutas med en symbol för det oskyldigt aningslösa och sårbara. De tre vita neonrören som är placerade över varje kolteckning uttrycker en nödvändig ambivalens. Delvis förtingligar de kroppen, delvis understryker de insikten om att det finns områden som är omöjliga att behärska eller närma sig. "Between me and my bed" skriver Frandsen med stora bokstäver över en sida i katalogen, intill en bild av kolteckningarna.

Hufvudstadsbladet 11 november 1992

Den osynliga kvinnan

Är hon vår? Jag känner inte att jag är den där personen. En version av mig. Med de här tre meningarna sammanfattar Louise Lawler, Cindy Sherman och Laurie Simmons sin utställning med retrospektiv betoning i Museet för nutidskonst. Perspektivet bakåt omfattar litet mer än tio år. Alla tre debuterade strax före 80-talet, under en tid som i många avseenden visade sig bli en vändpunkt i det amerikanska konstlivet.

Hur kommer det sig att det just då plötsligt dök upp en ny generation av kvinnliga konstnärer som började undersöka det kvinnligas plats i en asymmetrisk och fallocentrisk modell av såväl civilisationen som konsten? Synar man tidsandan vid övergången mellan 70- och 80-talet får man åtminstone tag på några rimliga ledtrådar. Europa steg igen en gång in på den amerikanska konstscenen; det var framförallt frågan om de tre "C-konstnärerna" från Italien (Cucchi, Clemente och Chia) och de tyska neo-expressionisterna. Dessa manliga målare, ofta skämtsamt kallade för "big boys", var sanna barn av sin tid och i konstboomens virvlar gick deras arbeten upp i skyhöga priser. Någonstans i marginalen började dock andra vindar blåsa. En grupp av unga konstnärer trädde fram; födda kring 1950, uppvuxna med TV och film, collegeutbildade och väl inlästa på konsthistoria, estetisk teori och psykoanalys. Denna generation, allmänt kallad för "The Pictures Generation" uppmärksammades tacksamt av poststrukturalistiskt influerade kritiker som från olika utgångspunkter försökte dekonstruera modernismens estetiska system. Termen det postmoderna, innefattande ett brett spektrum av betydelser, blev ett faktum.

I den postmoderna smältdegeln med alla dess inbakade dödförklaringar (subjektets, verklighetens, de stora berättelsernas, originalets m.fl.) föddes också nya insikter, den här gången bland teoretiskt influerade kvinnliga konstnärer bland vilka kan nämnas förutom Lawler, Sherman och Simmons också Sherrie Levine, Barbara Kruger, Jenny Holzer, Dara Birnbaum, Barbara Bloom. I motsats till 60- och 70-talens biologiskt förankrade "Moder Jord-feminism", som betonade kvinnan som natur, fokuserade man nu på det kvinnliga som en kulturell konstruk-

tion influerad som man var av en kritisk läsning av Jacques Lacans motsägelsefulla och svårtolkade texter.

För att undvika den snåriga, retoriska apparat som allt mer börjat vävas kring begrepp såsom blick/kön/skillnad/det andra refererar jag ett avsnitt ur konstteoretiker Kate Linkers artikel *Feminism och representation* där hon redogör för kärnan i sin Lacantolkning: I hans system är fallos det centrum kring vilket subjektivitet, social lag och språktillägnelse kretsar; mänsklig sexualitet bestäms, och levs därmed, i enlighet med den position man intar som innehavare eller icke av fallos, och med den har man tillgång till dess symboliska strukturer. Fallos intar i denna struktur rollen som betecknande, eller bäraren av betydelser, i förhållande till dess frånvaro, till bristen. Den senare positionen intas av flickan, som därmed kan påstås inta ett könsspecifikt och i sig problematiskt förhållande till språket i den fallocentriska ordningen. Lacans iakttagelser kan hjälpa oss att förklara överflödet av "bilder av kvinnor" i vårt samhälle: kvinnor är per definition uteslutna från språkordningen, de avbildar inte utan de avbildas (och naturligtvis då alltid som det manliga begärets bild).

Det viktigaste i Lacans lära är emellertid påvisandet av att sexualiteten inte är någon "naturlig" identitet eller något rent betecknat, utan istället effekten av ett betecknande, som härrör från yttre sociala bestämningar.

Alltså bilden av kvinnan är lika med kvinnan vilket är lika med att kvinnan inte existerar som subjekt eller verklig kvinna. Förstår man innebörden av det här får man också en förklaring till varför exempelvis Cindy Sherman och Laurie Simmons arbetar med ett fotografi som utgår ifrån de kvinnobilder vi ser i mediernas visuella flöde. Genom att fotografiet är meningsbärande *in potentia*: betydelserna fyller inte bilden som vattnet fyller ett glas utan uppstår snarare som ett resultat av att tolkande utnyttjas som ett distansskapande medel, ett påstående kan framläggas och samtidigt undergrävas. I Cindy Shermans händer blir kameran ett dylikt dubbelriktat vapen. Hon konfiskerar och imiterar mediernas bilder av kvinnan samtidigt som hon påstår något annat, att kvinnan inte är där, närvarande. I sin tidiga svartvita serie *Untitled Film Stills* (1977–80) rekonstruerade Sherman scener ur något som påminner om B-klassens filmer, själv spelar hon huvudrollen med noggrant utförd maskering. Tack vare kameran kan hon alltså spela en roll och i samma andetag säga, jag är inte den där personen. Således är det kameran som ljuger genom att den inte lyckas fånga skillnaden mellan att spela (att bli

en bild) och att vara.

Efter *Untitled Films Stills* följer färgfoton i större format där Sherman ställer fram ett eftertraktat byte för den manliga blicken, den unga oskuldsfulla flickan liksom ertappad av kameran. Följande steg blir en konsekvent reaktion på den förkroppsligade drömmen, ett abjektalt förkastande av idealet via konsthistoriska omvägar. Nu fokuserar Sherman på den klassiska porträttkonsten. Precis mot de områden av modellens kropp som varit föremål för konstnärens högsta idealisering riktar Sherman sin stöt. Låt oss exempelvis studera Shermans version av Rafaels berömda porträtt av sin modell Fornarina. De delar av Fornarinas kropp som Rafael mest lovsjungit har i Shermans rekonstruktion antagit en grotesk framtoning. Exempelvis Fornarinas bröst är ersatta med ett artificiellt och överdimensionerat bröstparti (ett maskeringshjälpmedel) som med synliga snören är fäst vid Shermans överkropp. Förkastandet av den idealiserade kroppen understryks av "kräkningsbilderna", hyperrealistiska färgfotografier av förruttnade matrester.

När Laurie Simmons säger "en version av mig" syftar hon med ett ironiskt tonfall på sina dockor och på den lilla flicka som identifierar sig med sin docka, omedveten om att spelets regler är givna och rolltillägnandet gäller repetition av färdiga mönster. Liksom barnets lekar följer också Simmons ett tydligt mönster och det råder ingen tvekan om vilket mönster som intresserar henne. I Simmons' värld har dockan växt upp och intar sin givna plats inom hemmets fyra väggar Plastdockan lever inte i hemmet utan hon är en del av inredningen, t.o.m. hennes kläder matchar färgmässigt den övriga interiören. När kvinnan är på resa som i serien *Tourism* är hon en tillfällig gäst i ett främmande landskap blickande ut över dess falliska monument som Parthenon, Eiffeltornet och Kinesiska muren. I de senaste fotografierna har dockornas överkroppar förvandlats till hus, pistoler, parfymflaskor m.m. Där Cindy Sherman driver upp känslorna med abjektala "kräkningsbilder" visar Simmons det motsatta, en långsam kvävningsdöd.

Den mest konceptuellt inriktade av de tre, Louise Lawler, ställer sig med sin kamera liksom i marginalen för att undersöka vad som händer med konstverket efter det att det lämnat den vita utställningssalen. Genom att tjuvtitta i konstsamlares hem, i museernas och galleriernas lager upptäcker hon hur kontexten förändrar konstverket. Det är således inte bara konstnären som skapar estetiska betydelser utan också en anonym skara

av samlare, betraktare och museianställda, och ytterst den kulturella apparat som dragit upp riktlinjerna för deras roller. Med ett diskret öga registrerar Lawler konsten som institution samtidigt som hennes fotografiska praktik just upprätthåller en distans till institutionsbegreppet. Finkänsligt skriver hon "Är hon vår? "ovanför sitt fotografi av Degas' lilla dansös eller så iakttar hon kyligt hur konstverken antar karaktär av marknadsprodukt i auktionskammarens bakre rum. Genom ett mycket exakt val av bildvinkel, proportioner och färgskala upprätthåller Lawler intrycket av att en objektiv observatör stått bakom kameran.

Hufvudstadsbladet, 21 april 1993

Orlan
Ateneumsalen, Helsingfors

På konferens med Orlan

Lördagkväll, klockan är 18.00 och den franska konstnären Orlan inleder sin "konferens" i Ateneumsalen i Helsingfors. Hon ställer sig bakom podiet och börjar sin föreläsning eller "intervention", som hon själv benämner det (på franska betyder order även operation).

Efter ett tag startar en videoföreställning på skärmen bakom Orlans rygg. Videon är ett icke editerat dokument av hennes sjunde operationperformance som tilldrog sig i New York den 21 november 1993. I operationssalen blir Orlan den "aktant" hon säger sig vara. Medan kirurgen omformar Orlans ansikte genom diverse ingrepp – fettsugning, omstrukturering av benbyggnaden, utfyllnad genom inlägg – är hon i satellitkontakt med sin publik, svarar på frågor, läser högt filosofisk text, pratar.

Som 18-åring inledde Orlan sitt konstnärskap i performance-genrens tecken. Under 70-talet, kroppskonstens gyllene tid, hanterade hon kroppsvätskor och övrigt "orent" material, som en förebådelse för den multimediala, interdisciplinära "köttsliga" genre hon idag arbetar med. Serien av plastikoperationer startades i Newcastle år 1990 på hennes 43-årsdag. Man frågar sig hur långt är det möjligt att gå i dylik "köttslig" konst? För Orlan

är strategin klar. När hennes liv medicinskt sett hotas, upphör plastikoperationerna och en annan process sätter igång, en juridisk. Orlan planerar att via den juridiska apparaten erhålla en annan identitet. Nytt ansikte, nytt namn och en kropp som kommer att skänkas till museum, detta är Orlans konkreta plan.

I Ateneumsalen skruvar publiken på sig, oroligt. Ungefär 18.30 är undertecknad (liksom många andra) tvungen att gå ut även om konferensen fortsätter. Illamående. Jag ser en flicka stappla ut och hon svimmar. Med en av yrsel grumlad blick tänker jag på Julia Kristevas intresse för ordet kadaver (på latin: *cadere*, falla), något som oåterkalleligen har fallit; död, förruttnelse, lik. Kristevas verbala association får en levande illustration när jag ser flickan falla ihop och vet vad som videon visar där inne i salen.

"Min kropp är min konst" och "jag har gett konsten min kropp" är två ständigt återkommande uttryck i Orlans retorik. När hon talar på så sätt provocerar hon fram, åtminstone hos mig, ett behov av gripa tag i termer som gräns och skillnad. Det är skillnad mellan det att bli illamående på grund av att man är tvungen att bevittna en blodig operation eller olycka, och det att titta på en video av det samma i en kontext där man ingår som publik. Manipulering i konstens namn? Visserligen finns det konst som rör sig i det abjektalas gränsmarker, på gränsen till den ursprungliga bortträngningen vars kroppsliga symtom är motviljan, äcklet, dvs. abjektionen, men med den skillnaden (i förhållande till Orlans praktik) att mediet står för den distans som överför "äcklet" till en nivå där också andra element så som skrattet, katarsiseffekten, ironin, kan passera och ingå.

När Orlan säger att hon ger konsten sin kropp frågar man, vilken konst, vems konst? Hennes egen? Om ett konstverk utraderar, liksom Orlans opererade ansikte, sin potential att vara en lek som just därför kan hantera och överföra sådant som i verkligheten är omöjligt, var hamnar man då? I ett vansinne som förverkligas med fullt förstånd?

Operationerna förbereds noggrant. Med hjälp av datamanipulering av konsthistoriska och mytologiska kvinnobilder (såsom Leonardo da Vincis Mona Lisa, Botticellis Venus, Gérards Psyche) har Orlan skapat en modell för ett självporträtt utgående från vilken plastikkirurgen arbetar. Orlan menar att hon sålunda genomgår riter som återföder henne som kvinna.

Under Orlan-konferensen i Helsingfors är det en märklig besatthet som blir det mest framträdande symptomet. Orlan är besatt, men av vad?

Hennes verbala utläggningar om sin konst lyckas inte helt svara på frågan. Nästa plastikoperation är planerad att utföras i Japan i syfte att konstruera en mycket stor näsa; den största näsa som tekniskt sett är möjlig att skapa (i relation till hennes anatomi) och etiskt sett är acceptabelt för en kirurg att utföra. Orlan håller på att skapa en mumie av det som i allmänna termer brukar kallas för det västerländska frihets- och jagbegreppet.

Hufvudstadsbladet 20 oktober 1995

Ars 95, Museet för nutidskonst, Helsingfors
Intervju med Louis Jammes

Konst dödar inte

Dagarna kring öppningen av *Ars 95* var det typiskt Helsingforsväder, småregn, blåst och grå ruggighet och man skyndade snabbt in. Därför kan jag inte säga exakt när Louis Jammes' fotografier blev uppsatta på fasaden, men när man en gång upptäckt dem vänder man inte bort blicken.

Vid den här tidpunkten kände jag varken till fotografiernas faktiska bakgrund eller Louis Jammes' verk i övrigt. Läser i utställningsguiden: "Louis Jammes är en fotograf som intresserar sig för hur människor utanför samhället lever, för marginalgrupper och kriser som drabbar hela samhället. Han har bl.a. fotograferat zigenarkolonier i Madrid och följderna av kärnkraftsolyckan i Tjernobyl. Sina motiv söker han på gatan och i vardagsvimlet, varefter han i framkallningsskedet bearbetar sina bilder. Hans senaste motiv har varit det belägrade Sarajevos bosniska barn." Sedan följer ett avsnitt om hur Jammes moraliskt engagerar sig i de livsförhållanden han återger, hur han med sina bilder också vill påverka det politiska planet … och texten börjar gå mot ett missvisande håll.

Jammes riktar inte i Sarajevo sin kamera mot den krigande skådeplatsen, fotografierna tar hand om enskildheter, ett barn, en person, och den färdiga bilden rör om i "fyrdelningen", sammanhanget mellan jorden, himlen, de dödliga människorna och gudarna. Det han visar kräver mindre att man tar hänsyn till dess mening, mer att verkningen iakttas. Här handlar verkningarna inte om det politiska planet utan vad som blir kvar då det skalas bort. Vad är en soldat utöver sin funktion som aktör i ett krig med privilegiet att ingripa i "fyrdelningen" jord, himmel, dödlig människa, gudarna (heliga värden)?

Roos Efter en relativt kort bekantskap med dina fotografier är jag övertygad om att de inte är realistiska på det sätt som guideboken insinuerar. Du använder ett slags estetik som har med en allmän skönhetsuppfattning att göra, t.ex. barn, krigets lidande offer förekommer i en infattning med änglavingar. Den här medvetna estetiken träffar en som ett hinder och jag kommer att tänka på vad som sagts om vår tid, konsten följer oss genom själens nya sjukdomar med symptomet – vi vet inte vilka vi är – men dina

fotografier får mig att göra tillägget, vi kan dock fortfarande igenkänna en änglabild. Därför blir bildernas estetik skenbart ambivalent: kontrasten mellan ett brutalt krig och föreningen ängel och människa. Det här får mig att uppfatta ett slags tredje skönhet, bilderna gömmer en dold, revolterande skönhet, för i konsten kan man frångå de vedertagna konstruktionerna enligt vilka krig, politik, nationalitet, självständighet m.m. får sina givna betydelser. Därför vill jag påstå, även om det låter paradoxalt, att dina foton är ett sätt för att uttrycka egentlig humanitär realism. I dem tänker man inte i termer av soldat eller offer, vinnare eller förlorare m.m. utan det de för fram är en nivå där vi kan dela våra tidstypiska sjukdomar oavsett vilken kategori vi tillhör. Kan du kommentera de här tankarna?

Jammes Mina fotografier är ingenting i namn av det som kan representeras, liksom titeln på den nyss utkomma bok som handlar om mina fotografier säger: "Sarajevo n'est en réalité le nom de rien qui puisse être représenté." Jag föredrar att visa hur jag ser, i motsats till massmedierna som låtsas visa verkligheten.

Roos Då kan man föra frågan vidare till följande, vad kan konst säga som exempelvis inte samhällsvetenskapen kan? Dina foton passerar ett visst hinder som är förbundet med relationen mellan ord som politisk konst, individuellt, kollektivt – de är ovanför dylika distinktioner och handlar i stället om den nivå där man kan säga, oberoende av om du är soldat eller offer är du människa i den bemärkelse att din existens förutsätter att någon annan människa gjort något för dig, tidigare. Kriget är ett sjukt hånskratt mot detta, ett symptom på att alltsammans gått fel.

Jammes Kriget betyder väl just det att en stor maskin kör över tillvaron, det finns ingen plats för individualitet, ingen plats för människan. Med andra ord, det handlar om ett berövande som äter upp essensen i att vara människa. I min bok finns ett kort avsnitt som talar om det här: kriget är inget öde, det är motsatsen, någonting som stjäl något från ödet, som rycker människorna bort från deras öden.

Roos Enligt min mening finns det ett slags revolt i dina bilder, men inte revolt på normalt sätt, som i politisk konst på 60- och 70-talet. Jag undrar om inte din revolt just uppstår genom att kriget som ett enda stort berövande får drag av universell sorg. Sorgen ger bilderna ett slags dold skönhet – men samtidigt låter det vanskligt att tala om skönhet för det gäller ju

kriget. Närmast avser jag med skönhet det jag relaterar ordet till, till den potential som trots allt finns någonstans hos människan.

Jammes Krig är död och döden betyder alla former av död (Jammes visar fotografierna på döda människor som finns i boken), därför finns dessa döda ansikten med.

Roos Hur länge har de varit döda?

Jammes Det varierar, några timmar, några dagar. I Sarajevo gick jag ofta till bårhuset, jag tog en hel del fotografier för det räckte länge innan jag fick fram det vad jag sökte, vilket jag inte exakt kunde förklara. I vilket fall som helst ville jag inte fotografera blod och blodigheter. Jag rörde inte vid de döda och upphörde omedelbart med fotograferandet när jag fann vad jag letade efter.

Roos Märkligt, vanligen sluter man den dödes ögon.

Jammes Nästan alla av dem har öppna ögon. I en krigssituation finns det inte tid att sluta dem. Det viktigaste för mig var att kunna visa verken i Sarajevo, att åka tillbaka med fotografierna. Fotona från kriget i Sarajevo skulle inte för mig ha den betydelse de har om jag inte haft möjlighet att visa dem i Sarajevo och det mest märkliga är att människorna där inte förstörde dem.

(Vi tittar i publikationen där fotografier visar verken på sin rätta plats på bombarderade och illa tilltygade byggnader i krigets Sarajevo. Jammes lyckades alltså med att montera upp bilderna i Sarajevo.)

Jammes Sarajevo är inte enbart i krig utan ett krigsfält och i denna situation är varje byggnad, varje plats under politisk kontroll, varje sak kan vara viktig och i synnerhet är detta systematiska bevakande viktigt för att upprätthålla den kämpande andan. Det sällsynta var att jag kunde sätta upp dessa fotografier på olika byggnader och ingenting hände, ingen angrep dem – i ett sammanhang där varje text, information, aktion är måltavlan för politisk reaktion.

Roos Och ditt liv då, har ord som glädje, lycka någon betydelse efter att man som du besökt platser som Tjernobyl, Sarajevo?

Jammes Det finns inte så mycket skillnad mellan mitt liv och mitt arbete. Jag upplever mig inte som intellektuell utan lever, arbetar och handlar

instinktivt och min besatthet gäller det vad jag gör.

Roos Du använder ofta barn i de här bilderna, var det ett instinktivt val?

Jammes Det är inte bara barn jag fotograferat, men en orsak är att då jag ville föra fotografierna tillbaka till Sarajevo förutsatte det en viss symbolisk nivå hos bilderna. Människorna i Sarajevo är mycket känsliga för symboler, t.ex. serberna använder ofantligt med tid för att förstöra symboler som bibliotek, minnesmärken m.m. och en bild med en ängel och ett barn finns liksom symboliskt sett ovanför den nivå som separerar allierad från fiende. I Sarajevo begås enormt mycket våldtäkter, kvinnor våldtas, barn våldtas. En ängel kan inte våldtas eller våldföra sig på någon.

Roos Alltså, det sätt du använder konceptet symbol på är anpassat till den verklighet som finns i Sarajevo.

Jammes En ängel reagerar inte med hämnd. Så därför tror jag att fotografierna är möjliga att visas på vardera sidan, och människor i Sarajevo förstod det här. Det finns en producent och regissör i Sarajevo som gjort en kort film om en soldat. Soldaten är ett monster enbart i det fall att du känner till vad han gjort. Han dödar med sina händer hundratals, våldtar unga kvinnor och dödar dem därefter. Men på ett annat sätt, och därför är den här filmen mycket intressant, förstår du att denna man också kunde vara på den andra sidan. Filmen visar hur han på några veckor blev ett monster genom att han blev soldat. Det är kriget som är maskinen, som skapar dylika monster. Kriget kan sluka nästan vem som helst och skapa ett monster av denna människa. Det är svårt att förstå grymheter såsom nazismen, koncentrationsläger m.m., men i denna film förstår man logiken enligt vilken en ung man som kunde ha haft en fullständigt annorlunda framtid börjar göra monstruösa ting. Jag lärde mig mycket av denna film. Kriget ger ingen en enda chans att vara mänsklig.

Siksi 1/1995

Death Angels on the Catwalk

Siksi 3/1996 (se den engelska översättningen sid. 97)

Damien Hirst
Gagosian Gallery, New York

Halali från la-la-land

När medlen saknas för att gå vidare tar man till något annat. Smärtan vänds inåt mot den egna kroppen, fantomsmärtan pulserar, signalerar fara. Något har blivit omöjligt att tala om och positionen är neurotikerns där ansatser till handling blir undangrävda innan de ens kommit halvvägs. Om en röst utifrån med ordet som spjutspets lyckas ingripa med frågor som hur, var, när, varför, om den lyckas med sin retroaktiva metod att ge den destruktiva transgressionen en förlösning, då upprättas ett möte utanför i ordet och berättelserna kan strömma fram.

Egentligen är det inte en utan två gränser som måste överskridas: destrueringen av lås och säkerhetskedjor samt upprättandet av nya gränser som finns till för att locka fram transgressionens lustfyllda potential. Precis detta är innehållet i det jaktrop man går ut med, en förväntning man önskar att konsten kunde infria. Minns filosofen Cecilia Sjöholms ord från symposiet i Malmö: "Om konsten är transgressiv är den det just därför att den inte intenderar att vara det. Upplevelsen av transgression föds utanför varje befintlig diskurs." En mentalt sett orörd plats där konturerna är så pass diffusa att de inte låter sig kontrolleras varken av konstvärld eller annan instans med legitimerande funktion.

Hade strax före symposiet sett Damien Hirst erövring av den amerikanska konstvärlden på Gagosian Gallery i New York. En smart, gigantisk framfart – ve den olycksalige skribent som lämnar galleriet med total snedtändning. Så mycket energi (och pengar) som mobiliserats och så litet som mentalt sett överförs och fortplantas. Ingenting – som att besöka en avancerad cirkus där varje nöjesmaskin fungerar med kalkylerad effekt. Inga diffusa kopplingar, ambivalenta känslor, sådant som tyder på att ett latent intresse trots allt gräver sig fram. I stället bara ett ingenting.

Misstänker att Hirst alltför väl lärt sig vad amerikansk pragmatism går ut på. Att säga att störst är synligare än större och stor synligare än mindre är inte driven ironi utan ett faktum att räkna med i ett samhälle där handling och funktion utgör de primära existensvillkoren. Således, Hirst har drivit upp sitt format. I centrum en enorm askkopp fylld med fimpar

(rökförbud i New York på restauranger och barer). På väggen mekaniska färgstänkande penselmaskiner (vulgarisering av pollockska metoden). Och styckad kreatur, bitvis inlagd i separata glasmontrar. Förvisso har ett brott begåtts, en regel för liv och död har brutits. Men det symptomskapande i den manliga psykopatologin är inte brottet i sig utan skräcken för det, och så länge brottet lever som gränslös mental föreställning får galenskapen sin näring. I korthet, utan att närmare gå in på psykoanalytisk teori, vad kunde vara mer intressant från en kvinnlig position sett än just insyn i den galenskap som finns på andra sidan av könets gräns? En kommunikation mellan hysterin och skräcken någonstans i la-la-landet.

När förråden töms, när man stirrar på fimparna i askkoppen och inser att det inte finns så mycket mer att tillägga är det spjutspetsen man saknar, ord och bilder som brutalt bryter mot oförmågan att överskrida just detta, gränserna.

Siksi 2/1996

Jan Hietala
Naturhistoriska riksmuseet, Observatoriemuseet, Galleri TRE, Stockholm

Jungfrulig mark

Sommaren 1994 deltar Jan Hietala i den svensk-ryska ekologiska tundraexpeditionen som åkte i spårvattnet av Nordenskiölds Vegaexpedition (1878–80) med målet att utforska Nordostpassagen. Hietalas reseskildring blev installationen *Terra Incognita* – obeträdd mark – i tre avdelningar på tre olika platser i Stockholm.

Sparade till en natt, långt efter mitt besök i Stockholm, läsningen av Hietalas skriftbok med dagboksanteckningar från färder samt tillhörande fotografier. Den svensk-ryska gruppen passerade 180 grader vilket gav en gudomlig, skugglös natt. Månne detta gett fotografierna deras märkliga delaktighet i annan luft, annan färg?

Resan har börjat: 940710

Meningslöshet… står på akterdäck… upplever innerlig meningslöshet… har ingenting här att göra… som en koncentration av hela mitt tidigare liv… genomskinligt och utan bestående nytta… värde… någonting som är sant och förmodligen det enda sanna omkring mig… åker över doftlöst öppet hav… oändligt och avgränsat endast av den konvexa horisonten… en blek sol… en lika blek himmel… kölvattnet bubblar fräser… lämnar ett spår över den annars lugna sjön… vad lämnar jag… vad är det jag inte längre vill se…

Expeditionen sker i vetenskapens namn. Medan forskarna fullföljer sina uppdrag går Hietala sin egen väg, för hans frågor uppstår i nuet, på platsen. Hans närvaro i expeditionen, så som installationen låter erfarenheterna genljuda, får i sin tur till stånd pinsamma frågor. Vetenskap. Vem är det som talar, vem ställer frågorna? När? Var? Och till sist, hur? En expedition är ju ett skeende med utrustning, fartyg, helikopter, kött, blod, skinn, fukt, värme, kyla, människor. Att droppa en vetenskaplig diskurs konkret ner i realiteten, att vara i världen, fungerar egentligen inte alls, vilket *Terra Incognita* får oss att misstänka. Konstellationen som kan utläsas blir följande: tundraexpeditionens forskare jobbade enligt sitt kontrakt med den vetenskapliga normen till skillnad från Hietala som spelade med realitetens villkor; förhållandet mellan *vrai* (sant) och *semblant* (liksom), som hos Hietala alstrar en delikat variant av *le vraisemblant* (det sannolika) vilket just förutsätter närvaron av någon som ger betydelse åt det upplevda, lärda och erfarna.

Tänker på de två föregående verk jag sett av Hietala, installationerna *Den gudarna älskar dör ung* och *Deixis*, jämför med *Terra Incognita* och tror jag förstår. I *Den gudarna älskar dör ung* är rummets väggar röda och små videoskärmar är upphängda. Blir litet illa till mods. Nästan som i pornografisk litteratur där texten är reducerad till några få element, gör det här, gör det där plus medföljande obscena beskrivningar. Återkommer. Och ser. Hietala har lyckats plocka bort ett slags imaginär nivå och istället låter han förloppet växla mellan det reala (syns inte, antyds) och det symboliska: Det finns rekvisita, det finns aktörer, två män i en soffa, en kvinna mitt emellan, och den frånvaro som finns i verket är verklig frånvaro och inte en närvarande symbol för frånvaro. Frånvaron och tomheten är liksom ingenting, ogripbart och symbolen (det vi ser på videon) är ett snitt ur något som kunde ha varit Leopold von Sacher-Masochs vardag, kylig, grym. Den röst som inte finns i verket, men som en lyhörd betraktare kan

förnimma, hörs så småningom tack vare videon som i närbild visar en monoton upprepning av det manliga könsorganet i den autoerotiska akten.

Deixis fungerar analogt. En paradox: det sägs ju att konstnärligt skapande utgår från upplevelsen av tomhet och det är tomheten som är drivkraften, det är tomheten som kräver en form, men Hietalas produkt innehåller den här tomheten, den är innehållet utan att visa någonting av tomhetens kretslopp. Installationen *Deixis*, där kroppen är HIV-smittad, fungerar som en injektionsnål som träffar rätt ådra. Man känner pulsen slå. Hör den.

Från sexualitet och interiör till tundra och vetenskap.

På tundran blir närvaron likväl frånvarande fastän på ett annat sätt... slås av att jag här precis som på andra platserna under resan... känner mig iakttagen... som följer någon min promenad... rör sig strax efter eller alldeles vid sidan om... kanske ett djur... en rad olika... upplever mig vara utsatt för examination... dissekering... snarare än att vara den som betraktar...

Alltså förloppet återknyts än en gång till frågan: Vem är det som talar? Vem är det som ser? På Naturhistoriska riksmuseet med Hietalas avdelning *Nesjkan – om den vetenskapliga resan*, finns ett fotoporträtt av expeditionens ledare ... ser en man som i sig själv bär medvetenhet om sin betydelse... Att han är centrum och drivkraften för sin omgivning... Och runt honom finns den starka utstrålningen som bara återfinns hos dem som har lyckats... Det övriga som Hietala visar i *Nesjkan* är det som expeditionens ryska forskare helst ville åka förbi: oljefat, föroreningar, glassplitter, "infödingar".

Pevek – om samlandet på Observatoriemuseet är installationens svåraste avdelning. Hietala som i detta verk hanterar tiden transversalt ställer fram objekt och mikroskop. Ibland har han gått så finkänsligt tillväga visavi museet att hans inslag nästan går en förbi. Hietala löper liksom linan ut genom att utnyttja den museipedagogiska rekonstruktionsprincipen, en utgångspunkt som i sig skallrar tomt. Realtiden är ju trots alla rekonstruktioner ändå frånvarande.

I Vega-rummet bland en kuliss avporträtterande Nordenskiöld, får man överraskande syn på två fotografier, diskret placerade intill dörren: ett manligt könsorgan, vackert och självklart, och ett annat fotografi som visar en ådrad, liksom rostad yta. Mitt i detta står alltså Nordenskiöld med

sitt självgoda upptäckarjag, han som överträffat alla andra män, som tillägnat sitt liv åt utforskandet av jungfrulig mark. Men ett sådant land finns inte och det är kanske precis därför det var så viktigt för Nordenskiöld att ta det jungfruliga i besittning.

> He has understood nothing of truth, nor anything of woman. Because, indeed, if woman is truth, she at least knows that there is no truth, that truth has no place here and that no one has a place for truth. And she is a woman precisely because she does not believe in what she is, in what she is believed to be, in what she thus is not. (Derrida, *Spurs*)

Är detta den nod som kan uppdagas både inom vetenskap och sexualitet? Den nod som gör sanningen till en förklädnad för ett oaccepta-belt bristbegrepp; lager på lager av transformationer och förvridningar. Vem var Nordenskiöld, varför ville just han konkret leva ut metaforen, att beträda Terra Incognita? I rummet längst bak finns arrangemanget *Förgät-mig-ej*: mikroskopet är ställt på ett underlag med ett foto av en ung tundra-kvinnas ansikte, ovanpå detta finns en torkad förgät-mig-ej-blomma. I mikroskopet hamnar ditt öga direkt, frontalt mot ett foto av det kvinnliga könsorganet.

Meningslösheten får sin upprättelse, det förlösande ordet kommer inte då du behöver det, det kommer oombett, senare. Sinnesorganen tar emot, doftar, ser, undersöker i installationen i Galleri TRE. Den begärande människan får ro för ett ögonblick. För det här verket har Hietala målat på akrylglas färger jag ser som tundrans. Fonden är en fotografisk upprepning av Wrangels ö betraktad från luften. Till skillnad från överbyggnadernas strukturer är strukturen i naturen faktiskt oproblematisk, den följer en rytm parallell till den samordning Hietala har skapat mellan målningarnas format, färger och sekvenser.

Siksi 2/1995

Intervju med Gertrud Sandqvist

Ett samtal om Privat i Alby

Galleri F15 som i år firar sitt 25-årsjubileum är något av en särling bland nordiska konstinstitutioner. Galleriet ligger litet avsides på den natursköna landsbygden utanför Oslo, inrymt i huvudbyggnaden på Alby gård som tidigare tjänat som hem för en skeppsredarfamilj. Då man tillfogar det faktum att galleriets uppgift är att visa angelägen nordisk och internationell samtidskonst bortfaller liksom av sig självt grunden för ett tänkande i termer som centrum och periferi, provinsiellt och urbant.

Gertrud Sandqvist inleder sin period som chef för Galleri F15 med utställningen *Privat*. De sex konstnärer som deltar i Privat fogar över var sitt utrymme i den nyrenoverade byggnaden och varje installation är gjord utgående från den specifika platsen. Videokonstnär Tony Ourslers talande dröm- eller fantomdockor befolkar som ett organiskt nätverk trapphuset. I nedre våningen vilar Olav Christopher Jenssens små vaxfigurer *Sovande Poeter*, ostörda av Marianna Uutinens ocensurerade teckningar i ämnet Napoleon. I övre våningen där utsikten öppnar sig mot havet har Lawrence Carroll lämnat sina nomadiska spår: en hög med hopvikt presenning, en trälåda, segelduk. Nina Roos serie av målningar går den motsatta vägen, de ger rummet en förankring, målningarna följer väggen liksom en panel. Utställningens enfant terrible, Anders Widoff representerar med sin installation den privata oredan.

Ordet privat får en att lystra till, det är ett ord man knappast alls under 80-talet hade anledning att använda i konstsammanhang. Med tentaklerna riktade mot 90-talet träffade jag Gertrud Sandqvist för ett samtal.

Roos Låt oss börja med den enklaste fråga: Vad betyder *Privat* och hur har den här speciella byggnaden, konceptet och konstnärerna funnit varandra?

Sandqvist När man blir förtrogen med en del konstnärer och deras arbeten börjar man se den enorma diskrepans som finns mellan det officiellt utsagda och de egentliga tankarna bakom ett verk. Man ser hur otroligt mycket det är som just har att göra med en privatsfär och att det är då, när denna sfär finns som någonting börjar hända också i verket. Överhuvudtaget kan man se hur konstnärer i sitt sätt att arbeta med konst

allt mer använder sig av de här brotten i vardagslivet.

Roos Vardagslivets brott aktualiseras väl också i relationen mellan verket och betraktaren, för det är ju frågan om ett område betraktaren har erfarenhet av?

Sandqvist Ja, det är nästan omöjligt att förstå de konstnärers arbeten som nu är intressanta om man inte som betraktare använder hela sitt register, alltså både det mest löjliga eller officiellt felaktiga eller absurda sätt att tänka. Den öppenheten, tänkte jag, skulle naturligtvis vara väldigt intressant att visa i en utställning. En annan rekonstruktion ligger nog just i det privata. Jag ville gärna öppna min första egna utställning med konstnärer vilkas arbeten betytt mycket för mig. Allteftersom fördjupades konceptet genom att själva byggnaden är så speciell som den är. I och med att den är ett hem som gjorts om till ett galleri, som dessutom har drivits som familjeföretag i många år, finns det väldigt många så att säga skavanker och speciella minnen som är förknippade med just den här platsen.

Det intressanta är då att man inte har en neutral institution att arbeta i utan det motsatta, en institution som är nästan nedsolkad utav olika föreställningar. Att bryta mot det här tror jag inte fungerar genom att sätta in en totalt ren utställning utan tvärsom, att arbeta mot det men med precis samma medel.

Roos Det verkar som om *Privat* skulle lyfta fram ett förhållningssätt som är i luften eller åtminstone på kommande. Kan du kommentera det här?

Sandqvist Bland annat tror jag att det är frågan om ett sätt att komma vidare från det som skett under de närmast föregående tio åren. För att undvika att hamna i en väldigt teoretisk språkspelsdiskussion eller i en schablonvärld där neoexpressionisterna arbetade, förskjuter många intressanta konstnärer perspektivet en aning och man ser helt nya delar, sådant som varit ointressant eller ansetts alltför privat för att våga plockas fram. Och så är det ju alltid med konst att det är de här förskjutningarna som är intressanta.

Roos Att arbeta med förskjutningar förutsätter en hel del av konstnären, framför allt en finkänslig hantering av medlen, processen och uttrycket vilket jag tycker är synligt i *Privat*.

Sandqvist Alla sex konstnärer arbetar med en väldig noggrannhet och

exakthet och det är en exakthet som inte har att göra med tilltron till en viss teori eller en viss analys utan det är frågan om någonting som arbetar i springorna mellan detta eller oavhängigt av detta. Då blir det också extremt spännande att följa med processen när konstnärerna gjorde sina installationer och att iaktta hur rummen blir knutpunkter för ett visst slags associationsfält och hur fälten liksom griper tag i varandra.

Men det som behövs från betraktarens sida är att man lämnar en del av den passiva, distanserade hållning som man blivit lärd att inta i konst-sammanhang, att man förmår släppa en del utav försvaren och också att man ger utställningen den tid den måste ha. Det är intressant att se hur många av konstnärerna mer eller mindre medvetet tvingat betraktaren att stanna en viss tid i rummet, vilket är väldigt viktigt för att man skall kunna se de här förskjutningarna. Exempelvis Anders Widoff gör det genom sin text på väggen. Marianna Uutinen har arbetat med en brutalare form av förskjutning genom att hon bara sänker taket i sitt rum och därmed tvingar betraktaren i en ovan position. Olav Christopher Jenssen sluter rummet kring sina vaxfigurer så till den grad att man blir helt isolerad. När man väl är där inne springer man inte ut direkt igen.

Installationerna här återfinner en närvaro som gör att det faktiskt är möjligt att se det man har runt omkring sig, även det som inte är förvän-tat. Det inte förväntade är kanske en liten skrovlighet i verket som inte är där man tänkt sig att den borde finnas. Under förutsättningen att man håller uppmärksamheten så blir man närvarande och då släpper natur-ligtvis alla tankarna på vem man är, vilka konstnärerna är, hur det här borde se ut.

Ett annat drag som kännetecknar *Privat* är att den saknar citat. *Privat* är inte en språklig utställning, den är svår att fånga i några precisa formu-leringar. Och just därför att den bara delvis är tillgänglig på en språklig nivå blir den undanglidande.

Roos Det här draget irriterar förstås dem som arbetar med prydliga kate-goriseringar?

Sandqvist Ibland kunde man ju nästan fråga sig inför en del verk under 80-talet huruvida de överhuvudtaget var intressanta att göra eller inte eftersom det de skulle visa var så väldigt styrt. Verken skulle tolkas precis exakt utgående från ett visst sammanhang och alla andra tolkningar blev felaktiga. Då har man ju egentligen tagit död på bildkonsten, det är ingen

idé att hålla på med bilden längre.

En annan aspekt av det privata har att göra med relationen till andra former av bildmedia, både till reklamfilmer, TV-filmer och vanliga biofilmer – alltså visuella medel som används för att tilltala så många som möjligt och som bygger på de enheter som är garanterat känsloframkallande för största möjliga grupp människor. De konstnärer som är med i *Privat* arbetar på totalt motsatt sätt, inte alls med det som är gemensamt för alla utan tvärtom. Ja, om inte bildkonst skall sugas upp i en allmän gegga av filmuttryck så tror jag nog att man tvärtom får säga att bildkonst är kanske inte till för alla, vid alla tillfällen, alltid, överallt. Det är viktigt att komma ihåg att det jag avser inte representerar någon form av elitism utan det är frågan om en helt annan nivå, en annan kvalitet på en erfarenhet.

Hufvudstadsbladet 3 maj 1993

Museum moderner Kunst, Frankfurt

Visionärt, dramatiskt museitänkande

En typisk tendens för de större tyska städerna har varit den att de insett behovet av medvetna, kulturpolitiska satsningar för att kunna hävda sig i ett europeiskt och internationellt sammanhang. Nya, moderna museibyggnader har vuxit fram i rask takt med den följd att just Tyskland kommit att fungera som föredöme och studieobjekt för den här typen av arkitektur.

Museet för modern konst i Frankfurt blev färdigt sommaren 1990. Byggnaden, som befinner sig på promenadavstånd från järnvägsstationen, har fått en exceptionell placering på en kilformad tomt mittemellan två livligt trafikerade gator. I den fullständigt urbana miljön har arkitekten Hans Hollein ritat en triangelformad byggnad som maximalt fyller ut tomten. Då man studerar den slutna fasaden framstår det som en gåta att byggnaden i tre våningar faktiskt omsluter 50 530 kvadratmeter. Holleins arkitektoniska lösning som utnyttjar gatuplanet är skräddarsydd för en urban miljö. Det är lika behändigt att stiga in i museet som i vilken som

helst affär. Betoningen finns alltså på det byggnaden döljer inom sig, ett antal rum i varierande storlek som utställningstekniskt är planerade med tanke på de krav nutidskonsten ställer.

De förväntningar staden Frankfurt har på sitt museum är intressanta ur en kulturpolitisk synvinkel. Museet får så att säga gå direkt på saken, att bygga ut sin samling innehållande verk alltsedan 1945 med aktuell nutidskonst som för fram de rådande pluralistiska attityderna. Ribban är högt ställd, det man satsar på skall vara intressant också i ett internationellt perspektiv.

Den här programförklaringen avviker avsevärt från det som vanligen ligger på ett statligt museums ansvar, att kartlägga nationella strömningar samt att presentera nutidskonsten utgående från dess historiska kopplingar. Symptomatiskt för detta är att uttrycket tysk konst inte en enda gång nämns i samband med museets linjedragning.

En annan fråga är den hur ett museum presenterar sin samling. Den utställning som för närvarande visas i Frankfurtmuseet ger man fulla poäng för, en professionell och kompromisslös sammanställning som fungerar som en bland många möjliga introduktioner till nutidskonsten. Museichef Jean-Christophe Amman, tidigare känd för sin verksamhet vid konsthallen i Basel, har tagit fasta på det som han uppgett som en av sina intentioner, att försöka visa ett representativt urval av enskilda konstnärers produktion istället för att koncentrera sig på en samling.

I synnerhet samlingens konstverk från 60-talet var enligt Amman problematiska – hur finna kopplingar till 90-talet som skulle motivera deras närvaro. Ett fint exempel på en sådan lösning är rummet med japanen On Kawaras "datumarbeten". Sitt första datumarbete gjorde Kawara i New York på 1960-talet. Därefter har han varje år fortsatt att måla ett visst antal av dem. Målningen är alltså lika med ett datum där tecknen alltid är vita och där bakgrundens färg varierar. För sin utställning har Amman förenat Kawaras äldre datumserier. Vanligen när man betraktar en konstnärs arbeten som sträcker sig över flera decennier lär man sig någonting om konstnärens utveckling; i detta fall är målningarna upprepningar via vilka man kan referera till sin egen utveckling.

Ett annat exempel på hur en konstnärs äldre arbeten följs upp av nyare är serien *18 oktober 1977* (1988) av Gerhard Richter, vilken museet lånat för tio år. Serien handlar om Baaders, Ensslins och Raspes död, d.v.s. om Röda arméfraktionens (RAF) ledare. Richter har målat de gråsvarta, fotorealis-

tiska arbetena på basen av polisens arkivfoton. Det är svårt att reda ut reaktionerna inför serien. En sekvens återger t.ex. Gudrun Ensslin med ett ofrivilligt leende på läpparna, uppenbart ertappad inför kameran. Samtidigt, som ett ofrånkomligt faktum, påminns man om att det är just de här personerna som blev nyckelfigurerna i det trauma som inte endast var en episod utan i högsta grad är en del av Tysklands historia. Såsom känt var det den 18 oktober 1977 som Baader, Ensslin och Raspe hittades döda i sina celler. Richters kontroversiella serie har endast två gånger tidigare visats för allmänheten.

Koreanen Nam June Paik, som räknas som en av videokonstens pionjärer, fyller ett av rummen med sin installation *Ett ljus* från 1988. Det som är intressant är att det här arbetet visar att Paik går mot en mer minimalistisk riktning, vilken kännetecknade hans tidigaste verk. I rummet finns ett enda brinnande, levande ljus, vilket videokameran återger genom otaliga, färgade projektioner. Paik menar själv att verket är ett uttryck för "antiteknologisk teknologi", ett ämne han för tillfället är upptagen av.

Rummet med popkonst väcker nostalgi, här är Andy Warhols Brilloaskar prydligt uppradade på en hylla intill en ung Marlon Brando. Under dessa trettio mellanår, har det egentligen hänt något banbrytande inom konsten? Såpass färska känns Warhols arbeten. Detsamma kan man också påstå om det 60-talsarbete av Claes Oldenburg som finns i ett närliggande rum. Under den här tiden sysslade Oldenburg med det amerikanska vardagslivets estetik – den sovrumsinteriör som Oldenburg rekonstruerat är ett typexempel på en stil som kunde betecknas som den amerikanska drömmens.

Bland de yngre konstnärerna finns två intressanta kvinnor representerade, Katharina Fritsch och Rosemarie Trockel. Fritschs installation är en mardrömslik scen där trettiotvå exakt likadana svartklädda män sitter uppradade vid ett bord i en exakt likadan ställning. De uniformerade figurerna fortsätter som en ändlös bild då man associerar till verklighetens oräkneliga förebilder, manliga sällskap vid mötesbordet. Trockel som jobbar med de mest varierande medel bidrar med ett arbete som består av vävnad i ylle med invävd text: Gör mig ingenting / Men snabbt. Ett enkelt utslag av den "kvinnliga logiken"?

Hufvudstadsbladet 12 juni 1992

Glamourös kulturnomadism

Flygturen från Helsingfors till Venedig är en smärtsam påminnelse om att resan leder mot hjärtat av ett Europa där politisk och social oro, upplösning och krigföring är en realitet. Under mellanlandningen i Tyskland är det omöjligt att utesluta det som händer utanför flygplatsens fredade ingenmansland. Och själva Italien så oerhört nära striderna i det forna Jugoslavien.

Resans egentliga mål, Venedig, som för 45:e gången är hemvisten för den internationella konstutställningen Biennalen, får genom sin exceptionella kombination av splittring och helhet en nästan symbolisk framtoning – byggd på en grupp öar i lagunen och sammanhållen av en enhetlig arkitektur vars fuktangripna byggnader i sig representerar ett slags sönderfallets estetik. Utan tvekan vågar man påstå att årets Biennal vuxit till en mammuthändelse som åtminstone under öppningsdagarna nästan hotade att spränga stadens mått.

Och man frågar sig om inte Biennalen i år närmar sig gränsen för sin egen upplösning vilket, ironiskt nog, påminner en om hur nära varandra begrepp som splittring och helhet egentligen befinner sig. Uppenbart är att mannen bakom årets projekt, den italienska konstkritikern Achille Bonito Oliva, har skapat en helhet som tycks värna om Biennalens position som prestigefylld institution; de nationella paviljongernas utställningar kring floden Giardini omges av otaliga andra runt om i staden.

Achille Bonito Oliva har döpt sin Biennal till *Konstens kardinalpunkter*, ursprungligen syftande på växelverkan mellan kompassens fyra huvudväderstreck. I stället för att föra fram ett begränsat, kritiskt synsätt, menar Oliva att temat utgår ifrån ett erkännande av kulturell nomadism och samexistensen av språk som format den samtida konsten – ett accepterande av "resans idé" med ett självklart refererande till "andra" kulturer.

Sitt bästa uttryck får idén på institutionell nivå där Olivas tendens till "avnationalisering" är mest synlig; korten gällande nationalitetstillhörighet och –gränser har på olika sätt blandats om, bl.a. har Oliva uppmanat kommissarierna för de nationella paviljongerna att inbjuda konst-

närer av annan nationalitet.

Sålunda finner man exempelvis amerikanen Joseph Kosuth (med ungerskt påbrå) i Ungerns paviljong och Hans Haacke (bosatt i USA) som inbjuden för den tyska och i den italienska paviljongens avdelning *Punti dell'arte* ingår namn som Beuys, Baselitz, Buren och Kirkeby. I det här avseendet innehåller Olivas ansats ett moraliskt värde som är oförnekligt i ett politiskt klimat där nationalitetstillhörighet är en av de stridbara frågorna.

I övrigt är det oklart vad Oliva egentligen avser med konstens kardinalpunkter, d.v.s. har temat någon relevans för innehållet, konsten? Frågan aktualiseras i synnerhet av det att en viss tillbakablickande tendens beträffande konstnärsvalen är uppenbar. Dessutom hedras konstens obestridbara kardinalpunkt Marcel Duchamp med en separat utställning i Palazzo Grassi (vilken inte hör till Biennalen).

Ännu dunklare förefaller frågan då man relaterar den till Olivas intention att presentera en Biennal som bygger på mosaikidén vilket i sig korrelerar dåligt med den överbyggnad av ordning, indelning och systematik som starkt präglar Biennalen som institution.

Efter flera dagars rundvandringar genom de olika utställningarna framstår mosaiktanken som allt mer problematisk. Man möter många separata bitar som är omöjliga att pussla ihop på grund av att varje enskild bit är av olika material och struktur och just därför skulle den behöva individuell fördjupning. Således, Olivas berömvärda tanke om "avnationalisering" skulle inte ha behövt lämna det faktum ouppmärksammat att det enskilda verket ofta är förankrat i en specifik plats och tillhörighet som formar dess kontext.

I detta mammutprojekt är det som om den kontextuella aspekten antingen glömts bort eller drunknat i utbudet och därmed uteblir också en av förutsättningarna för kommunikation mellan verket och betraktaren.

Konsekvensen blir den vi kunde förutse; de som bäst lyckas hävda sig är de välkända amerikanska och europeiska namnen för vi är ju bekanta med deras bakgrund. Försök att göra resor till andra sammanhang (etniska, perifera, marginella) är åtminstone under dessa förtecken ett omöjligt företag.

De två konstnärer som suveränt dominerar över Giardiniområdet är Hans Haacke och Ilja Kabakov. Vardera har på ett konstnärligt plan lyckats fördjupa det som Biennalens tema implicerar. Paviljongen problematiseras utgående från nationalitetstanken och därtill riktas kritik mot det institu-

tionen representerar. Dessutom påvisar båda konstnärerna att ställningsta-
gande konst år 1993 mer handlar om samtal än om svar och lösningar.

Hans Haackes installation i den tyska paviljongen (med texten
Germania ovanför sin entré) träffar direkt de ömma punkter landets historia innefattar. Då man stiger in i byggnaden möter man ett förstorat
fotografi av Benito Mussolini och Adolf Hitler taget i juni 1934 då Hitler
besökte Biennalen och bl.a. blev mottagen av en hel skara fascistungdomar.

Inne i paviljongen har Haacke företagit en enkel, aggressiv operation.
Marmorgolvet är sönderhackat och består nu av tusentals skärvor. Längst
bak på väggen finns ordet *Germania* textat med stora bokstäver. I all sin
enkelhet hänvisar Haackes installation till ett sammanhang som gömmer
en komplex problematik med outredda frågor – Haackes handling är lika
med en vägran att acceptera.

Ilja Kabakov, född i Ukraina, numera bosatt i New York, har ockuperat den forna sovjetiska paviljongen på kännspakt kabakovskt sätt, ömsint
och klarsynt. Byggnaden omgärdas av ett omålat träplank som fråntar den
varje uttryck av storhet (den närliggande tyska byggnaden representerar
nyklassisk stil).

Kabakov visar varken mer eller mindre än äkta bråte, byggnadens inre
ser ut som en uppsamlingsplats för all världens skräp. Då man går genom
den trånga gången närmar man sig ljudet av sovjetisk marschmusik som
kan härledas till en skrällig högtalare placerad i en rödrosa vaktbyggnad
på bakgården. Det befriande skrattet är också nu närvarande i Kabakovs
arbete.

Den andra intelligenta reflexionen över aktuella politiska frågor via
Biennalens historia utförs av fransmannen Christian Boltanski i den italienska paviljongen. Boltanskis svartvita fotoinstallation består av dokument av verk från Biennalen 1938. I en kommentar till sin installation
påpekar Boltanski följande: år 1938 tycktes ingen av besökarna vara upptagen av något annat än frågan, vem av konstnärerna skulle tilldelas The
Golden Prize. 1938 var det år då Hitler annekterade Tjeckoslovakien, då
det kinesisk-japanska kriget pågick och då den spanska republiken kollap-
sade under blodiga förhållanden.

Hur var det i år på Biennalen, hur många orkade mitt i värmen under
de glamourösa vernissagetillställningarna tala om exempelvis slakten i det
forna Jugoslavien?

Hufvudstadsbladet 28 juni 1993

Hur är det tänkt?

Finländaren har anledning att känna sig litet stolt. När man ute i världen drar in på utställningsprojekt är det finnen, vem annan, som sätter igång med att genomdriva en omfattande internationell utställning med nutidskonst. Otvivelaktigt har serien av Ars-utställningar (1961, 1969, 1974, 1983) skapat en betydelsefull institution för nutidskonsten. Ett exempel på det är att Ars-utställningen från år 1983 upprepade gånger under årens lopp dykt upp i diskussioner, den ena minns en sak, den andra något annat och poängen blir att vi delar nyckel till en "generationshändelse".

Ars 83 visade olika bitar av konstens fält, från jordkonst via nyexpressionism till transavantgardet. Och nu 1995, när konsten karaktäriseras av ett mitt-i-tillstånd, när nutidskonsten då den är som bäst lyckas skaka loss definitioner som blivit för trånga – hur tänker man på Museet för nutidskonst där uppgiften varit att arbeta fram den emotsedda Ars-utställningen? Man kunde tillägga: omtvistade. Det ligger i sakens natur att en dylik satsning skakar om i konstvärlden.

För egen del hoppas jag att det evinnerliga ältandet av fenomen inom "vår konstvärld" kunde läggas åt sidan då det för en gångs skull finns en unik möjlighet att uppleva, diskutera och analysera konstverk. Ars-utställningens betydelse ligger nämligen i det mycket primära; ett tillfälle att se sig omkring, att se konst.

Museichef Tuula Arkio, intendent Maaretta Jaukkuri och amanuens Asko Mäkelä (ansvarig för Ars-delen *Artificiell verklighet*) är alltså personerna bakom *Ars 95*. Jag träffar Maaretta Jaukkuri för att få svar på mina nyfikna frågor under det intensiva skedet då utställningen håller på och ta form i Ateneumbyggnaden. Vi samtalar om Ars som institution och Maaretta Jaukkuri kommer med ett klargörande.

Jaukkuri Ifall någon ifrågasätter *Ars 95* finns det ett enkelt försvar. Man får inte glömma bort att *Ars 95* har som uppgift att ge basinformation om nutidskonst isynnerhet till de betraktare som inte arbetar med konst och därför inte har expertens insyn i konstens nuläge. *Ars 83* fungerade på ett annat sätt genom att tiden var en annan. Den blev ett slags introduktör av

det nya, men idag då konstnärer och skribenter genom resor och tidskrifter är förhållandevis väl insatta i nutidskonsten har vi tänkt annorlunda.

Vi hoppas att utställningen fungerar som en förminskad modell av konstens "justnuläge", att betraktaren genom de enskilda verken kan skapa sig en helhetsbild som stämmer överens med nutidskonstens läge, att verken klargör och kompletterar varandra så att en möjlig kontext framträder för betraktaren. Utgår man från ett dylikt tänkande kan man påstå att *Ars 95* inte är en megautställning utan det motsatta, en modell i liten skala av den situation och den konst vi lever mitt i.

Roos I förhandsinformationen om *Ars 95* presenteras ett slags koncept med en tematisk indelning: *Individ, Samfund, Bild/språk* och *Artificiell verklighet*. Hur kom ni fram till det här och hur fungerar indelningen?

Jaukkuri Till en början, som igångsättande tankeredskap, dryftade vi identitetsbegreppet vilket ju de senaste åren varit ett nyckelord både inom konst och teori. Småningom klarnade våra tankar allteftersom vi reste omkring i syftet att välja fram verk för utställningen. Vi insåg att vi ville relatera begreppet till någonting, för just förmågan att relatera är specifik för konsten som uttryck – identitet är ju ingenting ifall den inte finns någonstans, har en plats.

Således gick det upp för oss att förhållandet mellan det privata (individen) och det offentliga (samfundet) är en adekvat axel kring vilken identitet och många andra aktuella begrepp kretsar. Jag kan ge ett exempel. Via konsten kan det mest privat upplevda föras fram offentligt och betraktaren som representant både för det privata och kollektiva kan genom den visuella framställningen bli delaktig i och kommunicera med en annan individs verklighet. Redan Freud insåg att då det privata/personliga artikuleras minskar skulden genom att ämnet förs upp till offentlig nivå.

Roos Det du säger leder till en intressant omsvängning av tematanken. Ett dylikt koncept för *Ars 95* innefattar en problematisering av själva "indelningstänkandet", det förutsätter ett flexibelt tänkande och kreativa övergångar mellan olika begrepp. Den tredje avdelningen som lyder under arbetsnamnet *Bild/språk*, vad avses med den?

Jaukkuri Benämningen *Bild/språk* refererar bland annat till en intressant iakttagelse. I dag är konstnären inte längre den heroiska typ som med eget språk berättar om sitt inre och sina känslor utan tvärtom, han använder

och utvecklar sitt språk utgående från det visuella språk som redan existerar. Jag tror att detta öppnar verket för kommunikation.

Det är faktiskt sant att konsten implicerar ett tillåtande, att verket genom sina specifika medel kan uttrycka saker och ting som det i verkligheten är omöjligt att offentligt föra fram. Och detta överträdande av gränserna mellan privat och offentligt, från vartdera hållet, ligger i tiden, t.ex. Kieslowskis film *Blått* berör ämnet och bl.a. Jonathan Friedman behandlar i sin antropologiska forskning just distinktionen mellan privat och offentligt. En viktig sak att påpeka beträffande utställningens teman är att de inte är avsedda att servera färdiga svar. Svaret får du själv som betraktare stå för.

Roos Det du talar om får mig att tänka på Documenta-utställningen som ju var en gigantisk manifestation av "hierarkiernas upplösning". Den lanserades som utställningen utan koncept, utan tema, och kritiken av utställningen svängde åt vardera hållet. Kanske utställningen ändock hade vunnit på att presentera ett enkelt grundläggande koncept som inledande arbetsredskap, åtminstone för betraktaren. Istället uppstod ett nytt förbud, en ny förnekelse.

Jaukkuri Den här typen av internationella utställningar blottar det problematiska ordet publik. Jag anser att man inte kan tala om publiken som en homogen massa, det är ju frågan om en ytterst heterogen grupp. Var och en som kommer till Ars-utställningen gör det i egenskap av individ och det är först på individplanet som den egentliga kommunikationen med verket sker, växelverkan mellan att ge och ta emot. Jag tror att 90-talet överlag är det årtionde som relaterar exempelvis ansvarbegreppet till individplanet.

En sak till angående temat *Bild/språk*. Formella uppfinningar i konsten är, enligt min uppfattning, så gott som omöjliga att finna. Därför blir det allt viktigare att lyssna till vad verket säger, hur det säger det och vilket uttryck som används. Det är kring den här aspekten det mest radikala inom bildkonsten i dag tilldrar sig och t.ex. konstnärerna i *Bild/språk*-avdelningen representerar denna strävan. De använder sig av ett existerande visuellt språk, men de använder det på ett sådant sätt att verket blir en syntes med något nytt som går utöver de formella elementen.

Roos En sista fråga, jag vet att de som är intresserade av "namedropping genren" sitter med listan på deltagande konstnärer och spekulerar. Finns

det säkra kort, för många eller för få? Eller för litet eller för mycket risktagning angående konstnärsvalen?

(Maaretta Jaukkuri småler – den där frågan ingår i det spel som spelas inom konstvärlden.)

Jaukkuri För mig personligen är den sällskapsleken fullständigt ovidkommande. Ser man på *Ars 95* utgående från konstnärsvalen måste man minnas att Ateneumbyggnaden sätter en fysisk gräns för antalet deltagare, visst hade man gärna visat ännu fler konstnärskap. Vi är dock nöjda över att s.g.s. alla vi inbjöd tackade ja. Dessutom finns det på utställningen ett antal konstnärer som faktiskt inte tidigare uppträtt internationellt, exempelvis företrädare för de baltiska länderna och i jämförelse med senaste Ars utan en enda inhemsk deltagare är situationen positivare för Finlands del, vi deltar med sex stycken konstnärer.

Intervjun avslutas med ett angenämt skratt. Maaretta Jaukkuri säger med humor i blicken:

Eller egentligen kan du skriva att vi inte tagit några som helst risker för här på museet kan vi skriva under att de utställda konstverken är av garanterad kvalitet – nutidskonst av förnämsta slag.

Hufvudstadsbladet 5 februari 1995

Smart Show
Wasahallen, Stockholm

"Smart" för andra gången

Smart Show hade sin debut i fjol, i år hörde man redan oroliga röster som undrade om evenemanget börjar bli för etablerat? Har fräschören förvandlats till smart manér?

Så här uttrycker sig initiativtagarna (en oberoende grupp svenska gallerister och utställningsarrangörer). "Precis som förra året vill Smart Show fungera som en katalysator för svensk och internationell samtidskonst. Vi

är övertygade om att det bästa sättet att vitalisera det svenska konstlivet är att bredda kontaktytorna mellan olika deltagare; vi vill gjuta nytt liv i den samtida konsten genom att skapa en ärlig, opretentiös och lagom stor träffpunkt där konstnärer och publik, samlare och gallerister, intendenter och kritiker kan möta konsten och varandra." Och showen rullade på i Wasahallen under fyra dagar så att det tidvis rådde brist på utrymme.

Knepigare blir det att ta ställning till den kritik som riktades mot Smart Show, d.v.s. att den nu som tvååring riskerar att "institutionaliseras", att bli förutsebar och mekaniskt infria de förväntningar som ställs på kategorin, den yngre generationen. Man får säga som ordstävet, tredje gången gillt, och vänta på det avgörande tredje året. Åtminstone ännu i år lyckades Smart Show profilera sig som alternativ i förhållande till den sobra Stockholm Art Fair som öppnade en vecka senare – ett tecken därpå är den diagnos en "etablerad" gallerist gav Smart Show: barnsjukdom.

Det angelägna i Smart Show är enligt min mening det som gäller den konst som visades av mässans fyrtio utställare (av vilka över hälften var från utlandet). Litet måleri, mycket mediakonst, sex, våld, brutalitet dominerade bland bildmaterialet. Och hela den stökiga blandningen har av en del kritiker kallats för bildkonstens *fast food*, av andra som tecken på den tendens som går under namnet *new reality*. Trots att man vet att galleristen på väg till en alternativmässa tenderar att plocka fram verk av det trendigare slaget, och trots att man vet att konst som visas under rubriken yngre favoriserar ett slagkraftigt uttryck kan man inte bortse från det faktum att de verk som visades på Smart Show de facto existerar, påverkar publiken och sålunda fungerar som symptom på det tidstypiska.

När man sedan undrar, hur definierar sig då det tidstypiska enligt en dylik kontext? ja då blir man nog litet oroad. Här avser jag inte det att verken visar sexualitet, våld och "anstötligheter" utan i stället det sätt bildmaterialet används och hur denna användning i sin tur fungerar som symtom på något tidstypiskt – hurudana är vi, hur ser vår verklighet ut, hurudan är vår värld? Frågorna blir relevanta isynnerhet om man kopplar dem till Julia Kristevas enkla tes om att konsten (liksom mycket annat) delar vår tids sjukdom.

Den insikt jag tackar Smart Show för handlar om hur ett missförstånd avslöjas. Hittills har jag trott att det aktuella uttrycket *new reality* (ny verklighet) betyder ungefär detsamma som ett nyvaknat intresse för realiteter, att fokuseringen ligger på det verkliga (även om detta förstås kan

uttryckas med abstrakta medel). Uppskruvningen av den här dimensionen på Smart Show får en misstänksam, bildmaterialet används så pass effektivt att intentionen knappast varit att visa "verkligheten". I stället tror jag att materialet syftar till en annan effekt, att så snabbt och skickligt som möjligt skapa konst som förför. Detta skulle förklara intrycket av att konsten hetsigt jagar visuellt material som med excessens medel tävlar om din uppmärksamhet. Då har exempelvis döden i en dylik bildanvändning förlorat sin förankring i en verklig upplevelse av död, den har blivit en visuell sensation bland andra – en ingrediens i menyn *new reality*.

För att beskriva det ovannämnda med ett läroexempel från Smart Show. Fascinerat granskade jag Wolfgang Tillmans fotografier som Daniel Buchholz, Köln, ställde ut. Efteråt blev de suveräna fotograferna med intima fragment av urbana verkligheter, på ett störande sätt kvar i minnet. Tillmans sätt att fotografera en person eller situation varierar beroende på ämnet och därför är varje bild fotograferad på ett specifikt, skräddarsytt sätt. Samtidigt undrade jag varför det känns som om jag sett alltsammans förut även om jag omöjligen kan ha bevittnat exempelvis den erotiska scen Tillmans fotograferat i närbild.

Det finns en möjlig förklaring. Tillmans fotografiska strategi kan jämföras med det sätt på vilket tidskrifter som Vogue och Elle manipulerar med fotografiet – varje fotografi eftersträvar maximal förförelse, ett reklamfoto för en parfym syftar till detsamma som inzoomningen av Kate Moss' höftben (supermodell). Det är detta fotografiska språk Tillmans suveränt behärskar och att han gör det så väl beror måhända på att han faktiskt började sin bana som fotograf för modetidningar.

En deprimerande insikt, för då är vi igen tillbaka i 80-talets citatkonst men med den skillnaden att citeringen nu är betydligt smartare utförd. På Smart Show fanns dock goda undantag. En ny bekantskap för mig var exempelvis Tracey Emins lilla installation i Galleri Andreas Brändström. Emin född 1961 och bosatt i London arbetar på den gräns där de visuella uttrycksmöjligheterna utmanas av en sällsynt kombination av personlig bräcklighet och styrka.

Hufvudstadsbladet 19 mars 1995

Taidetta
Finländsk samtidskonst i Stockholm, 1995

Helsingfors i dag – en internationell anmärkning

Häromdagen då jag promenerade längs med Arkadiagatan i Helsingfors, förstrött i mina tankar, höll jag på att krocka med strykbräden. En man, rysse, kånkade på ett antal splitternya strykbräden inpackade i genomskinlig plast, sju stycken. Ännu fler strykbräden, det här var bara början på paraden. En ryska orkade bara bära på tre stycken, hennes starkare väninna släpade på sex, dottern på ett. Strykbräden. Beslöt att spåra källan, ja, jag hade rätt, ryssarna höll på att tömma det närbelägna lågprisvaruhuset på strykbräden.

Generell nedtrappning och specifik uppbackning – ett uttryck som flög mig i hågen när jag grubblade över allehanda fenomen i tiden. Helsingfors är med avseende på strykbräden en internationell stad, ryssarna alltså, som för brädena till St. Petersburg. Och finnarna, de äldre damer som åker över till Tallinn för att fylla på förrådet med smör och mellanöl, vad kallar man dem där om inte provinsbor av första graden.

De här fenomenen känns varken nya eller gamla. Snarare naturliga. I finnarnas erfarenhetsregister har relationen till de östra grannländerna sitt eget kapitel, antingen den artikulerats under tiotals år av tystnad eller som nu, inledningsvis, genom handel och konsumtion. Sålunda, tänker man internationellt i riktning österut, är Finland mer aktivt än övriga nordiska länder. Roller som byts, positioner som förskjuts, kurser som skjuter upp så högt att de faller för en sista gång. Ett decennium genomlevs, för att nytolkas när följande tiotal inleds, och på nytt sedan när seklet är till ända. Relationer, tolkningar och bedömningar, i verklighet och nu-ögonblick.

Vilken eufori

1991 utkom verket *Koko hajanainen kuva* (Hela den splittrade bilden), där Marja-Terttu Kiviranta och Leena-Maija Rossi går igenom den finska konstens 80-tal. Väntan låg i luften, som om konsten befann sig i en stor bubbla i vars inre odlades allt det som skulle bli nytt, intressant. När bilden nu en gång för alla var splittrad så borde väl något avgörande hända med den finska konsten. Och med stor iver började man orientera sig bland

"diskurserna". År 1995 är behovet snarast det motsatta, vill man orientera sig i finsk nutidskonst, upptäcka angelägenheter, är det skäl att trappa ner på förväntningar som skall infrias utgående från generella termer och i stället skärpa sitt instrument för att kunna syna det specifika. Minns i samband med en intervju jag gjorde nyligen ett inlägg av Maaretta Jaukkuri, intendent vid Museet för nutidskonst. Hon citerade en filosof som menade att det intressanta just nu är att gå tillbaka till de första frågorna, inte med avseende på svaren i sig utan tillvägagångssätten som producerat svaren.

Ovannämnda replik signalerar något angeläget. Inför 80-talets bulimia: citatkonst, manipulerade bilder, iscensatta bilder, massmediala bilder, undrar man, är uttrycket symptom på att det finns en upplevd gemensamhet visavi verkligheten, eller är det så att generellt-internationellt visuellt uttryck är en befrielse både för konstnärer och kritiker? Konstnärens kreativitet handlar om att manipulera kodat material, inte att tänka utöver det, inte att "tänka i sig". Kritikerns aktivitet handlar om att upprepa. När han ser en avvikelse, en innovation, en främling som han inte kan repa upp med upprepning blir han tyst.

Om och kring det osagda

Många av de konstnärer som nu är aktuella i mitten av 90-talet slutförde sin utbildning i slutet av 80-talet. Och som finsk specialitet, bland angelägna konstnärsskap finns sådana som fick sin början redan på 70-talet. På Museet för nutidskonst visades hösten 1995 Pekka Nevalainens retrospektiva utställning. Utställningens äldsta verk var från 1976, ett fotografi av en performance där Nevalainen går genom ett snöigt landskap lämnande efter sig ett släptåg av primärfärger. "Jag var intresserad av måleri men använde ett annat medium, performance, för att uttrycka min idé om måleriet." Lakoniskt och enkelt. Nevalainens utställning sade väsentligheter om finsk konst. En mentalitet, en kultur som karakteriseras av det osagda, har gett positiva utkast för bildkonstens del; en finsk konstnär när han är som bäst gör sig till mästare över sitt medium, vare sig det är fråga om måleri, skulptur, installationer, fotografi. Den här precisionen gör att samtidskonstens stora teoretiska frågor avdramatiseras. Exempelvis den (internationella) tendens som eftersträvat en direkt förankring i konkret verklighet (som reaktion på 80-talets citatkonst), den blir liksom inbyggd i ett konstnärsskap som Nevalainens. När mediet förädlas hamnar det i direkt kontakt med det övriga innehållet – verket

blir verkligt oberoende huruvida det refererar till konkret verklighet eller föreställd sådan.

Ett annat exempel, Martti Aiha, som sedan 80-talet skulpterat i trä med en generös ornamentik som associerar till nordfinskt träsnideri. I sin bok om Aiha med titeln *Kotiinkaipuun kuva* (Hemlängtans bild) skriver Tom Sandqvist bl.a. följande: "Vitt står för livet, rött för blodet och det över allt närvarande våldet, svart för döden och sorgen, guld för det alkemiska hoppet – det är som om det vindlande, svindlande ornamentet sökte innefatta dem alla, täcka dem tillsammans med deras yttersta ursprung i det som kan blott visas, aldrig utsägas, aldrig sägas med ord på den diskursiva nivå där språket leker med dess olika betydelser, innebörder och hänvisningar till det som inte kan sägas."

Provokation

Gungflyn närmar sig, citatet ovan leder in på det kvinnliga i bemärkelsen av mentalitet, tillstånd. Att gå längre än ramen anvisat, att föreställa och uttrycka det som går utöver hierarkin av ordningar som i sin tur vilat på den första, den symboliska, språklig och given. I Uleåborg arbetar skulptören Reijo Hukkanen. Hans skulpturobjekt är nästan omöjliga att titta på. Man går vilse i dem. Organiserade anhopningar av diverse objekt, former, material, frånstötande och därför så lockande. Hukkanen liksom skrapar sig genom fernissan och lyfter fram ofärdiga klumpar av massa. Tänker härvid högt enligt Julia Kristevas terminologi, sådan abjektion, sådan helighet. Vad Hukkanen gör är att med välljud hacka sönder skulpturala stenblock av finsk natursten.

Och måleriet? Efter de finska krigen var återhämtningen långsam och det man vedertaget kallat det moderna genombrottet inföll relativt sent. Segt blev det. Den konkreta konsten (och modernismen generellt sett) spökar fortfarande utgående från sin position som grå eminens. När normen är stark kan just detta ge positiva utslag, vändas till en tillgång. Konstnärer som Silja Rantanen och Jussi Niva arbetar rationellt, de tänker i termer av konstruktion, arkitektur, färg, yta, primärperception. På sin utställning i Helsingfors konsthall hösten 1993 visade Rantanen en av sina höjdpunkter. Hon visade vetelängder i olika stadier av flätning. Det är inte motivet i sig som gör målningen när mediet suveränt driver vidare.

Och måleriets helighet? I finskt samtida måleri har det jag vill kalla verklig provokation just riktats mot den formella och expressiva behärsk-

ning och förutsägbarhet som karakteriserat området. Även det mest vilda, expressiva måleriet började ju under 80-talet, både här och i Europa, få ett karakteristiskt utseende, språket upprepade och upprepades. Bland målarna är det fram om andra Marianna Uutinen som slagit till. Uutinen gör det med en gest, en handling som kan vara både det konkreta att spruta färg på duken och ett hånskratt mot det måleri som petat med rutsystem eller försökt få det "inre" att fastna på duken. Andra gör något annat, det realas realism (i lacansk bemärkelse). Tiden i målningarna kan vara sekundsnabb, det gäller den sekund under vilken ett tillstånd hemma i det språklösa kan få massa och substans. Brottet blir brutalt, när man målar det som inte skall målas; förutsättningen för praktiken är ett totalt refuserande av välkända tillvägagångssätt.

På tal om provokationen så är det oftast Teemu Mäki som nämns som den finska 90-talskonstens "enfant terrible". Själv skulle jag snarast kalla honom för en sann existentialist. Liv och död utforskas genom sexualiteten. Hans egen kropp tjänar som resonansbotten för ångest, plåga, meningslöshet och njutning; precis den projektionsskärm som bl.a. naturen utgjorde i tidigt finskt måleri.

Fortsättning följer

Efter lågprisvaruhuset, ryssarna och strykbrädena nyktrar jag till och fortsätter mot mitt egentliga mål. Att besöka museerna i periferin kring Arkadiagatan där svenska konstnärer ställde ut hösten 1995 under rubriken *Strange Phenomena* – stannar upp för andra gången – vilka fenomen avses?

Pekka Nevalainen

Vad himlen var blå, vad bladet var grönt då, när man började lära sig att absorbera omvärlden i orden. Trevande försök att förstå att grönt är grönt, att himlen är hög, att jag finns i en kropp som är liten och i en värld som är stor. Upplevelsen av skillnader, nyanser, proportioner är verklig för barnet så länge hänförelsen över att ordna upp omvärlden sitter i, innan in- och underordnandet blivit liv med tvång.

Pekka Nevalainens retrospektiva utställning i Helsingfors heter på finska *Piiri*. Varje finne börjar, när han hör ordet piiri, tralla på en finsk barnramsa: *Pieni piiri pyörii lapset siinä hyörii*. Den beskriver en ringlek där barnen snurrar runt, en karusellek. På pärmen till katalogen för *Piiri* finns ett fotografi av Nevalainen sittande mitt i en cirkel han har ritat på marken med vit krita. Detta är egentligen det enda påstående jag sett av konstnären och ett viktigt sådant. Tänker på ett fragment ur Roland Barthes *Kärlekens samtal*. "Jag vill medvetandet självt till en drog, och genom den uppnå den restlösa visionen av det verkliga, uppnå den stora vakendrömmmen, uppnå den profetiska kärleken."

I ett av sina tidigaste verk, ett svartvitt fotografi, sitter Nevalainen på huk, naken och silar sand mellan sina fingrar och menar att varje sandkorn är en viktig del av verket, tillsammans formar de en helhet, ett litet berg av sand (Nevalainen citerad ur katalogen). En långsam och tålmodig process som markör för det systembyte Nevalainens konstnärskap grundar sig på. När konstnärskapet är en vakendröm är allt tillåtet, koherensens förutsättning är redan uppfylld för den som drömmer vaket är aktören, konstnären på den plats där processen skall (åter)upprättas, göras till vaken verklighet. Det första rummet i museet innefattar en hop av *Naturdokument*. Här finns det stora gröna bladet som liksom en skulptur sticker upp från golvet. Stammar av finska trädslag, skogsdjursskulptur av träbitar, måltavlor för prickskytte, naturdokument på video. Människokroppens mått blir i relation till dokumentet som ett tänjbart gummiband som justeras beroende på var i rummet man står.

De sandkorn Nevalainen silade mellan fingrarna år 1976 blev betydelsefulla i hans arbete med den indiska mandalan där trianglarna fyllts

av olika färgpigment. På den retrospektiva utställningen är "mandalarummet" med det hemlighetsfulla, orangegula tältet från år 1982 solens, blommornas och evighetens rum. Det intressanta är att så här kan man uttrycka sig om Nevalainens konst och avse just solen, blommorna och evigheten utan anstrykning av kliché eller slentrian. Generöst målade blommor på glas (*Löv*) står radade längs med den ena väggen, redo för den bibliska uppmaningen: gån ut i världen och föröken Eder. Blommorna gör det med ett roat leende, inte för att det är plikt och tvång utan njutningsfullt. Nevalainens mandalarum ser lika självklart ut som vilket som helst kök.

Den bärande Bilden i Nevalainens installationer är en vacker bild, vacker för att den är aningslös. Kanske det är därför jag oupphörligen tänker på Barthes och hans fragment i *Kärlekens samtal*. Fragmentet "Jag vill förstå" slutar med en parentes.

(Tänk om medvetandet – ett sådant medvetande – vore mänsklighetens framtid? Om medvetandet en vacker dag, genom ytterligare ett spiral-varv då all reaktiv ideologi försvunnit, äntligen bleve ett avskaffande av det uppenbara och det underliggande, av skenet och det fördolda? Tänk om kravet ställdes på analysen att inte krossa kraften (inte ens korrigera eller rikta den), utan att bara utsmycka den, som en konstnär? Kan vi föreställa oss att förbiseendenas vetenskap en vacker dag upptäcker sitt eget förbiseende och att detta är: en ny och oerhörd form för medvetande?)

I installationen från 1991, *På bilden är Anton så modig och energisk*, springer barnet Anton från sin mammas famn mot kameran. Fotografiet handlar om detta, om ögonblicket som bevisar att ännu då fanns kraften, ingenting är ännu krossat. Nevalainens tillit till att hans eget konstnärskap kan fortsätta härifrån, från Antons position, ger oss förströstan. Kraften är lätt och samtidigt allvarlig, som lekens.

Siksi 4/1995

Intervju med Jaan Toomik

Tomorrow is a New Day

Siksi 3/1996 (se den engelska översättningen sid. 129)

Marjatta Oja
Galleri Lilla Agora, Helsingfors

Mor och dotter

Vad är en videoinstallation? Efterlyser man en saklig definition kunde den beskrivas som ett verk som grundar sig på interaktionen mellan en videobild och en omgivning konstruerad av konstnären. Betydligt intressantare är det att granska installationen som en mötesplats för motsatta aspekter av ett medium – t.ex. en förening av konst och teknologi, videorutans bildrum och det fysiska rummet, subjektiv vision och apparatens konkreta volym.

Marjatta Oja arbetar med det här mediet på ett sällsynt fruktbart sätt. Premisserna aktualiseras och utnyttjas enbart till den grad som är nödvändigt för att innehållet skall kunna gestaltas. Sålunda avdramatiseras den tekniska aspekten genom att den integreras med innehållet.

Videoinstallationen *Mami* studerar förhållandet mellan mor och dotter utgående från begreppen nära och fjärran, vilka placeras i relation till tiden och rummet. Dessa fyra begrepp är nästan konkret närvarande då de också korrelerar med installationens tekniska uppbyggnad. I galleriet finns avgränsat ett litet fyrkantigt rum med hjälp av lakan. I rummet projiceras en köksvideo. Dottern (i naturlig storlek) rör sig i sitt kök. I det fysiska rummet har därtill placerats en monitor som visar hennes mor. Denna sitter i en länstol och pratar om sin barndom. Samma monitor syns också i köksvideon. Alltså då dottern i sin tur sitter i sitt kök kan hon synkront betrakta videon där hennes mor talar.

Den ständigt närvarande modern är det tema som effektivt iscensätts. Bilderna blir dokumentära, verkliga på samma sätt som ett foto alltid kan sägas vara ett med sin referent. Den här autenticiteten är intressant i kombination med det att själva problematiken tilldrar sig på det psykologiska planet och dessutom är uttryckt genom tekniska manövreringar av tiden och rummet. Modern i sin länstol finns i dotterns kök samtidigt som den faktiska tiden producerar ett allt större tidsmässigt avstånd mellan dem. Här ligger skillnaden mellan minnets bilder och bilderna i monitorn. Minnets bilder existerar utanför nuet i motsats till videon som brutalt föråldras i takt med tiden.

Efter ett tag börjar man ge akt på ljudeffekterna. Vad säger modern? Man hör knappast någonting för hon överröstas av köksljud från dotterns kök. Det finns antytt oförenligheter; dilemmat med den närvarande modern? Vad säger dottern? Är hon den dotter som enligt Julia Kristevas termer har två alternativ. Antingen att identifiera sig med moderns kropp utan röst eller språk, eller med en röst utan kropp, en "ordjungfru", i en position från vilken det är omöjligt att gå utöver talets givna gränser, omöjligt att trotsa auktoriteter.

Det känns som en lättnad att gå in i galleriets andra rum för där finns en installation med samma kvinna (dottern), men nu sitter hon och målar framför ett fönster. Det psykiska och konkreta planet är förenat i något som kunde sammanfattas under rubriken: ett eget rum.

Hufvudstadsbladet 25 oktober 1991

Konstnären Anna Ghéczy, forskarna Marja-Liisa Honkasalo och Terhi Utriainen
Porthania, Helsingfors universitet

De sista orden

Kvinnor som självmördare, tiden som kryper allt närmare den avgörande handlingen som blir den absoluta gränsen mellan ett före och ett efter. På vardera sidan befinner sig självmordsmeddelandet, före handlingen, i efterhand avsett att läsas av de anhöriga.

Utställningen i Porthania är underordnad en annan intention än den konstnärliga, den vill ge talan åt de kvinnor som begått självmord. Vitt tyg är installerat som väggar mellan smala korridorer, på tyget finns textat i svart simuleringar av de budskap som kvinnliga självmördare lämnat till avsked. En omedelbar trivial association är lakan på tork.

Konceptkonstens förkärlek att använda t.ex. framförallt truismer, har gett oss en viss vana att handskas med verbalt innehåll i konsten. Beträffande dokumentaritet i konsten av i dag kan man säga att den håller på att omvandlas till fiktiva iscensättningar. I relation till det här får installationen i Porthania fördubblad effekt. Det man ser är verkligt, det är sant

i ordens ursprungliga betydelse. Och man undrar vilken är den verklighet som döljer sig bakom texterna.

Tyvärr är forskarna Honkasalo och Utriainen i detta skede ännu inte klara med sin jämförelse mellan män och kvinnors självmordsmeddelanden. Hälften av gåtan är således olöst. De har dock rätt i det att det är mannens självmord som framförallt intresserat forskarna i Finland, förhållandet mellan män och kvinnor beträffande självmord är för övrigt 4:1. Hurdana är då den finländska kvinnans självmordsmeddelanden? De är vanligen kortfattade och innehåller kombinationer av olika konfliktfyllda element; kommentarer över livet, lämnandet, avfärden, omsorg om de anhöriga. Direkt hänsyftning på den förestående döden är ovanlig. Avfärden uttrycks indirekt: hälsningar, adjö, måste bort. Däremot berättar meddelandena om kvinnans liv och framförallt om hennes familjeliv. Det är som om hennes värld krympt till vardaglig trivialitet präglad av en ångestladdad atmosfär. In i det sista är hon fylld av vardaglig omsorg.

Honkasalo och Utriainen har funnit ett återkommande innehållselement i meddelandena som de kallar testamente. Ordet gäller såväl konkret fördelning av egendom som anvisningar om de anhörigas inre relationer. I den sistnämnda betydelsen kan testamentet innebära begränsningar för andra människors liv, skapa skuldkänslor. Testamentet får en intressant aspekt om man ställer det i relation till det budskap som ofta förekom samtidigt, att inte orka mera. Genom sitt testamente lämnar kvinnan efter sig ett absolut sista ord, vilket betyder att hon efter sin död kommer att framstå som ett aktivt subjekt. Att inte orka mera är ju motsatsen, maktlöshet, att vara objekt för omständigheterna. Kan således döden för kvinnan vara något som fördriver en upplevd jaglöshet och därigenom bli en initialrit som möjliggör representationer kring ett själv: en resa mot ett subjekttillstånd.

Antropologiska studier av kvinnliga mystikers upplevelser har visat sig vara fruktbara också för tolkningen av kvinnors självmordsbudskap. Den avgörande iakttagelsen gäller kvinnomystikernas övergång till klosterliv. Dessa bytte nämligen inte lika radikalt som sina manliga kolleger roller då de lämnade ett liv för ett annat, vilket bl.a. framgick ur det språk med vilket de här kvinnorna tolkade och artikulerade sina liminalupplevelser (visioner om Jesu och Maria lidande). I motsats till männen bibehöll de ett vardagligt språk som var förankrat i deras egen kroppsliga erfarenhetsvärld. Kvinnornas religiösa liminal innebar alltså en yttersta

fördjupning av vardagliga grundupplevelser. De gled smidigt över från ett sammanhang till ett annat. Det här överensstämmer med iakttagelser om kvinnliga författares självmord. Virginia Woolf sjönk ordlöst med stenen i fickan ner i floden. När mannen Kirilov i Dostojevskijs roman begår självmord är det för att visa att hans vilja är starkare än Guds. Den ryska poeten Marina Tsvetajeva skriver något helt annat inför sitt självmord: Jag vill inte dö. Jag vill bara inte vara.

Kvinnor kan begå självmord utan tragedi, till och med utan dramatik, utan att ge intryck av att fly från en välbevakad gräns. Som handlade det om en naturlig, oundviklig, oemotståndlig övergång.

Hufvudstadsbladet 8 november 1991

Olav Christopher Jenssen
Museet för nutidskonst och Nordiskt konstcentrum, Helsingfors

Brist på minne

Olav Christopher Jenssen, en norsk målare som sedan 80-talets början varit bosatt i Berlin, visade senaste år i Kunstnernes Hus i Oslo en uppmärksammad utställning, *Lack of Memory*, bestående av 41 stycken målningar. I Museet för nutidskonst är nu fjorton av målningarna utställda och bildar ett slags gammaldags bildkabinett; tre av rummets väggar är från golv till tak täckta med de stora dukarna som mäter 275 x 255 cm.

Tidigare målade Jenssen lager på lager av färg som mer eller mindre täckte varandra. Det dolda och gömda var en väsentlig del av innehållet, vilket möjligen var en anledning till kritikens tendens att behandla Jenssens arbeten som en bekräftelse på allt det man önskade läsa in och ur "det nordiska". Målningarna i *Lack of Memory* har en annan vinkling som inte nödvändigtvis kan förklaras enbart genom en jämförelse med de tidigare arbetena. Riktningen kan också vara den motsatta, det nya kastar ljus över det föregående.

Serien handlar om det enskilda, den upptäcker och för fram komplexiteten i den enskilda utsagan med en oerhörd respekt för dess integritet:

Mycket är tillåtet, skiftningar allt från ömsint klumpighet till gracil finkänslighet. Genom målningarnas vägran att låta sig inordnas i en tillrättalagd harmoni omvänds skillnad och olikhet till häpnadsväckande styrka. "Jag tänker motarbeta spekulation med alla hederliga vapen som finns. Man kan inte lösa livet som ett taktiskt problem", säger Jenssen själv i en intervju i tidskriften F15 Kontakt.

Många recensenter har talat om den gåtfulla närvaro verken besitter. Det gåtfulla gäller snarare frågan om hur en konstnär lyckas skapa en närvaro som så totalt öppnar sig mot betraktaren att erfarenhet kan delas utan dolda hemligheter och hänvisningar. Närvaron i sig är inte gåtfull utan generös och öppen. Varje målning talar utgående från sin egen förutsättning, förankrad i den uppenbara skicklighet med vilken Jenssen hanterar bildens formella verkningsmedel. Och det är precis här som kritikerns problem börjar. Försök att placera målningarna i kategorier viker undan; figuration, abstraktion, symbol, metafor är begrepp som i detta fall leder till begränsningar i stället för att ge förklaringar.

Namnet *Lack of Memory*, brist på minne, innehåller betydelser man knappast kan undgå att relatera till målningarna, deras närvaro, öppenhet och rörlighet. Motsatsen, att hålla sig till minnet, betyder ju att måla som man lärt sig att man borde göra. Utgångspunkten är då en definierad plats med en överordnad uppsättning av strukturer som måleriet sedan försöker gripa tag i. Öppenheten i Jenssens verk tror jag har att göra med konstnärens kodifiering av platsbegreppet genom ett slags rörlig fragmentering. Platsen är inte längre ett unikt fastslaget ställe utan den skiftar så att dess överbyggnader splittras sönder.

I *Lack of Memory* finns dock en given plats, platsen för måleriets början. Och att börja är här detsamma som att utsätta sig för en tomhet och ge den gränser som fyller den med möjligheter. Det är dessa möjligheter vi möter i Jenssens måleri.

Avsaknad av minne kan förliknas med en glömska som inte bortför utan bevarar händelser man varken kan minnas eller helt förskjuta; obeskrivligheter som ger överraskande tonfall, röster, stämningar, färgsättningar och nivåer åt det vi medvetet förstår och uppfattar. De fjorton målningarna beskriver sådana obeskrivligheter.

Åker man ut till Sveaborg, till Nordiskt konstcentrum, blir sammanhanget mer intimt. Galleriets rum har förtätas och förminskats genom mellanväggar där Olav Christopher Jenssens utsökta teckningar är placerade

tätt intill varandra. Upphängningen och atmosfären får mig att tänka på familjefotografier i vilka förhållandet mellan de uppställda personerna förmedlar något väsentligt beträffande deras inbördes relationer.

Världen som inrymts i galleriet är sin egen men ändå möjlig att ta del av tack vare att teckningarna är autentiska, de är sitt medium trogna. De är inte skisser till målningarna utan deras uttryck lever i närheten av ett liv som levts och lever. Genom att teckningarna omfattar en rätt så lång tidsperiod blir det just deras föränderlighet som vittnar om den här förankringen. Ett fotografi kan i efterhand betraktat kännas som en spök-bild medan teckningens här och nu är omistligt genom den formskapande handens närvaro.

När Jenssen tecknar tecknar han inte av något utan han ger något en karaktär. Man kan skriva ett brev genom att teckna, eller förundra sig över maten i New York eller undersöka hur en liten plump på pappret kan växa till en organisk form. Jenssen lyckas, liksom en virtuos skribent som Roland Barthes, att utgå från det personliga och sedan föra det till en nivå där det skapas ett sammanhang som överträffar den första impulsen eller intentionen, för en teckning kan tillkomma i ett ögonblick av plötslig distraktion.

Ett spretigt streck eller en mjukt formad slinga i Jenssens teckningar kan vara exakt det minsta möjliga uttryck för kvaliteter som är större än orden förmår beskriva.

Hufvudstadsbladet 1 juni 1993

Georg Gudni
Galerie Artek, Helsingfors

Molnet, himlen eller luften

Inför storslagna landskap, som griper en till kropp och själ, har jag ofta undrat över vad det är man egentligen ser. I alla fall är det inte det landskap som postkortet avbildar. Reproduktionen saknar något väsentligt, den åstadkommer ingen bild på näthinnan då man sluter ögonen – en bild

som t.o.m. kan återkalla hur den fuktiga luften i ett disigt landskap doftar.

Islänningen Georg Gudni (f. 1961) har sedan början av 1980-talet målat det isländska landskapet, framför allt fjällen kring Reykjavik. I början avbildade målningarna porträtt av de kännspaka siluetterna som omger staden. Spår från den här fasen finns också med på utställningen i Artek. En serie bestående av små arbeten på papper anger hur konstnären arbetar med landskapet som bokstavligen utbreder sig framför hans ögon. Småningom förändrades målningarna, Gudni övergick till att beteckna höjderna med mjuka kurvor. Genom att betecknaren blev en annan förändrades också målningarnas relation till den yttre verkligheten. Abstraktionen blir alltmer uppenbar. Endast i några av de utställda arbetena finns en linje som anger horisonten, i övrigt är de helt abstrakta, liksom bilden som uppkommer på vår näthinna.

Tre målningar, samtidigt monumentala och transparenta, på var sin vägg i galleriets ena rum speglar sig i varandra. Den glänsande ytan får den blå färgen att se nästan genomskinlig ut – en substans såsom luft och vatten som svävar och flyter utan motstånd och specifika gester.

Gudnis målningar existerar i regioner svåra att rekognoscera för där skymtar bilden fram i ett tillstånd som föregår avbildningen. Den innefattar fortfarande möjligheter på samma sätt som våra förställningar, den går utöver synsinnet.

Yves Bonnefoy räknar upp ord i ett av sina prosapoem: Det första ordet var "molnet", det andra var också "molnet", det tredje, det fjärde etc. var "molnet", eller "himlen", eller "luften", man visste inte så noga. Men redan det sjunde brast sönder och plånades ut, det skiljde sig inte längre från andra som brustit och plånats ut längre ned, från andra i det oändliga, andra som var aska… Ifall molnet, himlen och luften också tillåts vara metaforer för bilden kan man säga, för att parafrasera Bonnefoy, att Gudnis måleri handlar om de sex första.

Hufvudstadsbladet 15 mars 1992

Våg, andning, kyss

Ange Leccia arbetar cirkulärt. Den mest kortfattade karaktäristik jag kan tänka ut angående hans verk är följande; de placerar sig som punkter i en cirkels mitt. Först när punkten är uppmärksammad ser betraktaren det som fnns mellan den och omkretsen – exempelvis att Leccias arbete kan vara en videoprojicering eller bestå av två grävskopor som står med gapet mot varandra framför ingången till ett konstmuseum. Hur noggrant man än reder ut förfarandet i Leccias praktik förblir det sekundärt i förhållandet till, ja, till vad?

När Leccia var inbjuden till Japan för att ställa ut ville kuratorerna att han skulle göra en utställning inspirerad av landets teknologi. Men i Japan började människorna däremot intressera honom och resultatet blev istället ett verk (fotografi) med en pojke och flicka. Ansiktena möts och läpparna, de nästan möts sekunden före kyssen. Sekundens förhållande till repetition – i ett annat arbete låter Leccia kameran om och om igen upprepa Maria Callas' sista andetag då hon avslutar sitt sånguppträdande.

Leccias verk på *Ars 95* finns ovanför väggen till huvudingången vilket gör det möjligt för betraktaren att växla den höjd från vilken han vill se på videoprojiceringen, som i sin enkelhet är extremt njutningsfull, man förlorar sig i vågornas ändlösa upprepning. I tankarna kallar jag verket *Vågorna* men märker att titeln är *Hav*.

Roos Finns det någon skillnad mellan benämningarna?

Leccia Jag föredrar att kalla verket *Hav* för det gäller kontakten mellan ett stycke land och havet och rörelsen som ständigt pågår dem emellan. I kontaktzonen där havet möter landskapet finns den aktivitet, den rörelse jag är intresserad av. För mig innebär den en konkret akt med vida betydelser, konstnären försöker vidröra systemet och han åstadkommer vågor, skapelser. Ständig flukturering, rörelse är lika med kraft.

(Leccia tar fram papper och penna och börjar rita.) Här är havet, här är stranden och den här gränsen rör sig hela tiden och den är alldeles vit. Jag gillar den vita färgen, för mig är den densamma som kreativitet, som en

vit duk eller ett vitt papper. Samtidigt är havet aldrig detsamma, det förändras från dag till dag. Därför krävs det lång tid för att uppfatta havets betydelse och för mig handlar det också om zenfilosofi, om att befinna sig rakt framför. Just nu är jag framför dig, men för att jag skall förstå dig och du mig behövs dessa vågor. Hav är ett verk om kontakt, kommunikation.

Roos Det problem *Hav* ställer mig inför har att göra med min synvinkel. Då jag inte anser det vara ett symboliskt arbete (däri ligger en av dess förnämsta kvaliteter) undrar jag hur jag skall tala och skriva om det. Eller är hela denna ambition i sig en omöjlighet, någonting som redan antyds av den abstrakta bild verket väcker trots de expressiva vågorna, en stilla mittpunkt i en cirkel. Minimal, exakt, absolut på rätt plats, d.v.s. måhända är mitt lingvistiska problem en följd av det att du lyckas föra ditt konstnärliga uttryck just till denna enkla, orubbliga punkt?

Leccia Om jag fortsätter med min demonstration kanske du får en vink. Här är stranden, här är havet och jag står här uppe på toppen av berget. Plötsligt gick det upp för mig att jag vill ta en bild med kameran svängd i onaturlig vinkel. Varför vet jag inte, jag har i tjugo år vistats vid den här stranden i Korsika där jag har mitt hus.

Roos Intressant, för när man ser på verket tänker man inte alls på hur det är gjort, tekniskt. Men det finns alltså en liten onormal svängning, vinkling som får den normala scenen litet ur spåret, just så litet att man knappt uppfattar det som en avvikelse.

Leccia För mig är det en demonstration av hur en vanlig situation blir ovanlig med en annan betydelse.

Roos Är det en speciell insikt som har med zen att göra, den lilla svängningen som gör det vanliga upptäckbart, klart framträdande?

Leccia Mina verk handlar om att utgå från mycket vanliga omständigheter och via små förändringar få dem att fokuseras, bli tydligare. Förskjuta en aning för att något skall framstå klarare. För mig handlar inte zen om mystik utan närmast är det en liten svängning, att svänga på kameran. Jag känner en forskare i matematik som berättade för mig att man inom den nya matematiken undersöker turbulens. När han såg mitt arbete såg han en parallell just till den nya matematiken. Och här kan man dra en parallell till våra egna liv, i princip har vi miljoner möjligheter. Att sitta på stolarna

här i cafét är något av det mest vardagliga man kan göra utan att man reflekterar över det. För mig kan just en dylik situation vara mycket stimulerande att arbeta med konstnärligt sätt. Det behövs så litet för att en ny betydelse skall ta överhand. Jag arbetar snabbt och betydelserna upptäcker jag först efteråt.

Roos Jag undrar varför den visualitet som finns exempelvis i verket *Hav* är så inspirerande. Är det för att ens uppskruvade visualitet år 1995 verkligen välkomnar något som förmår avlasta sinnet från det överflöd av visuellt bildmaterial som finns där? Rening?

Leccia Det är säkert helt korrekt att kalla Hav för ett slags rengöringsapparat. Det placerar sig före filosofin, före resonerandet, det är primärt, enkelt och rent. Och därför är det väl också möjligt att se en mängd betydelser i det.

Roos Det vanliga är ju att ett verk, även om det uppfyller de där kriterierna, gör dig som betraktare enbart uttråkad, ingenting händer. Med *Hav* sker motsatsen utan att man behöver anstränga sig för att uppbåda någon form av intresse.

Leccia (Skrattar till) Det är konstens magi.

Intresserade mig fortfarande för det arbete jag omtalade i början av texten, sekunden före kyssen och ställde Leccia den enkla frågan: *The kiss work?* Leccia tog ånyo fram pennan.

Leccia Det är, jag förklarar, två spotlampor som lyser mot varandra. En mot en, ljuset går inte ut, det belyser inte som brukligt är en situation utan här möter ljus ljus och konstellationen är för mig zen.

Nu förstod jag att förklaringen gällde ett annat verk som faktiskt hette *The Kiss* och att sekunden före kyssen är ett annat arbete. Felsägningen hade det oaktat rätt, vardera verken kan på en viss innehållsmässig nivå sägas handla om samma sak. För att ta till min inledande relatering om mittpunkten och cirkeln menar jag att just detta är utmärkande för Leccias praktik. Verket når samma abstrakta nivå, mittpunkten, även om det visuella framställningssättet kan variera på det mest överraskande sätt.

Siksi 1/1995

Anne Katrine Dolven
Nordiskt Konstcentrum, Helsingfors

Från yta till rum

Då Anne Katrine Dolven senast, för tre år sedan, ställde ut i Helsingfors deltog hon i Nordiskt Konstcentrums grupputställning *Det grønne mørke* med ungt, norskt måleri. *Det grønne mørke* förde fram den tendens som genomgående utmärkte nordiskt 80-talsmåleri, en återupplivning av den romantiska traditionen inom landskapsmåleriet. Dolvens arbeten hade då färger associerande till naturen och formerna anknöt till arkaiska symboler.

Under de här tre mellanliggande åren har Dolvens måleri förändrats på ett spännande sätt. Borta är nu element som kunde uppfattas som representationer och därigenom kopplas till betydelser. Färgen har också förändrats. I sina målningar laborerar Dolven med den vita färgens nyanser, vilka framkallas genom den teknik varmed färgen bearbetats. På så sätt genomgår färgen en transformering och blir en aspekt av målningens materiella utsträckning. Ibland har ytan en struktur som påminner om ett tunt lager gips, ibland ser ytan ut som vit, hård sten utskuren med kirurgisk precision. Svaga toner av gult kommer in i bilden just på de ställen där det vitas variationsmöjligheter är uttömda. Målningarna domineras av horisontella och vertikala fält uttryckta på samma stränga, knapphändiga sätt som färgerna.

I det här avseendet kommer Dolvens måleri nära den modernistiska konstens anspråk på renhet d.v.s. en konst begränsad till enbart det vad den i sig förmår uttrycka. I analogi med detta förnekas representationen och övriga betydelsebärande tecken. Men detta förnekande behöver inte vara entydigt, det kan också innebära det att konsten närmar sig det absolut hemliga språket, att konsten hänsyftar på det man kan tänka och föreställa sig men inte förevisa. Dolven har upprättat en struktur som uttryckligen fungerar genom den här typen av paradoxal negation. Strukturen hänsyftar på något man kan föreställa sig men den förevisar det inte. Vi möter den yttre sidan av något och genom att igenkänna det yttre impliceras föreställningen om det inre.

Trots att Dolvens måleri är fritt från artikulerade hänsyftningar och i denna bemärkelse rent möter man dock en fiktion, som inte är av litterär

utan av rumslig art. Det är denna koppling till det rumsliga som leder Dolvens måleri in på spännande områden. Målningarna pendlar mellan sin yta och objekt utanför och härigenom ingår de i samma rum där betraktaren befinner sig eller tvärtom uttryckt, betraktaren blir en del av målningens rum. Vad händer i skärningspunkten mellan betraktarens rum och den fiktiva rumslighet målningarna framkallar?

Platslösa platser, slutna förbjudna rum, korridorer som leder till fler korridorer; ett långt, smalt rum som en tunnel, i vilken närmande och avstånd dras till varandra och går isär i en oändlig rörelse. Rum där talet och skeendet står utanför det som sägs och inträffar. Det verkligas ödemark som det inres outforskade zoner.

Hufvudstadsbladet 7 juni 1991

Anders Tomren
Galerie Artek, Helsingfors

Positivt i vitt

Anders Tomrens utställning är en positiv överraskning på skulpturfronten, hans verk har funnit sin integritet och utgående från den arbetar de sig fram till en plats och ett mentalt tillstånd där någonting väsentligt händer, både i förhållande till skulpturbegreppet som medium och konsthistorisk kategori samt i förhållande till betraktaren och dennes referenser visavi relationen mellan konkret verklighet och föreställd sådan.

Effekten av Tomrens skulpturer är extremt multidimensionell, det känns som om skulpturerna hade osynliga motorer vars verkningar utsätter betraktaren för korsdrag. Omedelbart när man stiger in i galleriet händer något, det annars så sobra galleriet ser nästan litet sjabbigt ut i jämförelse med Tomrens kliniskt vita objekt i melamin och annat industriellt material. Ytan är ren, hård och brutal utan spår av hantverk, handens närvaro eller hänvisningar till det organiskt fysiska.

Tänker man på objekten i relation till sin kategori, skulpturen, kan man snabbt dra några slutsatser som bevisar hur svåra Tomrens verk är att

135

placera inom kända klassifikationssystem för skulpturen. Skulpturen som historiskt sett bär tyngden av att vara en av de stora gestaltande konstarterna uppnådde sin position genom sin förmåga till avbildning utifrån från vilken dess estetiska värde mättes. Marcel Duchamp gjorde vid 1900-talets början en negation av detta. Urinoaren han ställde ut som konstverk var ett ready-made objekt utan medvetet estetiskt värde, ett bruksföremål. Tomrens verk som refererar till möbler utmanar inledningsvis vårt beroende av språklig tolkning, ett verk liknar ett spegelskåp, ett annat en hylla, men de signalerar något mer som gör att man kan påstå att verken inte är möbler, inte heller ready-mades, för de är unika produktioner tillverkade av konstnären. Inte heller hör objekten hemma bland minimalistisk skulptur som syftade till att agera direkt med betraktaren, i ett slags drama i rummet, genom att den distanserande piedestalen utelämnades. Minimalistisk skulptur fungerade direkt i rummet, Tomrens verk har alla ett underrede: de tre säckarna på golvet ligger på en cirkelformad plattform, "spegelskåpet" i verket *Nude* har igen en rektangulär bas och exempelvis *Realm II* vilar på en bastant sockel. Å andra sidan kan man inte heller påstå att Tomren är en renodlad konceptualist, för i konceptkonsten ersatte verkets betydelse och intention processen att skapa verkliga objekt i rummet. Däremot har det unika i Tomrens skulptur sin avstamp i det att verken är mycket påtagliga, verkliga objekt i rummet, en annan sak är sedan det att språket inte kan sortera fram ett begrepp för vad man kunde kalla dem. De avbildar inte föremål från realvärlden utan producerar fram ett slags egen realism som lever i sin unika ordning. Här kunde man som instrument tillämpa Jean-Francois Lyotards analys av figurens ordningar. Lyotard analyserar fram tre stycken av vilka de två första är förankrade i modernismen. Den första gäller det optiska, det vi empiriskt sett säger att vi ser, objektet bundet av sina konturer. Den andra ordningen var den modernismen eftersträvade att nå, att finna de formella förutsättningarna för att framkalla "ren" form, att finna en osynlig struktur som lyfte fram den rena formen.

Den tredje ordningen kallar Lyotard för matrisens. Det är den som intresserar mig visavi Tomrens verk emedan skulpturerna för en vidare till något okänt som går utöver deras existens som konkreta objekt i rummet. I synnerhet verket *jag, jag, jag* antyder om detta. Tre säckar i kliniskt vitt finns på var sin låga plattform på golvet med en rubrik som refererar till en föreställning om jaget. Matrisens ordning opererar enligt Lyotard

under jorden, osynlig men levererande impulser upp till ytan som stör de påståenden som det konkreta och synliga lägger fram. Tomrens yta är systematisk och sammanhållen av träffsäkra former vilket underbygger det matrisen uppnår, ett slags konstans i det mentala flödet. Matrisens verksamhet går ut på konstans i det mentala flödet. Matrisens verksamhet går ut på att "slå till", och det är denna enhetliga puls som finns i Tomrens verk. För att citera Lyotard, fantasin må vara i konstant rörelse, dess föreställningar och innehåll markeras av instabilitet, men under detta finns en form: en rytm, en puls. Den här sällsynta varianten av formbegreppet är den Tomren arbetar med, skulpturernas synliga form uppdagar matrisens ordning där formen via dykningar i föreställningarna kommer upp som rytm, puls.

Hufvudstadsbladet november 1995

Marja Kanervo
Helsingfors konsthall

Skiftningar i rummet

Marja Kanervo (född 1958) debuterade 1981 och har sedan dess flitigt jobbat med både separat- och grupputställningar, bl.a. deltog hon i São Paulo-biennalen år 1989.

Konsthallen, planerad av Hilding Ekelund på 20-talet, är beträffande sin interiör en plats med ett påfallande drag av högtidlighet. I synnerhet de många trapporna som leder upp till själva utställningsutrymmet väcker en känsla av att man är i färd med att stiga in i ett slags konstens tempel. För en konstnär som arbetar med installation är det uttryckligen rummet med alla dess egenskaper som blir utgångspunkten. Det är således ingen lätt uppgift Kanervo haft att lösa – att finna en kombination som sammanför den anrika Konsthallen och 1990-talets installationskonst, speciellt som den senare baserar sig på begrepp som tid och rum.

Förutsättningen för att en installation skall fungera är att betraktaren blir närvarande, att hon tas i besittning på ett sådant sätt att hon i fysiskt

avseende upprättar en relation till rummet. Någonting måste hända beträffande rumsligheten så att betraktaren involveras och reagerar med skärpt känsla för detalj, kontur, struktur och nyans. Upplevelsen kan förlikas med den instinktiva, plötsliga känsla genom vilken man på ett fysiskt plan kan uppfatta närvaron av en annan person, innan ögat hunnit bekräfta saken. Det är ingen tvekan om att Kanervo suveränt behärskar det här området. Man reagerar omedelbart på hennes lösning för trappuppgången vars väggar hon täckt med vaxplattor som var och en försetts med ett avtryck av hennes egen rygg. Den monumentala uppgången förvandlas med en gång till konturer av något mänskligt som lockar genom sin frånvändhet. Det fragmentariska och splittrade fångar uppmärksamheten effektivare än en icke-tvetydig helhet. Ser man tillbaka på Kanervos produktion märker man att hon ofta använt sig just av det här draget, upprepning av enheter vilka ibland också bildat serier.

På väg upp för konsthallens trappor reflekterar jag över Ekelunds förtjänstfulla planlösning som får besökaren att omedvetet vika av till vänster, till rummet med det vackra, långsmala fönstret som sträcker sig från golvet till taket. Också Kanervos installation följer den ekelundska riktningen för i detta första rum sker en avgörande tematisering av rumsligheten med den konsekvensen att Kanervo lyckas frånta Konsthallen dess karaktär av konsthall (institution). Tidigare har man exakt vetat var rummets gränser legat, nu är de oklara. Var börjar rummet? Var slutar det? Rummet har transformerats till transparensens och återspeglingens rike. Den arkitektoniska helheten är upplöst. Kanervo har reproducerat rummets fönster samt detaljer man i vanliga fall inte fäster sig vid och därefter placerat fotografierna under plexiglas i olika nyanser. T.ex. på golvet rakt under det långsmala fönstret finner vi dess struktur upprepad i mörkviolett och svart. Då vi tittar ner ser vi hur det verkliga fönstret återspeglas i fotografiet.

En form av överskridning har inträffat. Den upphävda strukturen i det första rummet färgar av sig på upplevelsen av de övriga. Man är beredd att orientera sig i en rumslighet som fungerar enligt de betingelser Kanervo skapat; själva Konsthallen hamnar i skymundan. I det följande rummet är det mörker och ljus som kontrasterar varandra. På nästan hela golvet finns utplacerade brinnande ljus som reflekteras i mellanliggande glasytor. På väggarna finns bilder av tegelbitar som förmodligen härrör sig ur innerväggarna.

Inför Kanervos tidigare ljusinstallationer har jag känt mig en aning svävande, ambivalent. Visserligen är det vackert, men kommer det för nära det patetiska? Här i Konsthallen förändras dock inställningen en aning genom att utställningen tack vare sin omfattning synliggör ett betydelsefullt drag i Kanervos strategi. Speciellt påtagligt är det i verken där materialet utgörs av t.ex. olja eller fågelfjädrar indränkta med samma förödande vätska. Det är alltså som om den yttre världen skulle komma in i arbetena via materialet, t.ex. oljan som påminner oss om ekologisk katastrof. Utgående från den här synvinkeln är det inte så långsökt att uppfatta ljusen som minnesbilder för kollektiva trauman.

Det bakersta rummet är likaväl ockuperat av ett koncept som helt och hållet tagit det i besittning. Den ena väggen är täckt med silkespapper som indränkts i matolja vilket förvandlat papperet till en transparent hinna. En del av oljan har runnit ut över golvet, som också är beklätt med samma slags papper. De genomskinliga fläckarna på golvet blottar prydliga rader av siffror som anger olika mått för ifrågavarande byggnad. Det inslag av levande process som ofta förekommer i Kanervos installationer får här ett hotfullt uttryck. Allt efter hand som tiden framskrider förändras rummet genom den svarta oljan som långsamt droppar ur två kar. Då utställningstiden går ut har det vita golvet troligen helt förödats.

Epilogen infinner sig i de mindre rummen – en epilog som är lika förtätad som utställningen i övrigt. Ryggavtrycken i trappuppgången får en motsvarighet som går ut över det privata, cirkeln sluter sig. På väggen hänger en rya som knutits av fågelfjädrar impregnerade med olja. Oljekaret placerat intill har en ogenomtränglig, svart yta. Det är inte svårt att föreställa sig vilket drama ur verkligheten detta kunde handla om.

Hufvudstadsbladet 28 augusti 1992

Eva Löfdahl
Kemiska övningslaboratoriet, Stockholms universitet

Abstraktion och rum men också, och också

När man skall uttrycka sig om Eva Löfdahls verk med språket som medel är det bäst att så snabbt som möjligt acceptera sitt underläge. Det blir ett stammande och ett adjö till välljuden (eller till ens beroende av dem).

Vill använda uttrycket "klippa bland orden", ungefär som att klippa till pappersdockor och hoppas att konturerna blir så pass lyckade att det ser ut som om det skulle finnas ett skelett bakom som ger volym åt de platta bitarna. Beslöt mig att försöka klara av detta med minsta möjliga ordapparat. Endast det nödvändiga.

Det jag fick till uppgift att tala om var begreppet rum i relation till Eva Löfdahls verk. Det är viktigt att här säga begrepp för vad jag snart insåg var att det man menar med bildrum i ett verk, och dess relation till verkligt rum inte alls finns eller är aktuellt i Eva Löfdahls verk. Alltså, hon arbetar inte med bildrum i den konstvetenskapliga betydelsen, rumsbegreppet visavi hennes praktik har en annan betydelse. Något annat. Vad?

Jag har en längre tid sysslat med att titta på Jacques Lacans diagram, eller grafiska framställning av tankarna, och i synnerhet när texten blev frågetecken var det en lättnad att studera diagrammen. Ofta frågade jag mig varför diagrammet säger något annat än det som skriftsidorna säger. Att förstå samma sak på olika sätt, genom olika, i sig begränsade medel. Och framförallt att diagrammen började påverka min tolkning av Lacans teori, de började säga något mer om den – om lagen, strukturen, ja ni känner till vokabulären. Dessa begrepp för det givna, för förutsättningar, och för bas, öppnar sig plötsligt åt olika håll för att abstraktionen hamnade i ett rum, blev tredimensionell, visuell.

Med erfarenhet färsk i minnet från innebörden av modernismens rutsystem, menar jag inte det slag av system som ju var avgränsande, uteslutande, autonomt och syftade att skapa en essens i mig när jag talar om figur och diagram och ordning. Jag menar detta som medel för att få fram att en abstraktion kan ha som förutsättning det att den ger ett rum att existera i, d.v.s. att den görs tredimensionell. När man exempelvis hör nämnas Eva Löfdahls verk finns ofta ordet absurd skulptur med. Absurd betyder

förnuftsvidrig, vilket hennes skulptur inte alls är. Nog så lätt att presentera som sådan om man enbart utgår från utseendet och jämför hur den ser ut i förhållande till annat i verklighten.

Referenser. Lyotard har diskuterat ordningarna. De två första känner vi till. Den första, det vi empiriskt sett ser, objektet som det ses, objektet bundet av sina konturer. Den andra ordningen, har att göra med formella möjligheter som villkor för det visuella i sig, hur det låter sig framställas, den nivå där ren "form" opererar som princip för koordinering, enhet, struktur: visuella men osynliga. Detta ville modernismen behärska.

Men den tredje får mig att tänka på abstraktion i rum och också det som därför införs och kommer till, får mig att tänka på ett verk av Eva Löfdahl. Den tredje, alltså, kallar Francois Lyotard för matris, med vilken han menar en ordning som opererar utanför räckhåll för det synliga, en ordning som arbetar helt och hållet underjordiskt, utanför synfältet, och här vill jag tillägga med tanke på Löfdahls verk *in space*, dvs. i beroende-förhållande till rummet, tredimensionalitet. Hur förenas en fenomenolo-gisk och psykoanalytisk rumslighet?

Lek med orden. *Spatium* betyder mellanrum, *spatiös* med stora mellan-rum, *spatel*, litet spadformigt verktyg (för att göra mellanrum) och *tesked* då? Vad gör den? Den fångar också upp fyllningen för att det skall bli rum, inte bara mellanrum.

Underjorden. Och upp. Och ner. I Eva Löfdahls verk är det balansgång mellan rumsligheter. Bitar av former kan anta gestalt och bli synliga igenkännbara, och den tredje ordningens rum kommer in som rummet (*space*) för det omedvetna. Det här rummet är "oföreställbart" men det finns framställt I Löfdahls verk: ett block av motsättningar. I verkligheten finns detta som projektioner av varierande "figurer" som kommer upp till ytan från "djupet" av detta "rum": felsägning, dagdröm, fantasi etc.

I Löfdahls verk är dessa figurer inte projektioner utan förverkligade som den tredje ordningen, som i princip arbetat underjorden men som kan då när abstraktionen förverkligas som tredimensionalitet få synlighet, konkretion.

Föreläsning 1 november 1995